Youth Work

Professi... ...e theory
learned i... ...ort. This
compreh... ...; people
become ... ...ing and
intervent...

Divid...

- prov... ...work;
- expl...
- dem... ...l impact
  on th...

Engag... ...g about
working ... ...des case
studies, t... ...nections
between

Jason W... ...f Social
Sciences ... ...erests in
the relati...

Sue Wes... ...: at De
Montfort... ...heories
and prin... ...rk and
developing professional practice.

Gill Thompson is a freelance trainer and youth and community worker and previously
worked as Senior Lecturer in Youth and Community Development and Field Placement
Co-ordinator at De Montfort University, UK.

Youth Work

Preparation for practice

**Jason Wood, Sue Westwood
and Gill Thompson**

Routledge
Taylor & Francis Group

LONDON AND NEW YORK

First published 2015
by Routledge
2 Park Square, Milton Park, Abingdon, Oxon OX14 4RN

and by Routledge
711 Third Avenue, New York, NY 10017

Routledge is an imprint of the Taylor & Francis Group, an informa business
© 2015 Jason Wood, Sue Westwood and Gill Thompson

The right of Jason Wood, Sue Westwood and Gill Thompson to be identified
as the authors of this work has been asserted by them in accordance with
sections 77 and 78 of the Copyright, Designs and Patents Act 1988.

British Library Cataloguing-in-Publication Data
A catalogue record for this book is available from the British Library.

Library of Congress Cataloging-in-Publication Data
Wood, Jason, 1978–
    Youth work : preparation for practice / Jason Pandya-Wood,
    Sue Westwood and Gill Thompson.
        pages cm
    1. Social work with youth—Great Britain.
    2. Youth—Services for—Great Britain.
    I. Westwood, Sue.   II. Thompson, Gill.   III. Title.
    HV1441.G7W66   2014
    362.7'2530941—dc23
                                                    2014000293

ISBN: 978-0-415-61985-1 (hbk)
ISBN: 978-0-415-61999-8 (pbk)
ISBN: 978-1-315-76737-6 (ebk)

Typeset in Sabon
by Keystroke, Station Road, Codsall, Wolverhampton

Contents

Figures

Tables

Acknowledgements and dedication

This book builds on our experiences of working with students, practitioners and colleagues involved in youth work over a number of years. We are very fortunate to be able to draw on their numerous accounts of practice, which have shaped our thinking. We are therefore grateful to our students and colleagues both at De Montfort University and Nottingham Trent University for their encouragement and support with this project. A number of people offered advice and suggestions on some of the chapters and structure, and we are thankful in particular to Bob Payne, Hazel Kemshall, Zora Visanji, Alex Rafter, Alexander Cotton and Russell Thompson. External advice was appreciated from Jean Spence (Durham) and Steve Bullock (Gloucestershire), who read and commented on some early drafts. Thank you to many of our students who allowed us to use their valuable experiences as case studies within the chapters. You know who you are and we are very grateful to you for sharing your stories.

This book is dedicated to the many youth work practitioners for their continued commitment to making a difference to young people's lives, particularly in these challenging times. We would also like to extend our own dedications.

Jason: for Raksha and Jasmine

Sue: for Tim, Billie and Ella

Gill: for my amazing husband and ever-expanding family, who support, inspire, advise and encourage me, and particularly for Eloise and Imogen in an ever-changing world.

How to use this book

Like all those who write a textbook for students, we hope that this will provide a useful volume to assist your studies. We also hope it will be a living document and throughout we have provided a number of case studies to bring some of the issues to life. We have also included two interactive ways for you to engage with the text, either on your own or with your colleagues, peers or supervisor:

- **Reflections:** these are designed to encourage you to think about your own experiences in relation to the context of the chapter. You may find these useful for relating your own personal and professional experiences to your practice placement. These activities can usually be done on your own but you may also find benefit in discussing your reflections with others.
- **Tasks:** the book contains a number of tasks that are designed to put some of the book's ideas into practice. Here, you may be encouraged to apply models, develop sessions or follow multi-staged processes that could assist your work with young people. In all cases, the tasks are designed to enhance your studies and practice, but all are suggestions – we would encourage you to use, develop, critique and refine the tasks to suit your own circumstances.

1 Introduction

Whether you are just about to embark upon your journey into youth work or have been a practising youth worker for a number of years, undertaking an assessed practice experience can prove rewarding and challenging in equal measure. Youth workers today enter increasingly diverse settings and contexts, contributing to sometimes contradictory or complementary policy objectives. They are arguably more skilled, more knowledgeable and have more resources than at any other point in the history of the profession.

Youth work itself has been subject to intensive political reform with increased measures of accountability, targeted approaches to work with young people 'at risk' and an emphasis on accrediting outcomes for young people (Tyler 2009). Whereas once youth work was predominately located in dedicated youth services and social work, youth workers today will engage with a number of agencies and statutory partnerships that did not exist ten years ago (Wood and Hine 2009) and will be required to make contributions to policy objectives in health, crime reduction, and inclusion in education and employment. Furthermore, at the time of writing, statutory youth services in England are under the threat of unprecedented cuts resulting in the withdrawal of youth work from mainstream local authority provision (Spence and Wood 2011). Student placements increasingly reflect these diverse contexts and varied policy priorities. As a result, it is vital that emerging practitioners can identify their own contribution as youth workers in contexts where the principles of youth work may be tested.

This book is designed to provide you with a companion through the process of undertaking your practice placement. It is built around three important and interconnected components of youth work: principles, context and practice skills.

What do we mean by youth work?

Defining precisely what is meant by youth work poses challenges as it 'has remained an ambiguous set of practices, pushed in different directions at different times by different interests' (Bradford 2005: 58). The work itself is diverse 'whether by the different forms the work takes, the perspectives adopted, the setting, organisational arrangements, or even ideology' (Payne 2009: 217). Indeed, youth work may not mean the 'same thing to every volunteer, youth worker, youth work manager or policy maker' (Batsleer and Davies 2010: 1). Consequently, a range of practices loosely defined as 'youth work' flourish in a wide range of settings delivered by numerous organisations. Like all other human services, youth work is influenced by the social, political and economic context in which it operates, taking on different 'guises' according to 'varying conceptions of youth need' (Bradford 2005: 58). Despite this ambiguity and debate, there are some key principles, values and methods that can enable us to distinguish professional youth work from other forms of work with young people.

A useful starting point for student youth workers would be to consult the appropriate occupational standards for our work. For example, youth work is defined in the English National Occupational Standards for professional youth work as '[Enabling] young people to develop holistically, working with them to facilitate their personal, social and educational development, to enable them to develop their voice, influence and place in society and to reach their full potential' (Lifelong Learning UK 2008: 4). What does such a statement mean? How do we differentiate youth work from other forms of practice that may also seek to work 'holistically' with young people to enable them to 'reach their full potential'? There is obviously much that youth work shares with other forms of work with young people, but some features are worth distinguishing.

Youth work is an educational practice

Youth workers are primarily educators who engage with young people in diverse settings, using different methods and activities to stimulate informal education and learning (Chapter 5). They build and sustain open and trusting relationships in order to create the conditions for learning and, wherever possible, young people will choose to engage in the learning relationship. Informal education is distinguished from other types of educational practice by its values and methods. The approach relies on starting where young people *are at* instead of using pre-determined learning outcomes and didactic teaching methods. It is primarily concerned with young people's personal and social development but we reject the rather passive concept of 'facilitation' outlined in the occupational standards definition above. Youth workers *purposefully intervene* in young people's lives, creating opportunities, activities and conversations that aim to enable young people to think, feel and act differently towards their social world.

Alongside the use of informal education, youth workers also undertake a wide range of other personal and social education work that may be pre-determined but is notable for its creativity and diversity. For example, practitioners will find new and engaging ways to impart important information about health risks through participative games or arts-based activities. Whilst this is not informal education, it is often found in the educational practice of youth workers and offers a valuable contributory dimension to the role.

Youth work is a social practice

Increasingly, many youth workers will adopt 'case-work' approaches to working with young people, for example through the provision of personal information, advice and guidance work. However, youth workers seek to prioritise working with groups in order to nurture collective *association* amongst young people (Chapter 12). The reasons for this approach are numerous, not least the fact that young people themselves generally associate with their peers in groups and this provides a useful starting point for engaging with them. Social practice also enables young people (and practitioners) to test their values, attitudes and behaviours in the context of *being with others*: the essence of something called 'pro-social modelling'. Therefore, youth workers will either convene groups or work with existing peer groups.

Youth workers actively challenge inequality and work towards social justice

A key ethical standard that underpins youth work is the 'promotion of social justice for young people and in society generally' (Banks 2010b: 10). Most youth work takes place in the context of social injustice, often with young people and others who are on the margins, excluded by a number of personal, cultural and structural barriers (Thompson 2006). Chouhan (2009) makes the distinction between anti-discriminatory practice (working within society's legal framework) and anti-oppressive practice: 'understanding of oppression and power, commitment to empowerment and the ability to reflect, critically analyse and change . . . practice' (Chouhan 2009: 61). Crucially, this positions the role of the youth worker as one who seeks to address power imbalances rather than merely say or do the right things to avoid unlawful discrimination. In Chapter 14, we explore this distinction further and establish some of the ways in which these principles can translate into practice.

Where possible, young people choose to be involved

Young people have traditionally chosen to be involved with youth work, rather than participating because they are compelled to. Whereas young people have little choice in attending school (and may be severely penalised for not doing so), their interaction with youth work is based on a voluntary engagement between practitioner and young person. This is perhaps one of the most contentious points of debate around whether newer forms of work with young people can be considered 'youth work'. For example, youth workers increasingly engage with young people in a variety of settings where they are compelled to attend (such as the school or a compulsory programme run by the local youth offending team). What then does the youth worker do in these circumstances? It is our view that youth work and informal education not only takes place in these environments, but can make a distinct and positive contribution to the personal and social development of young people.

Payne (2009) argues that the voluntary principle has always posed challenges. Whilst young people may have chosen to attend less formal environments such as youth clubs, their choice was located in the context of pre-determined rules and peer group norms. Put simply: they attend because their mates do, and when they get there the encounters are somewhat constrained. Whilst voluntary attendance is desirable to be sure, it is the *quality of engagement* and *extent to which young people can shape encounters* that are more important (Ord 2007).

Youth work seeks to strengthen the voice and influence of young people

Youth work has a long history of describing itself as strengthening the voice and influence of young people. Various terms have underpinned this work: empowerment, participation, active citizenship and democratic engagement. According to the National Occupational Standards for Youth Work, practitioners encourage and enable young people to 'influence the environment in which they live' (Lifelong Learning UK 2008, value 10) and through the use of educative processes, practitioners seek to move young people from a position of limited power to one where they can exercise influence and make decisions (Wood 2010a). Practitioners create opportunities for democratic behaviour to flourish (Jeffs and Smith 1999) in order for young people to 'claim their right to influence the society in which they live' (Young 1999: 22). This work takes place at a number of levels using different methods to stimulate formal and informal democratic thinking and behaviour (Chapter 5).

Youth work is a welfare practice

It is the contention of this book that youth work is a *welfare practice* that, alongside its primary education role, promotes 'the welfare and safety of young people' (Banks 2010b: 10). Youth workers often, though not always, work with young people experiencing greater needs or in areas of higher 'deprivation'. It is possible to balance the educational goals set out in Chapter 5 with welfare interventions designed to address personal or social behaviours and circumstances that may limit the opportunities available to young people to flourish. If youth work contributes to pre-determined and overarching agency objectives (e.g. a school requiring young people to attend classes or a youth offending project's need for young people to adhere to licence conditions), then this is an additional bonus that extends the role of the youth worker, rather than limiting it. We are yet to meet a youth worker who would promote exclusion from school or engagement with crime as desirable outcomes.

Finding the balance between working towards pre-determined welfare-oriented goals (such as 'doing' a teenage pregnancy reduction project) and the promotion of informal education is a difficult one. Key to effective working is to avoid framing our work as primarily about solving 'problems' even if we work in agencies where this may be their sole purpose. The value of our educational approach and its emphasis on working with young people in a holistic way enables us to counteract the view that young people comprise 'problem' categories that need to be managed.

Youth work works with young people 'holistically'

In Bradford's (2005) analysis, the shifting sands that characterise youth policy have led to youth workers often defining their work in the context of what problems they can address. For example, youth work *may* contribute to the reduction of anti-social behaviour in a local community and, as a result, be perceived as a 'fix' to problems in 'hot-spot' areas. However, the difficulty for us is when this becomes the *primary* driver for youth work. Youth workers can be heard describing their work with 'young offenders', 'teenage parents' and 'NEETs'.[1] Despite the pressures from policy and the challenges of working in different agency contexts, using these labels to describe young people with whom we work should be resisted at all costs. We work primarily with young people because they are *young*. Young people encounter difficulties or pose particular challenges and these are often situated in precarious structural or environmental circumstances, and, as we acknowledge above, our contact with them is often in situations of higher deprivation or need. However, this is but one part of their complex, interesting, multi-faceted lives, and to focus only on the narrow policy-defined problem is likely to result in, at best, a limited impact (Yates, S. 2009) or, at worst, further demonisation of young people (Hine 2009). So Tyler (2009) is right to show that youth workers can and do make contributions to various social policy objectives (the welfare approach) but this work is most effective when it takes place *because of the primary work that youth workers do*.

What makes a good youth worker?

Reflection 1.1

- What do you think makes a good youth worker?
- What knowledge, skills, attitudes and values are characteristic of youth workers you have met who you consider to do a good job?

As a young person, one of the authors encountered two very different detached youth workers. The first was a fairly young man, dressed in fashionable clothing, loved talking about chart music, smoked and was even known for being able to purchase alcohol for young people if they asked. He was undoubtedly popular with young people! The second knew little about pop music, wore quite old clothes, told young people about the risks of smoking and drinking and was often subjected to light-hearted mockery from young people. These are, of course, two extremes. The comparison helps though to debunk a common misconception about the right type of youth worker. Whilst it is important to relate to young people and to communicate respectfully, a worker neither has to be young nor cool to engage them. The first youth worker was quickly forgotten after the local authority dispensed with his services; the second had a lasting impact upon a particularly challenging group of young people. The first condoned problematic behaviour and, to some extent, encouraged it. The second continuously challenged young people to consider their behaviours and the possible alternatives available to them. In the end it was the second who tapped into the creative interests of the group and enabled them to make a film about the neighbourhood they lived in.

Young people value youth workers firstly because they are trusted adults. The McNair report (1944) argued that a youth worker acted as a 'guide, philosopher and friend' to young people and that this role was dependent on their character and integrity. In the above two examples, we see the first youth worker embodying the surface-level friendship qualities that, arguably, young people are already able to access in abundance from their peer group. The distinctiveness of the second was in his desire to operate as a 'role model' to young people, and as a 'critical friend', able to respect and relate to young people but with clear professional values and boundaries that guided his interventions.

To act with integrity and to maintain a professional role requires a number of key factors that are explored throughout this book. Good youth workers:

- have a well-developed sense of 'self' and can use reflection to understand how their own identity impacts upon their understanding of and work with others (Chapter 3);
- recognise the distinctiveness of their educational contribution and commit to their own lifelong learning (Chapter 5);
- act ethically, both by adhering to professional codes of conduct and to broader virtue ethics and values (Chapter 4);
- seek to promote social justice and equality through anti-oppressive practice (Chapter 14).

Becoming the professional practitioner

The character of a youth worker, their integrity and their willingness to act as a role model and critical friend are vital. Alongside this is the commitment to learning and development described throughout this book. As a student embarking on a qualification towards professional practitioner status, you will be expected to meet assessment criteria that satisfy the expectations of your awarding institution and the professional body for youth work.

An emerging professional practitioner takes account of good practice that is inherent to all services that work with people. Many supervisors we have spoken to will cite being trustworthy, reliable, consistent and punctual as the minimum expectations they have of students. These might be described as professional behaviour and attitudes, and are somewhat supported by the policies and procedures of the organisation we work with. They are qualities that, alongside integrity and respect, are seen as most important to young people (Yates, S. 2009).

However, we also believe there are a number of other commitments that professional practitioners need to make in order to enhance their learning experience, their thinking and their practice. These include using reflective practice (Chapter 11) and supervision (Chapter 10) as processes to foster learning and practice development. Some student youth workers (and placement supervisors) can struggle with moving beyond thinking of these as instrumental processes that monitor a person's tasks or workload. Supervision and reflective practice is best when it encourages the practitioner to attend to their feelings, question their practice and think about alternatives for engagement. In order for this to happen, practitioners must be *open to learning*.

Whether you have joined your professional youth work course with decades or weeks of experience behind you, it is worth reflecting on the extent to which you consider yourself 'open'.

Focus of the book

This is a book primarily for undergraduate students embarking on professional practice placements during their youth work training course, though it will also be very useful for students on allied courses, postgraduate students and practitioners. It is designed to support readers as they engage with testing their skills, drawing the links between theory and practice, engaging with difficult situations and successfully completing placements: it will be the core companion to field practice placements. Through three parts, it is a book that:

Establishes and locates the prerequisite principles required for practice

In changing contexts and challenging practice situations, the developing student practitioner requires a firm footing in terms of the principles, values and distinct features of modern youth work practice. Though not designed to be an exhaustive exploration of values and principles, there is a need for the placement student to locate themselves and their professional identity in relation to the placement they are about to undertake. Part I of the book revisits key themes of youth work theory: the importance of self-awareness and the impact of identity on our work (Chapter 3); the commitment to ethical practice (Chapter 4) and the recognition that education is the 'business of youth work' (Chapter 5). All of this work is situated in the context of the reader using and developing skills in reflective practice (Chapter 11) and being prepared for practice (Chapter 2).

Explores the importance of understanding the context of work

Work with young people is affected by numerous contextual factors and three are explored in Part II of the book. First, the importance of 'local knowledge' is revisited through developing an understanding of the community (by which we mean neighbourhood, estate or village) in which the practitioner is working (Chapter 6). Second, we examine how social policy contexts can shape, support, challenge and sometimes hinder effective work with young people (Chapter 7). Finally, in an era of increased partnership working, Chapter 8 attends to how a youth worker identifies and asserts confidence in their role when working with others and also gains a better understanding and appreciation of different professional roles.

Sets out the core skills required for effective work with young people

Having set out the core principles and contexts of modern youth work, Part III examines what we would consider to be some of the core skills of a youth worker who intends to engage meaningfully with young people, their families and their wider community of people. The chapters will enable you to:

- develop frameworks for assessing, planning, implementing and evaluating work with both groups and individuals (Chapter 9);
- be an effective listener and converser – someone who can utilise effective communication skills to engage with different groups of people (Chapter 13);
- understand and apply models, principles and processes of working with groups (Chapter 12);
- apply principles of anti-oppressive practice to effectively challenge discrimination and use educational skills to help young people and others to transcend prejudicial views or discriminatory behaviour (Chapter 14);
- create the conditions where young people can move from passive recipients of service provision to active participants and leaders (Chapter 15);
- use supervision and reflective practice effectively to work towards professional range skills, learn and grow in terms of professional practice, and help develop ethical and value-based practice (Chapters 10 and 11).

Taken together, the three parts form an important narrative for guiding a modern youth work placement student. In order to work effectively with young people, student practitioners require an understanding of and commitment to the *principles* of youth work; an awareness of how *contexts* shape their work; and the core *practice* skills that are required to make a meaningful impact on the lives of young people.

Note

1 Not in Education, Employment or Training (NEET).

Part
I

Principles

Youth workers who make a meaningful impact in their work with young people do so by using more than their practice skills. They embody a commitment to professional and personal values that put young people's needs, interests, hopes and anxieties at the heart of what they do. This section of the book revisits some of the guiding principles that underpin good quality youth and community work.

Since this book is primarily aimed at those students undertaking their fieldwork placements, it would be remiss of us not to discuss some of the core expectations of engaging in practice learning. Chapter 2 provides an overview of issues such as professional formation, workplace learning and the expectations that supervisors have of their students, and vice versa. The reader is encouraged to think about how best to prepare for placement and how to tackle difficulties if they arise.

In Chapter 3, we present an account of how and why our own identities, histories and past experiences inevitably shape our encounters with others. Given the diversity and complexity of young people's lives, deepening our understanding of the 'self' is a good step towards appreciating the viewpoints and experiences of others. Situating this understanding in a broader ethical context opens Chapter 4, which briefly reviews aspects of ethical practice. In this chapter we provide an overview of the ethical codes that support youth work practice and explore one of many strategies that can help to nurture ethical dialogue.

One of the challenges associated with the more diverse forms of work with young people that have taken shape over the past two decades is the potential for us to lose sight of our distinctive contribution. Chapter 5 seeks to address this challenge by restating that youth work is an educational intervention. It is also possible that youth work practice can flourish even in environments where informal education is not the focus.

Taken together, we hope these chapters help the reader to locate their own principles and values in a wider body of work that firmly defines youth work and the role of the youth worker.

2 Preparation for practice learning

Introduction

Many readers of this book will be embarking on assessed practice, a learning journey that takes place primarily in a workplace setting. For some of us, this setting may be familiar. In other cases, we may be working with a new organisation for the first time. Whether we are new students or established practitioners, taking time to explore our own professional formation within the context of work-based learning is a valuable exercise. In any practice setting you will be supervised and your competence assessed alongside agreed assessment criteria. This process will not only support professional and skills development but will be pivotal in your ultimate development as a competent workplace manager who understands and is able to support and manage staff and resources. This chapter aims to support students and supervisors in understanding these processes. It will explore:

- professional formation;
- preparing for practice;
- the context of workplace learning;
- expectations of students and employers; and
- the nature and dynamics of working relationships.

Professional formation

Undertaking a youth work placement in an appropriate setting is a significant and distinct learning experience that will contribute to your professional formation. Perhaps more than at any other time, your experience in the workplace will be characterised by its emphasis on specific learning goals.

Practice experience is valuable, not only from the perspective of the student but also from that of employers and colleagues. In a multi-agency, integrated services context where many youth and community workers practice, there is a need to understand not only the dynamics of the multi-professional team and the skills that others bring, but also to have a clear understanding of the youth worker role and the unique skills, values and working methods they can bring to the team. Being aware of one's own professional skills and role allows for more effective partnership working, which ultimately benefits the service and its users.

From an employer's point of view a skilled and professional worker who operates within the structures, values and ethos of an organisation and demonstrates a clear understanding of their role is an asset that will support consistent service delivery and development. This is particularly important in an environment where work is increasingly target-driven and where successful funding applications are key to the sustainability of many organisations in allowing them to deliver appropriate work and maintain a professionally qualified workforce.

Therefore we need to look at who we are and what we bring as individuals to the workplace learning environment, and to understand the impact of our level of engagement.

> Workplace learning is fundamentally individual because learning is always related to the learner's background and experience from their previous life course and their hopes and expectations for the future. In particular work place learning is influenced by learners' fundamental attitudes to work as they have been formed through socialization in the family, in the school and education system and in later experience at work.
>
> (Illeris 2011: 38)

Illeris suggests that an awareness of self and ones life's experience is important in work-based learning, a theme which will be explored in Chapter 3. Thus, it is important to recognise that you are on an individual learning journey, based on your own unique life and practice experiences. Who you are and what you bring to the assessed workplace experiences will be different to peers in the same setting. Having self-awareness and recognising learning and experience to date will help in allowing you to see the potential and opportunities for further learning and professional formation.

In all reading, whether it be a novel or academic book, we take the content then analyse and blend it alongside our experiences, thereby making sense of what we read and in so doing creating our own unique picture of the content. During the practice experience and when reading this chapter it is important to match your picture, experience and understanding alongside the practice assessment requirements you are working towards. A clear understanding and ownership of these requirements is important if you are to succeed. Preparation for practice is essential – we would not set off on a journey without all of our travel documents, passport and currency, so in the same way we should avoid embarking on a practice experience without preparation. Remember that in your chosen area of work, the abilities, talents and experience you bring contribute to your development as a professional on the journey to qualified status.

As professional formation progresses, you will be supervised and assessed by someone who is ideally a competent and experienced practitioner who understands and has an overview of staff roles within the organisation, and can therefore support you in locating your role within the agency framework. They should also have an understanding of work-based learning and reflective practice. This person assumes the role of 'guide':

> It is true that the guide should be professionally qualified and well integrated in the work, while the learner starts the process in a much weaker and more marginal position. But it is decisive that the relationship between the two is equal and friendly.
>
> (Billett 2011: 90, cited in Illeris 2011)

An 'equal' and 'friendly' relationship is ideal in supporting progression but one should be aware that in reality this may not always be the case. Equally, within a working relationship there needs to be professional boundaries that transcend friendship. Working alongside colleagues deepens our learning; reinforces professional identity, principles and values; and is fundamental in helping to interpret and understand the building blocks that construct professional formation and competence.

Through the process of professional formation in the workplace, you will come to understand the importance of effective and reflective practice (Chapter 11) and supervision (Chapter 10), and be aware of how it may differ in a range of settings. As multi-agency and interprofessional working increases you may find that you can be in more than one setting for assessed practice. Increasingly employers need youth work professionals who can transfer their skills into a range of settings.

Preparing for practice

The conscious competence ladder in Figure 2.1 overleaf is a useful tool when beginning to consider your starting point for practice. Developed in the 1970s, the ladder is designed to help us think about the various stages we go through in developing new skills (Adams, undated). In this context we will use it to focus on experience, knowledge and awareness of practice skills before work-based learning begins.

Looking at the four levels, how is the ladder interpreted?

Level 1: Unconscious Incompetence (You don't know that you don't know)

At this level you may lack necessary knowledge and skills in areas you are required to work in. However, key to this is being unaware of this lack of skill. Essentially, this might be like sitting behind a steering wheel for the very first time, having never even been a car passenger. Our confidence at wanting to be a great driver will not be matched by knowledge and skills. Looking at the dashboard of a car will bamboozle us as we try to work out what each of the controls might do. However, given that we have never even seen a car function – we do not yet know what we don't know!

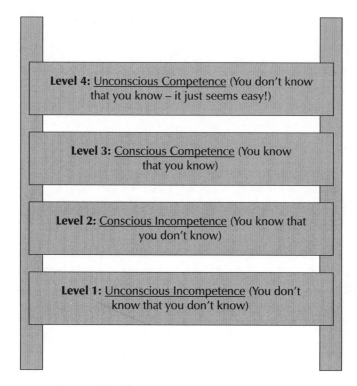

Figure 2.1 The conscious competence ladder

Level 2: Conscious Incompetence (You know that you don't know)

At this level you realise that there are skills you need to learn and may be surprised to see that there are others much more competent than you. As you realise your ability is limited, your confidence drops. You go through an uncomfortable period as you learn these new skills to develop the competence others may possess. You might wonder if you are ever going to get to grips with the requirements of the work. Think of the driver who tells their friend of their struggles to reach the balance between a clutch and accelerator whilst the friend speaks confidently of their own mastery of the car's controls.

Level 3: Conscious Competence (You know that you know)

At this level you acquire the new skills and knowledge. You put your learning into practice and you gain confidence in carrying out the tasks or jobs involved. You are aware of your new skills and can work on refining them. You are still concentrating on the performance of these activities, but as you get ever more practice and experience, these become increasingly automatic. As we prepare for our driving test, we may be attuned to the small mistakes we make or the ways in which we need to perform better behind the wheel.

Level 4: Unconscious Competence (You don't know that you know – it just seems easy!)

At this level your new skills become second nature and you perform the task without conscious effort and with automatic ease. This is the peak of your confidence and ability, and because you learnt competence consciously you can now apply the rules habitually and unconsciously. Newly qualified drivers therefore can balance clutch and accelerator, but they can also get distracted when driving as their confidence levels increase. The challenge for new drivers and for youth work practitioners at this level is to remain focused on reflective practice to avoid becoming complacent.

Reflection 2.1

- What is your starting point on the conscious competence ladder as you embark upon your first practice experience?
- At what level is your understanding of practice requirements and expectations?

When starting a workplace learning experience it is common for students to have a sense of uncertainty and to feel out of their comfort zone, but as skills develop and they integrate into the staff team and organisational structure, their confidence grows alongside the new professional skills they are developing. Below are reflections from a student, following her first assessed practice experience:

> When I first went into the organisation it was very daunting because it was in a new city, a new environment and new type of youth work in a context that I had never worked in before. I was also conscious of the age of the young people as they were a similar age to me if not older. It unnerved me because I wasn't sure if they would accept me as their youth worker. Throughout my placement the staff team was friendly. In the beginning I think they were wary of me coming to the project as they had preconceived ideas of a student. Throughout my time at the placement they aided me with different difficulties I was having and I built a good relationship with them. I believe that the key to having a good placement is building relationships with the staff team and putting 100 per cent into working, because 'what you put in you get out' and I believe this ideology helped me have a successful placement.

> The overall placement was brilliant. I have learnt a lot about myself, about people and how to work effectively with them but also about parts of society that I had never experienced before. I feel that the experience will help me throughout the rest of my career as a youth worker. Be organised – it's tough, hard work but definitely worth it!

Organising your workload is essential as poor organisation and time management can lead to feeling stressed and potential failure or breakdown of practice. Combining classroom teaching time and academic work with placement hours can be challenging. There can be a sense of urgency to get on and tackle individual tasks when the workload is great. This however can lead to compromising time needed to reflect on work in order to improve practice and develop skills. Good planning at the start of the process and having an overview of all of the required tasks within a given time frame will give a sense of well-being and control.

It is important to recognise what our individual attitudes are to learning. Would you describe yourself as an 'active' or 'passive' learner? Passive learning can be seen as accepting without question, hearing but not absorbing, learning by rote, cramming before assignments and lectures, waiting for instruction, being disengaged, doing the bare minimum. Active learning can be defined by questioning, thinking, reflecting, regular reading, engaging, seeking and learning from feedback. Dynamics in the classroom and workplace will differ but learning is the primary focus of both. In Chapter 3, we explore the value of thinking about your own 'learning identity' but a message when preparing for practice is that 'there are no short cuts to high quality learning. It is important to immerse yourself as much as you can' (Moore *et al.* 2010: 6).

Structured induction into the practice agency plays an important part in being able to deliver the work in a confident and informed manner. Doel describes the process as: 'orientation . . . Because it differentiates your introduction to the placement from induction that a new worker might receive' (2010: 48).

The team you will work with need a clear understanding of your role with them and to consider the difference in focus between a volunteer in the organisation and a student on placement.

Effective and structured induction into the agency is important before face-to-face work and other duties begin. Poor induction can lead to poor practice, leaving the worker unable to fulfil their duties in an empowered and confident manner. If there is uncertainty around policies, agency structures and values the worker can feel oppressed and overly dependent on their supervisor and other workers to make sure they 'get it right'. This blocks learning and personal development and could lead to serious consequences for the student who unknowingly works outside of a policy. For example if when working with an individual they disclose abuse to you and you respond inappropriately and outside of the safeguarding policy, then the outcome for the young person could be compromised and you could face disciplinary procedures. You also need to be aware of a whole range of other policies including risk assessment, lone working, confidentiality, expenses and other finance claims, use of email and social media sites, dress code, behaviour codes and sanctions, sick leave and lines of communication, management structures and lines of accountability, to name a few. Being aware of the importance of induction will allow you to help guide and influence the process in the practice agency.

Working with supervisors and workplace dynamics

The word 'supervision' has many definitions and interpretations, for example we may talk about carefully supervising children at play to minimise risk. Supervision orders are used to monitor the behaviour of offenders; we have lunchtime supervisors in the school dinner hall. For some people it can have negative connotations suggesting that a person has to be watched to make sure they do not step out of line. 'Supervision is one of those irritating words that holds a particular meaning for certain people, and quite different associations for others' (Marken and Payne 1987: 23). Therefore as we explore the supervisory element of practice we need to be clear of its meaning and the value it holds in the practice process for youth and community workers: 'Effective Supervision can often be the difference between: success and failure, stress and job satisfaction; worry and reassurance; good practice and excellent practice. Its significant role should therefore not be underestimated' (Thompson 2007: 157). We need to know what to expect from supervision and have a clear understanding of the roles of all who are involved in the process. Roles and models of supervision are considered further in Chapter 10. Your supervisor is the person who will guide you through the practice experience and help you to reflect on your work, so the relationship you have with them will be a significant one.

There are probably as many ways of approaching the supervision process as there are supervisors in the world! Above all it is important that the process is transparent and collaborative where all parties understand their role and that the model of supervision is agreed from the outset: 'the wrong balance, for example where there is an over-emphasis on accountability, may lead to a situation where workers feel unable to share problems or openly discuss their practice' (Pugh 2010: 151). Individual supervisors will have different approaches and some may not have a background or qualification in youth and community development work. With this in mind, it is important that you begin the process in an informed and confident way, making sure practice and personal requirements are met.

Because we bring our individual strengths, skills and attitudes into the workplace, understanding and capturing our learning can be difficult. Fenwick (2009) highlights the various layers of complexity when she discusses:

> how to conceptualise and assess professional learning in ways that honour the complexities of practice and expertise, and that acknowledge more fully the important connectivities among different learning actors, among actors and tools, routines and architectures structuring their work; among actors and the institutions of professional associations, workplace and academic disciplinary knowledge; and among actors and the emerging collective knowledge and action in which they are enmeshed.
>
> (Fenwick 2009: 237)

This suggests that the dynamics of workplace learning are complex and will differ according to the people involved and the context of the practice. If we consider the different settings where work with young people takes place we can begin the possible impact of dynamics. For example, consider these two different settings:

- *An alternative curriculum provider* where young people spend perhaps three days a week out of their usual school setting. It may be that some of the young people display challenging behaviour. Within that setting there is likely to be a structured curriculum and the participants will not engage voluntarily. There could be a team of professionals involved, for example teachers, social workers, youth offending team, youth workers, educational psychologists and speech and language therapists. The youth worker will need to use his or her informal education skills in order to effectively build a meaningful relationship with the young person. They will need to contribute in such a way that allows for informal education methods, values and principles to be integrated into the more formal structure.

- *A local authority Youth and Community Centre.* This provision offers youth clubs five nights a week. Young people engage voluntarily and are supported in the sessions by Youth workers and additional invited specialists who contribute to the informal learning curriculum. The student will work alongside other youth workers and may deal with the premises officer and other local authority personnel as required. The programme is developed in consultation with the young people and based on their identified needs. The ethos of each session is based on informal education methods, principles and values, and whilst there may be contact with other professionals working alongside a young person, or contact with their family, this would all be secondary to the main focus of the work.

From these two examples it is clear that each workplace setting will have a different dynamic which the student will need to adapt to and find their role within whilst at the same time working within the values and principles of youth work.

As informal educators whose primary focus is the welfare and well-being of young people and communities, we expect to see effective collaborative relationships in the workplace that acknowledge issues of power and have anti-oppressive practice at their core. It would be naïve not to recognise the tensions and power struggles that can occur within organisations and potentially within the supervisory relationship. Therefore, a positive pro-active approach is needed from the outset of practice in order to develop and maintain good working relationships: 'Power can be a constraint on open conversation and has the potential to undermine the critical capacity of dialogue. It is therefore essential for supervisors and supervisees to raise the issue of power' (Kogler 2012: 101, cited in Ord 2012).

To understand issues of power we can refer back to Illeris's suggestion that awareness of self and one's experience of life is important in the learning process. Thompson's (2001, 2006) PCS model explores how oppression operates at personal, cultural and structural levels (see Chapter 14 for further discussion). Appling this analysis to our own work context can help us to understand and identify how power might influence workplace dynamics.

Some organisations may not place a high value on or measure the effectiveness of good supervision in workforce development or professional formation. There can be differences between the sectors where work is located. In some organisations there may not be a culture of regular staff supervision and this can cause difficulties for a student who is placed there, as they can be disadvantaged by not being supported and assessed adequately. This highlights the importance for placements to be vetted and protocols agreed. Your practice supervisor should be someone who is committed to the process as defined by your training institution and is able to timetable regular supervision sessions with you. You should expect to be assessed in a fair and rigorous way so that at the end of the practice there is clear evidence of competence as a youth worker at the required level.

We will consider the roles of two key people in the practice experience: that of the student – the supervisee; and that of the member of staff who will supervise and assess performance – the supervisor.

What makes a good supervisor and supervisee?

> Tell me, and I will forget.
> Show me and I may remember.
> Involve me and I will understand.
>
> (Confucius, 450BC)

The role of the supervisor

Openness and transparency in the relationship is important, with the learner having a say in selecting their supervisor.

> this works best if the learner chooses his or her own guide . . . at the very least the learner should be able to freely express an opinion on the appointed guide, because, if learner and guide do not get on well, a reasonable learning process seldom gets under way.
>
> (Billett, cited in Illeris 2011: 91)

This however poses problem as few students have a choice in who will supervise and assess their learning but we may also find other peers or colleagues who support in this 'guiding' role.

As would be expected, the majority of managers and supervisors in the workplace are professional in their approach to the supervision responsibilities they have either agreed to undertake or those that are given as part of their role in the workplace. Having agreed to a student placement there is an expectation that they will follow the requirements of the practice, offering constructive feedback and regular supervision sessions. How will you know what to look for in a good supervisor?

Table 2.1 overleaf suggests some of the attributes you would expect from an effective supervisor.

However – what if you come across a supervisor who does not display these attributes? One student shared a particularly challenging case:

> My supervisor seemed under a lot of pressure and was late when I had my initial placement interview, but she was keen to have me in the youth centre as they were short staffed. She agreed to come to the training at university but at the last minute had to go to a meeting, so was sent the pack of information. We met to develop the

Table 2.1 An effective supervisor

An effective supervisor is someone who . . .	✓
Has the relevant qualifications and experience in the field of work.	
Is competent in and has experience of supervising and assessing students on placement.	
Is committed to anti-oppressive practice.	
Understands and practices the values, methods and principles of informal education.	
Understands the dynamics of a multi-agency context and within that is able to support the unique role of the youth worker.	
Is active in reading, understanding and facilitating the specific practice requirements thereby supporting professional formation.	
Can negotiate and support development of the plan of work for the placement to meet the practice requirements and time frame.	
Is clear about their own role within the organisation and their accountability within the management structure.	
Is aware of professional boundaries, potential conflict of interest and confidentiality.	
Understands the importance of protecting supervision time and meeting space so that they are free from interruptions, thereby allowing progress and assessment of the student's performance in the workplace to be discussed in a meaningful way.	
Knows the purpose and importance of recording supervision.	
Will attend institutional briefing or training sessions as required and is willing to liaise with academic and support staff from the training institution.	
Knows the importance of induction into a new organisation and facilitates this for the student, thereby allowing them to work in an empowered way within the organisational policies and values.	
Identifies as a role model and resource for reflective practice.	
Is able to meet the time demands that a student placement makes and has the support of their manager or organisation.	
Is aware of race, gender, disability or sexuality issues for the student and possible implications during practice.	
Identifies as a learner.	

practice plan but because she had to answer a number of phone calls she suggested I go away and do a draft and send it to her via email. The project is a busy one and although we timetabled supervision sessions as part of the plan, I am now half way through the practice and have not had a formal supervision session. I am worried as I am not confident my supervisor can accurately assess my performance and write a true interim report to be sent to my tutor. There is little opportunity to reflect on my work or consolidate my learning and for me to know how I am doing. Others in my group in different settings seem to be having a much better experience than me.

Reflection 2.2

- How is this student disadvantaged?
- What actions should this student take?

In the above scenario we see a supervisor who wants to support a student on placement but is struggling for time to engage in the required way. In such a case the student could communicate their concerns directly to the supervisor and if it was difficult to speak to them then an email would suffice. Their academic tutor should also be notified that the supervision and support being given is not adequate. If things do not improve then the tutor could instigate a concerns meeting.

In setting up the supervision process there is potential for difficulty, and the reasons may be complex and unavoidable. Thompson and Thompson (2008: 150) suggest that: 'We can ignore that culture and make sure that our own actions are not unduly influenced by it. In doing so, this gives us the opportunity to lead by example'. Cultures are not easy to ignore or change when on placement but by staying focused on what should be taking place, professional formation and learning is possible even in difficult situations. To lead by example is to stay focused and try to reinforce best practice where possible.

The role of the student

Table 2.2 overleaf will support the student in effectively fulfilling their role and help them to influence the learning culture.

In the same way that some supervisors fall short of expectations, supervisors can also recall situations where students have had a negative impact upon their placements. One supervisor told us of one such example:

Initially the student seemed very enthusiastic and keen to please. We negotiated supervision times to fit around their part-time work and placement demands. The student has been consistently late and is unprepared for the sessions. He does not appear to see himself as an integral part of the team or seem to see the need to take responsibility for himself and the work.

Table 2.2 An effective student

An effective student is someone who . . . ✓

Has attended all of the practice teaching sessions and is familiar with the practice requirements.

Can identify their learning needs alongside the practice requirements.

Takes ownership of their practice experience.

Takes induction seriously and can locate themselves and their role within the agency context.

Is aware of the meaning of professional engagement and endeavours to implement the agency's policies and values.

Understands the role and purpose of supervision.

Has a concept of self and understands the experience they bring to the practice setting.

Contributes in a meaningful way to developing a professional working relationship with their supervisor and workplace colleagues.

Has a clear understanding of what is meant by reflective practice.

Understand the methods, values and principles of informal education.

Understands and demonstrates anti-oppressive practice in all aspects of their work.

Can demonstrate how reading and theory impact on their practice.

Reflection 2.3

- What are the issues that need to be addressed by the student?
- What actions do you consider the supervisor should take?

In this scenario it would seem that the student is not taking the practice experience seriously, does not see themselves as an employee and has not grasped workplace expectations. It could be concluded that the student does not want to be there. Perhaps they enjoy the theoretical part of the coursework but do not want to engage in the practice hours. It could be that they are having difficulties of some kind. Whatever the reason for the poor engagement there needs to be a meeting with the supervisor and tutor to discuss the situation.

In conclusion, if both supervisor and supervisee are aware of their roles and approach these in a professional manner, the result will provide the best opportunity to develop a mutually beneficial learning relationship.

Reflection 2.4

- What is your understanding and experience of supervision in the workplace?
- How similar or different is this from supervision requirements for practice?
- What are your expectations from the relationship with your supervisor?
- What do you think the workplace supervisor will expect from you?

A professional approach to practice

There are particular expectations of professional workers. There are a number of definitions of the term 'professional' but in this context we draw on Banks (2010b: 5), who identifies 'youth work as a specialist occupation'. Any specialist, whether it is a teacher, nurse, doctor, social worker or youth worker, brings the right mix of skills, attitude and conduct to inspire confidence and offer appropriate support to the people they are working with.

For professionals, ethical dilemmas and problems can occur on a daily basis and the challenge is how well equipped we are to deal with each situation as it arises (see Chapter 4). In the workplace there can be situations that demand the full use of your abilities and skills, so in order to make a success of practice you need to be aware of what is expected of you as a professional. How we conduct our relationships with others plays an important role here. In the example of practice experience of a placement student given earlier in the chapter, she was concerned about being close in age to the young people she was working with. This can present dilemmas with regard to how best to conduct and present yourself. How do you build effective relationships that develop trust? Above all, being aware of professional boundaries both with young people and colleagues will support effective working practices (Chapter 4).

Getting ready

As stated earlier, the practice experience can be a confusing and complex one; therefore, organising and managing oneself is pivotal to success. The IPAC model (see Table 2.3 overleaf) is a useful tool to help with structured planning and preparation.

- I – Introducing (Before practice begins)
- P – Preparing (Getting ready for face-to-face work)
- A – Acting (Delivering the work)
- C – Consequence (Learning gained from the experience)

Table 2.3 The IPAC model

Introducing	**Before practice begins** • Getting to know your supervisor and colleagues within the working team. • Agreeing supervision model and structure. • Induction into the organisation policies and values as well as those of service delivery partners. • Agreeing the plan of work-days, times and tasks. • Awareness of management structures and funding streams. • Awareness of the community context of the agency where practice is located. • Awareness of potential issues of power, hierarchy and the working dynamics of the organisation. • Locating your role within the university's practice requirements. • Setting up and agreeing effective communication methods with your institution's tutors and others who are supporting you.
Preparing	**Before each session** • Are you clear what your role will be in the session? • Who will you be working with? • Have you done the planning required? • Are you appropriately dressed? • Where is this work located in your practice plan? • Will the session allow you to demonstrate the required level of work needed for practice? • What assessment criteria do you hope to meet in this session?
Acting	**Throughout the session** • Are you fully engaged with the young people and colleagues? • Are you working collaboratively where appropriate? • Is the work going according to your plan? • Are you managing time within the set limits? • How are you feeling about your role in delivering the work?
Consequence	**Following the session** Make notes in a reflective diary following each session and consider: • How did I feel during and after the session? • Did I receive any feedback from colleagues about my performance? • Have I made notes on the session which I can develop and take for discussion to supervision? • What might I do differently next time? Why? • What learning did I gain? • How do these learning gains sit with practice assessment requirements? • What skills have I refined or developed in the session? Could I have gained more? If so how? • What further actions if any do I need to take following the session?

Reflection 2.5

Consider a past workplace experience you have had. Look again at that experience alongside the IPAC model. On reflection how well prepared were you in that work? What similar strategies will you use in this new workplace experience? What might be different?

Conclusion

This chapter began by looking at the workplace as a learning environment and considered how our past experiences, attitudes and learning can influence the process of skills development and professional formation. Supervision expectations, workplace dynamics and the importance of developing professional relationships were considered.

Workplace learning will be most effective if the student is motivated, manages their time well, can make the links between theory and practice, uses reflection as an aid to professional and skills development and is an effective communicator.

In time and with the use of our guides along the way, good practice can become embedded and we may find ourselves climbing the conscious competence ladder.

3 | Locating the self

Introduction

Sydney J. Harris, the journalist, once said:

> Ninety percent of the world's woes come from people not knowing themselves, their abilities, their frailties, and even their real virtues. Most of us go all the way through life as complete strangers to ourselves – so how can we know anyone else?

What makes you who you are? How do you understand the world? What is your place in it? And why are these questions important for youth and community workers? It is the premise of this chapter that skilled practitioners need to know who they are in order to be able to practise effectively. They need to be aware of their values, attitudes and beliefs because there is a correlation between these and how they engage with, experience, understand and interpret the world, including the context and relationships of practice. In order to understand and work effectively with others, we must first understand ourselves; to undertake what Whitaker (1989: 193) calls our 'internal work'. This necessitates taking an active and critical stance if we are genuinely seeking new self-knowledge. The primary focus of this chapter is to take the reader on a journey by means of undertaking three exercises. Through these tasks we will explore:

- how we define ourselves and the implications of these definitions;
- our place in society and the impact this has on us; and finally
- the significance of our life experiences and how they help shape who we are.

Throughout the chapter, it is vital for the reader to engage with the information presented, taking into consideration three different but core perspectives, namely:

- how to better understand yourself; which will then help you to
- better understand others; in order to
- positively develop your practice.

Defining ourselves

'Who am I?' On the surface this appears to be a deceptively easy question. Surely we know ourselves better than anyone else? It is only when we try to answer the question that we recognise how difficult it is. Physically, as humans, we are all essentially the same but we like to think of ourselves as being unique individuals with a distinct identity.

Let's begin by exploring how we see ourselves.

Exercise 1

Write down 8 sentences that begin with, 'I am...............'

Ask your colleagues or peers to do the same

For example, if I did this task I might start with:

'I am the author of this chapter'

I am..

I am..

I am..

I am..

I am..

I am..

I am..

I am..

- How have you defined yourself and how did your colleague/peer define themself?
- What are the similarities/differences and what does this tell us?
- Do any particular patterns or categories emerge?
- Are some more important or meaningful than others?

Exercise 1 helps us to begin the process of understanding how we see ourselves and others through the various descriptions and categories we use. Psychologists have found that age, sex and race are the primary categories when we think about other people; they occur automatically, being 'spontaneous, unreflective and uncontrollable and cannot be avoided' (Blaine 2007: 22). One of the reasons for this may be that they are visible physical characteristics and easily identifiable categories that help to organise and simplify the great many stimuli we encounter all the time within our social world. This tallies with our understanding of perceptual processes (Glassman and Hadad 2013). Perception is an active and complex process whereby we:

- select certain stimuli from the millions available to us everyday;
- categorise them so that the incoming information is more manageable; and then
- interpret the information based on our prior experiences and expectations – what we see is not a passive mirroring of the world but an active ordering.

Hence we tend to categorise groups of people under one simple heading, for example, 'woman' or 'disabled' and then we interpret these categories, that is, we have a view about what they mean, with expectations for behaviour. This links to stereotyping, which is essentially a special case of categorisation that involves an exaggeration of similarities within groups and of differences between groups (Brown 2010). The key issue for us as practitioners here is that our expectations of other people's personalities or capabilities may influence the way we treat them, thereby impacting on our ability to practise anti-oppressively. This may in turn influence their behaviour in such a way that confirms our expectations. There are also evident dangers and inherent inaccuracies in defining anyone by one simple heading, one single dimension of identity, when the reality is that we can all claim multiple and shifting dimensions that encompass our identity.

Reflection 3.1

Read Chapter 1, 'Behaviour and Psychology', in Glassman and Hadad's (2013: 5–13) *Approaches to Psychology*. This is a very accessible introduction to the processes of perception and the interaction of these processes with our life experiences.

In this chapter, we are introduced to the idea of naïve realism and to the idea that the relationship between ourselves and the outside world is more complex than we might initially think. So, when you read these pages, consider the following:

- Before you read this, did you believe that what you saw was a true representation of what was out there, rather like how a video camera records a scene? How far were you guilty of 'naïve realism'?
- Can you begin to recognise how far your previous experiences and expectations influence what you see?
- Have you ever misjudged someone when you first met them? How far was this due to a stereotype, or a personal schema?

Alongside the primary categorisations mentioned earlier, other likely categorisations you may have used for Exercise 1 include:

- Physical characteristics, e.g. tall. These aspects of our identity are what make us unique as individuals.
- Social roles, e.g. student. We all play a number of different roles throughout our lives. This relates to our memberships of groups.
- Psychological traits, e.g. outgoing. These traits are not necessarily permanent and may vary within different contexts; they are personal characteristics developed within a social environment.

How many of these factors were in your eight sentences from the 'I am . . .' exercise? What are the importance and relevance of this to your practice? For example, how far are you influenced by stereotypes associated with physical characteristics? How might this affect your view of someone who has a very different identity to yours?

If the research is correct, then it is likely that you had some if not all of the three primary categories in your list. This is important because it is not the identification and salience of these factors per se that is significant, but rather the meanings that are attached to them; there are no aspects of our social identity (a concept we will return to later) that are value-free. For example our sex provides us and others with a major part of our identity, given the cultural and historical weight of meaning given to it. 'Whether a child is a boy or girl shapes our expectations of its behaviour, activities, interests, feelings, emotions, sexuality, self-identity, ways of relating to other people and its future' (Burkitt 2008: 111). Reflect for a moment on this. How far do you agree with such a statement in terms of your own perceptions and expectations of others? How far do you think other people use these social categories as a means of understanding others?

Certainly, we are all raised with the shared cultural knowledge of what it means to be a male or female within our society. This then suggests that many of the features with which we choose to identify ourselves are not simply descriptive but also *prescriptive*, that is, they inform us about how we should be acting. Indeed, how society decrees we should be acting in a certain role both influences and constrains us. Consider the example of a parent/carer. Our expectations are that they will be nurturing and put us, their children, before themselves. But when do we begin to see our parents as individuals in their own right? Or in another role such as an employee, a lover, a friend? How far do we constrain them in their role as our parent/carer?

It is evident that within society we have a shared understanding and expectation of given social roles. This in turn can lead us to make judgements of others based on our perception of their performance in those roles. However, it is our duty as practitioners to actively work against falling back on such shared social and cultural stereotypes. If we do not, we are in danger that such stereotypes may serve to limit our expectations and allow us to underestimate the potential of some of the young people we work with.

Personal and social identity

Thinking about your answers to Exercise 1, 'I am . . .', now try to categorise them by identifying which are personal to you and which are shared with others.

Personal	Shared

The idea here is that, essentially, we can develop two principal identities that can define who we are and which we use to develop our sense of self in the world:

- A personal identity, which refers to self-knowledge that derives from the individual's unique attributes, for example their physical characteristics or psychological traits.
- A social identity, which encompasses information derived from membership of social groups to which they belong. Some social identities relate to enduring social categories, such as ethnicity or nationality; other social identities relate to dynamic groups, such as sports teams or clubs, in which membership is not necessarily permanent.

There are three interesting considerations when thinking about these aspects of our identity.

(1) Facets of our identity vary in the extent to which they are actively chosen by us. For example, we can choose whether to be a Tottenham Hotspurs fan but we have no (or limited) choice over whether we are black or white, male or female, and, as has been discussed previously, these labels are value-laden; they have a significant impact on how individuals see themselves and how they are perceived and treated by others.

(2) Regarding our social identity, some labels are ascribed to us by others through what they see, as with the three primary categories of age, sex and race. However, the extent to which we identify with and accept the label will vary (e.g. Jenkins 2008). This can cause conflict. One example is that many young people with disabilities struggle against being defined by their disability, yet social categorisations often occur based on distinctive features we cannot help but notice (Blaine 2007), for example a physical disability or wheelchair use. So for most people, this will be the key salient factor and the one they use to determine how they relate to a young disabled person. They will draw on the shared social script regarding the role we play with people in this 'group', often falling back on stereotypes to guide their behaviour (French and Swain 2004).

Task 3.1

Read French and Swain's chapter in *Youth in Society* (2004) entitled 'Young Disabled People' (Chapter 22, pages 199–206). Here, they discuss how stereotyped ideas of young disabled people adversely affect their self-image and self-confidence. Consider these ideas in the light of your own practice.

(3) How far does your identity change and what are the factors involved? How we present ourselves to others may vary from one setting to another (think of how you behave in a pub and in a theatre) and with who we are with (consider your behaviour with your boss versus your partner); and we change and develop as we come into contact with different people with different ideas (for example, when conversing with other students or indigenous people from other countries). 'In the modern world we are engaged in so many activities that take place in a variety of contexts with a mixture of people, we become many different things to different people' (Burkitt 2008: 1).

In essence, we form and re-form who we are through comparison with others and this helps us to define and refine ourselves; this can be a conscious or unconscious process. Indeed, much of what we know about ourselves comes through interaction with others. Our social identities and our behaviour and thinking are influenced by others; we react to and learn from other people's expectations. Further, we act and speak according to our assessments of the expectations of others and the roles we inhabit. We are therefore not always consistent as we perform differently in different circumstances. Therefore, part of the 'internal work' we need to do is to try to become more aware of the impact and influence other people have on us and the consequences of this for our own values and behaviour. This will help us develop our self-awareness. It is also important to understand and acknowledge how social interaction influences how we perceive others, for example, what do we presume of new people we encounter? Let us summarise some of the earlier points to help us answer this question.

In Britain, when we meet someone for the first time, a question often asked is, 'What do you do?' This tells us: whether the person is employed or unemployed; how much they might earn; their social class and status; and their likely lifestyle, skills and possibly interests. From the answers to this seemingly simple question, we feel that we can make an informed judgement about the sort of person they are and our feelings towards them. The problem with such judgements is that they are based on stereotypes which often include biases and distortions. This seemingly inoffensive question might also unwittingly make those whose work is deemed low in status feel uncomfortable and unhappy in having to identify themselves in such terms.

Our tendency is to use easily accessible categories or labels, usually based on dimensions of social difference (Blaine 2007). Although you may not know an individual personally, you make assumptions based upon their visible membership of a social group or groups, and these social categories are tools for viewing and evaluating them. Therefore, belonging to a group within society, for example being a member of a particular political party or a supporter of a football team, can be a highly significant aspect of our sense of identity.

As practitioners, we need to be aware of our use of such stereotypes and work hard to (a) bring them into our consciousness and (b) avoid making judgements about people based on these over-simplistic categorisations; instead, we need to find out about them as individuals. How often have you been misjudged? How did you feel as a result?

Membership of social groups will affect us in complex ways, some of which are positive because they add to our sense of self and belonging; others are more negative because they have the potential to undermine our self-confidence and limit our opportunities, depending upon how they are perceived by others. For example, the label of 'young offender' is likely to be detrimental to an individual's psychological well-being as well as their future prospects.

Playing a role

Our behaviour and that of others can be understood by considering the roles and scripts we perform daily. These roles are not a fixed part of our identity but are dynamic and evolving; they are part of who we are and, to an extent, we can choose which role to play and when. This draws on the seminal work of Goffman (1959), who uses the metaphor of drama to explain how we choose to present ourselves to others through the roles we play, and how the 'self' in this sense is socially constructed. Beckett and Taylor (2010: 167) invite us to ask ourselves some questions to help us to consider the various roles we play. The following task uses some of their questions:

Task 3.2

- What roles do you play currently in your life? For example, student, daughter.
- Which are the most important roles for you? Why?
- Which ones are you most comfortable with? Why is this?
- Which do you find challenging? Why do you think this is?
- Are there any roles which you would like to play but don't? Or from which you feel excluded for any reason?

The metaphor of drama can be extended to the use of a mask, which is the front we portray to others, with our private thoughts and feelings underneath, out of sight. However, we can choose to 'lift' the mask in order to examine the hidden thoughts, feelings, attitudes and beliefs in an attempt to achieve a deeper understanding. Let us consider how this may work in practice.

During supervision, a student confided that she had experienced an uncomfortable situation whilst on practice, working with refugees and asylum seekers. During a conversation about employment, one of the young people had asked what her partner did. She felt she could not tell the truth about him being a soldier and so made up what she considered would be a socially acceptable job to these young people.

There are many problematic issues here but two key considerations are:

- The student's dishonesty: being honest, genuine and authentic are key values that ought to underpin all practice with young people (Banks 2010b; Jeffs and Smith 2010). The student felt that she could not 'lift her mask' and share with the young people her feelings of discomfort; she felt she needed to detach herself personally and to maintain a professional distance. The consequence of this was that she lied to them, a questionable decision if she wants to develop effective working relationships with them, and by lying, she denied them all the opportunity to engage in some potentially powerful exploration and learning about roles, beliefs and values.
- Resorting to assumptions and stereotypes: the student assumed that all refugees and asylum seekers have problems with soldiers and the army, and that to admit to a relationship with a soldier would therefore jeopardise her working relationship with them. This stereotype adversely influenced her understanding of these young people, thereby limiting the work she did with them by underestimating their ability to engage with the issues. In practice, we are in a position not only to lift our own mask but to help and encourage others to lift their masks where appropriate: 'looking behind the mask encourages us to look beyond the automatic assumptions; beyond that which is obvious about ourselves and others' (Baim *et al.* 2002: 20). In this instance, the student denied the young people this opportunity.

This is an important process for practitioners where being genuine and authentic is critical to developing effective and honest relationships. In order to achieve this, it is necessary to understand the role you are playing and why, whilst recognising your 'hidden' thoughts and feelings, and perhaps sharing these where relevant and helpful to do so. This does not deny the complexities involved concerning the matter of self-disclosure. Practitioners must judge when it may be appropriate to share and when it may be acceptable to lie. The issue of personal and professional boundaries is complex (see Chapter 4). Essentially, recognising why someone may be asking you for personal information and why you may or may not be willing to tell them is crucial.

Social context

The number of characteristics that can be used as the basis of identity is almost unlimited, as we are sure you discovered from undertaking the first task 'I am . . .'. In reality, a whole range of different factors contribute to making us who we are, acting as a complex interlocking web, where it is often difficult to assess the respective contribution of each factor (Green 2010). So far we have explored some of the most common categories and definitions used to identify who we are and some of the implications of these. The next step in the journey is to begin to explore how the social context into which we are born and live has a significant influence on the person we become. The following reflective exercise illustrates this point.

Reflection 3.2

Boy A

Boy B

Figure 3.1 The social context of young people: Boy A and Boy B

Source: © Shutterstock

Boy A is from Glasgow. He left the local comprehensive school at 16 with no qualifications and no job, and his prospects of finding work are poor; neither of his parents is employed.

Boy B is from Guildford, Surrey. He has decided to continue his education at a well-known public school in order to realise his ambition of going to Oxford, like his father. Both parents are doctors.

The life experiences and life chances of these two British white boys are likely to be extremely different.

- Why do you think this is?
- What are some of the likely differences?

Again, there are a number of potentially important factors to consider here. These include:

- genetic inheritance;
- the extent to which they have access to financial capital;
- upbringing, early relationships, position in the family, parental attitudes and values;
- social history, e.g. growing up during a time of significant economic depression;
- location within the social and structural hierarchies of gender, age, race and social class;
- location and roles within the institutional orders of religion, work and community;
- geographic context, e.g. region of the country, rural or urban, and so on;
- membership in and relative identifications with various social groups.

Indeed, the position into which we are born and live, which is the culmination of the above factors, will have a significant influence on the person we become. For example, a child born in a Glasgow suburb can expect a life 28 years shorter than another living only 13 kilometres away (WHO report 2008). The crucial point here is that none of these ways of categorising ourselves and others is value-free, so how we perceive ourselves, how we are perceived and how we perceive others are hugely important. Specifically:

- Such categories can lead to very different social conditions. Consider what it would be like to be born as boy A or boy B.
- When in a particular social group there are consequences, that is, expectations about how you look, how you behave, how you are perceived. Just look at the photos above to see the reality of this. What judgements might you make about boy A or boy B?
- What judgements might boy A make about boy B and vice versa? What might inform these judgements?

- These social identity phenomena are closely linked to power and wealth. Consider the likely employment prospects of both boys and the almost inevitable power and wealth differentials that will result from this.

In this sense, life is rather like a card game where you begin with a particular hand. Some start with a very good hand and are thereby at a significant advantage (boy B) and others start with a very poor hand and are in a relatively highly disadvantaged position (boy A). Thus, where and to whom we are born affects our life chances in so many ways. It shapes how we perceive ourselves and are perceived by others. This is especially important given that some labels are powerful forces of social exclusion.

This leads us to Exercise 2. This task aims to help you to further develop your understanding of who you are by placing you within your social context, in essence to help you to map out your social identity.

One of the aims of this exercise is to provide a framework for understanding your own and other people's lives. We live in a diverse and changing society and yet many people believe that who they are within their social location is 'normal'. Undertaking this mapping exercise allows you to understand your own unique web of identities, and that everyone has their own specific web. Look at your answers:

- What do they tell you about yourself?
- Are you surprised by anything?

For the majority of us, we can locate ourselves simultaneously in positions of oppression and privilege. How far is this the case for you? For the young person you work with?

- What are the differences between you and the young person you work with, and how significant are they?
- What do you/have you taken for granted in your life that gives you power and opportunities that are not available to others?
- What judgements did you make about other people previously?
- How might these change having undertaken this exercise?
- What have you learnt?

Being aware of ourselves and our social location can help to militate against some of what might otherwise be the inevitable value judgements we make about other people, and which can get in the way of effective interactions. It can help us not to judge other people but rather to try to understand the reasons why they feel, think and act as they do and to open up our understanding to the possibilities of change. Indeed, 'we can never view ourselves or others in ways which are value-free, objective or neutral because our perceptions will always be filtered through the many layers of our own experience' (Crosby 2001: 55). Continuously undertaking 'internal work' may diminish some of the potentially negative consequences. We typically bring into our interactions with other people a set of beliefs and expectations about them. These operate in two ways: first, they guide the way we act towards others; and second, they influence the way others act towards us (Blaine 2007). As effective practitioners, we need to submit ourselves to a

Exercise 2

- What 'hand' have you been dealt? Locate yourself using the categories discussed. Add any others that you feel are important.
- Do the exercise again, but for a young person with whom you work.
- Where you position yourself in certain categories may change over time, so it might be interesting to consider how far your position has changed over the last five or ten years.

Category	Your position	Position of a young person with whom you work
Genetic inheritance		
Access to financial capital or resources		
Upbringing, early relationships, position in the family, parental attitudes and values		
Social history, e.g. growing up during a time of significant economic depression		
Location within the social and structural hierarchies of gender, age, race, disability, sexuality and social class		
Location and roles within the institutional orders of religion, work, community and dominant political ideologies		
Geographic context, e.g. region of the country, country vs town		
Membership in and relative identifications with various social groups		
Other relevant factor		

continuous process of reflection, checking and analysis, based on our understanding of our own and others' social location alongside the concomitant power differentials.

Life experiences

We can see that who we are has been constructed within a specific context (see Exercise 2). Although this provides a valuable insight into helping us to understand ourselves, by itself it is not sufficient. Most of those factors are relatively static and historical in nature, that is, they make up the particular 'hand of cards' we have been dealt. Arguably as important are the ongoing experiences we encounter throughout our lives. Such experiences help to shape the way we think about ourselves, others and the world in which we live, and some make us re-think/re-shape the way we see things. Given the potential importance of such experiences, reflecting on our own life experiences is a valuable exercise for a deeper self-understanding and personal-professional development.

Exercise 3 will provide you with the opportunity to think about the important events you have experienced and the effect those events have had on your thinking and your view of the world.

Our life experiences inevitably shape not only our personal worldview but the interactions we have with others through our work. One student on placement in a residential home for looked-after young people described how she was experiencing difficulties in this respect. She was struggling to become part of the staff team due to constant 'battles' with various members of staff. One example was that within the home, there were strict rules and regulations. The student consistently sought the views and opinions of the young people about these rules, wanting them to have their say; however, the staff felt that the young people needed these firm boundaries and that they should not be open to debate. The student was a care leaver herself and this was having a significant impact on her assessment of the placement and her evaluation of the needs of the resident young people. She felt strongly that the young people should be treated as she would have wanted to have been treated; she remembered strong feelings of disempowerment, having little say, with decisions being made for her.

A reflective and honest discussion during the midpoint assessment of her placement allowed the student to explore the impact that her experiences in care were having on her practice. It also enabled the staff team to understand why she was acting the way she was. The ensuing discussion resulted in finding a positive and mutually acceptable way forward.

Conclusion

It is evident that although some facets of our identity are relatively constant, we are continuously changing and developing in the light of life experiences. An analogy that may be useful is that who we are can be embodied within the contents of a rucksack that we carry with us through life (OSDE undated). The initial contents of this rucksack are those factors identified in Exercise 2 but we continue to add content to this

Exercise 3

Construct a significant life events chart. Mark on it what you would consider to be your most important and memorable experiences, both positive and negative. These may include experiences:

- you choose, e.g. to go to university, enter into a relationship
- outside your control but expected, e.g. leaving school
- outside your control and unexpected, e.g. bereavement, accidents, lottery win
- expected but not inevitable, e.g. becoming a parent, getting a home of your own
  (see Beckett and Taylor 2010: 17).

Your chart could be in the form of a timeline, starting from when you were born and then recording any significant life events in order of when they took place, for example:

———→

| May 1986 –
Born | Jan 1996 –
Dad left home | June 2000 –
Mum | Sept 2012 –
I went to uni
as mature |

Or, it may simply take the form of a table. Here, the life events might be in order of significance to you, in chronological order, or just randomly; whatever best suits you:

Date/time: when it happened	Significant life event	Description: why is was significant to you

Consider:
- What impact have your significant life events had on you?
- Have any of them changed the way you see yourself, others or the world in which you live?
- How far have past events affected your current thinking?
- How have you coped with change or with adversity?

rucksack as we go through life (Exercise 3), and our current rucksack is filled with the content of our life journey so far i.e. our knowledge, attitudes and values gleaned through our experiences, social context, history, upbringing, education, religion and so on. In this sense it is clear that no two people's rucksacks can hold exactly the same content because even if some parts of our identity are shared with others, our thoughts and experiences will differentiate us.

Our upbringing and life experiences mould our individuality. Nevertheless, through these experiences and our relationships with other people, we can learn to question our values and beliefs, to modify and change our actions and behaviour, and to develop our views of the world and our place within it. Through a questioning and critical stance, it is possible to recognise that previously taken-for-granted or unconscious stereotypes, unknown prejudices and ill-informed opinions can be challenged. It takes time and effort to examine our attitudes and behaviour in order to adapt what we experienced as a child into appropriate adult thinking and behaviour but an effective practitioner is one who knows what is in their rucksack and how it got there, and who is able to periodically unpack it in order to decide whether its contents are what they want and need. In this way, they can choose to:

- keep some of the content, e.g. positive traits of pro-social behaviour;
- discard some of the content, e.g. unhelpful stereotypes and prejudices; or
- borrow some content from others, e.g. attempts to learn strategies to enhance resilience.

For the best practitioners, this will be a continuous and ongoing process with clear links to effective reflective practice. Certainly, it is impossible to separate the actions of a worker from the thinking, attitudes and values that generate those actions (Carter *et al.* 1995), so to develop our self-awareness is an essential foundation of good practice. Individuals do not exist in a social vacuum; being self-aware therefore incorporates being socially aware, attuned to the wider contexts in which we work. Workers need to understand the world as it appears to those they are working with, each of whom has their own distinct rucksack; but in order to achieve this, they need to have done this work for themselves. It entails 'recognising and managing their own opinions and feelings so that they don't get in the way' (Crosby 2001: 55). People in professions such as youth and community development have to draw on their understanding of what makes us who we are and behave as we do, in order to assess situations and decide on actions. We have to draw constantly on our own resources (skills, knowledge and values), that is, our 'use of self' (Thompson 2006).

> When I do not know myself, I cannot know who my students are. I will see them through a glass darkly, in the shadows of my unexamined life.
>
> (Palmer 1998: 2)

This is what we are trying to help all practitioners to avoid.

4 | The ethical practitioner

Introduction

When we ask the questions 'Why do we do youth work?' and 'What do we hope to achieve?', we begin to encounter the questions of ethics. Ethics are the moral principles that govern our behaviour, and youth workers engage with young people for their own personal ethical motivations as well as their professional ones. Our work takes place within an 'ethical context' where young people face ethical issues on a daily basis. We encounter ethical dilemmas and ethical problems that can restrict what we are able to achieve. To guide us in making ethically sound decisions, we have a number of resources at our disposal.

This chapter reviews the 'everyday ethics' of youth work and provides an overview of some of the ethical codes of conduct that are designed to ensure ethical practice. Such codes are useful to establish the boundaries of youth work but in practice we also need to develop ways of nurturing ethical dialogue. This chapter therefore invites the reader to consider how to develop such dialogue in a placement or workplace context.

Everyday ethics

Banks (2010b: 3) argues that 'ethical issues are endemic in youth work'. We operate within an ethical context imbued by questions and difficulties of power, authority, consent, rights, control and participation. Our engagement with young people is as much concerned with promoting their rights and upholding principles of social justice as it is protecting them from possible harm. We start these engagements on the basis that young people are immeasurably less powerful than adults, on account of their age, resources and other characteristics. Our relationships with young people are also arguably more ambiguous than those that other professionals occupy: youth workers, for instance, may meet young people in informal settings unbound by formal rules and conventions that operate in school settings. As Sercombe (2010: 78) acknowledges: 'the informal nature of youth work means that often there is no space or time boundary around the action: it is not a fifty-minute consultation in a counselling room with the door closed'. These, and many other issues, tensions and dilemmas, mean that, for youth workers and young people, ethics is an 'everyday' issue. Consider the following example:

> *I recently started a new role working with a group of young people in North London. The group of men I was working with lived in an area of considerable deprivation, were intensively monitored by local police and often had fractious relationships with other family members. As we began to develop our working relationships with one another, some of the group told me that they were involved in the London 'riots' that took place in August 2011. Two of the group had never been charged . . .*

Within this example, we might identify a number of issues that we would consider to have an ethical dimension. The first is the nature of the relationship we have formed with young people. This relationship is built on principles that should enable us to operate ethically. We will have built up the conditions of trust required for the young men to disclose sensitive or difficult issues to us and perhaps we have recognised that for many of them, we may occupy a 'privileged' role of being one of the few adults they trust. In thinking about the young people we are engaging with, we are sensitive to the wider context of their lives: the structures, relationships, cultural norms and other factors that either promote or limit their capacity to exercise rights and so on. In this case, we will be mindful of the broader social and economic context within which the August 2011 disturbances occurred and the place of young people in society more generally. We might pay particular attention to the identities of the young men: how might aspects such as 'race', class and gender be important in understanding the experience of young people?

All of these questions and considerations help us to form an understanding of how our work with young people operates within an ethical context. An ethical context is something that recognises that we do not work with young people in a vacuum. Our encounters with them and interventions are shaped by a series of ethical issues concerning:

- our identity and the identities of the young people we work with;
- the rights of young people;
- the balance of power between adults and young people;
- our legal responsibilities and organisational policy obligations.

It is probably helpful to think of ethical issues as operating at three levels:

- *Macro ethical issues*: the broader legal, social and cultural context of young people, the wider socio-economic context of our work and so on. Macro ethical issues might put the balance of power away from young people and we may constantly find ourselves as advocating for young people's rights in the face of antipathy or hostility. The government of the day may deem that a policy proposal is in the best interests of young people whereas we might determine, through our encounters, that the reverse is likely to be true. Therefore, to understand the macro context, we ask questions about young people's relative position in society. To what extent are their rights upheld and supported by laws and institutions? Do we determine that the government and other structures work in favour of young people? Why? What other macro forces have an impact upon young people? Further exploration of these issues in discussed in Chapter 7.

- *Meso ethical issues*: the immediate cultural and environmental factors that shape the experience of young people, their relationships with family members and other members of the local community and so on.
- *Micro ethical issues*: the characteristics of an individual's experience and those factors that shape our individual interactions, especially how our own identity or experience can promote or inhibit good practice (see Chapter 3). We are also concerned here with how the identity of an individual young person may shape their worldview based on their own perceptions or experiences.

Task 4.1

In discussion with your tutor or practice supervisor, reflect on the particular ethical context or ethical issues you operate within. Try to group these under macro, meso and micro issues.

Having established that all practice occurs within an ethical context, we now turn to two further defining features of understanding everyday ethics. These are ethical dilemmas and ethical problems.

Ethical dilemmas concern those situations where we may have to make a difficult decision or choice, with each decision resulting in a less-than-satisfactory outcome. Through a process of deliberation, we arrive at a conclusion that looks for the *least bad* outcome or the 'lesser of two evils'. Examples of ethical dilemmas in youth work practice abound and can cause disagreement and tensions between those involved in a situation. Take the example at the start of this chapter. Some practitioners might argue that, having learnt about the young people's criminal activity, a worker should take action to notify the police. Without doing so, they may be seen to be condoning criminal activity or they might diminish the impact of the disturbances on victims. They may also feel that they are somehow an 'accessory' to a criminal event and find that this can cause much personal consternation. On the other hand, some practitioners might argue strongly that they have engaged with a group that may be on the margins and with limited contact with trusted adults, and that this may be an opportunity to build meaningful relationships that in the longer term will hopefully reduce the feelings of isolation and exclusion. They might stress that contacting the police may result in irreparable damage to the conditions required for a trusting relationship to flourish. In all the years of facilitating ethical conversations, we have yet to encounter immediate consensus amongst a group of students exploring scenarios similar to this one: hence the term 'dilemma'. The judgement we make about this case needs to be underpinned by careful and thoughtful reflection. Those who argue that it is straightforward on either side are in danger of arriving at quick judgements that may ultimately result in negative outcomes for the young people concerned.

Task 4.2

In discussion with your tutor or practice supervisor, can you identify a recent example where you or others have encountered an ethical dilemma? Reflect on why the dilemma occurred and what different options might have been considered. What decision was taken? What was the outcome or impact of that decision?

Ethical problems are different: they concern situations that you are powerless to change but which you know are inhibiting young people. For youth workers, it is commonplace to come up against seemingly immovable ethical problems. For those young people who are in contact with welfare agencies, the bureaucratic machinery and seemingly cast-iron rules often work against young people's interests, neglecting to take into account how individuals experience welfare in very different ways. We are often faced with an uncomfortable situation where we have to reinforce decisions that we believe to be plain wrong. Sometimes we can challenge these, resulting in a better position ethically. Other times, and perhaps all too often, we find ourselves either being in a position of upholding rules we are uncomfortable with or attempting to work in contexts that we believe may be damaging.

An example might be as follows:

> I was working with a young man who left school and is not currently in work or further education. As he has reached the age of 18, he is now entitled to access the welfare payment linked to job seeking. I'm aware of his many caring responsibilities that limit him from working. However, when asked to contribute to his assessment for an alternative benefit, I was unable to confirm he has a physical or other disability that would qualify for a benefit that does not require him to seek work. He's got to attend a number of sessions preparing him for work or he'll lose his benefit entitlements, even if this has a detrimental impact on his caring responsibilities.

In this example, the best interests of the young person and the family may not be best served by compelling him to attend work programmes that take him away from his caring responsibilities. Since the young person does not qualify for an alternative benefit, we have no choice but to accept a difficult ethical problem and comply with it.

How we respond to immovable ethical problems will vary from case to case. In the case above, we might want to support the young person with identifying other sources of support for his caring responsibilities. We might look to identify possible work opportunities that will accommodate his needs. These are called mitigation strategies and may offer some comfort or relief to young people. In other cases of ethical problems we might simply have to accept that this is not much we can do. Here is another example that was recently put to us:

> *I was working with a young guy who was involved in some alcohol-related violence. It was really a terrible one-off incident that should not have happened. He was at a crossroads when he went before the judge. His family promised to put in mechanisms of support, the local church and youth club sent letters of support promising to link him into programmes of volunteering. He had even received letters of support from the victims involved. Yet, despite this, he was given a short-term custodial sentence to be served in 2–3 jails far away from his family and support networks. I am 100 per cent certain that if he had remained in the community, we could have really tackled the issues that underpinned his offence. Now we've got a bigger job on our hands – keeping him linked to his positive networks (rather than the negative ones he's forming in prison) and thinking about how best to challenge his post-custody behaviour.*

A young person who has been charged, convicted and is in custody *may indeed* be better off in the community in order for certain needs to be met. However, in the case above, a judgement has been made that cannot be altered, so we must find ways, no matter how limited, of redefining how we work with the young person in question.

Task 4.3

In discussion with your tutor or practice supervisor, can you identify an ethical problem you have encountered? How did this problem impact upon the young people you worked with? How did it affect what you were able to achieve?

So in summary, all youth work practice takes place within a context imbued with ethical issues. As practitioners we need to have a good understanding of this context in order to begin and maintain our relationships with young people. Sometimes these relationships are challenged by ethical dilemmas, situations where we need to make difficult choices. Others are bound by ethical problems; invariably these are circumstances where we know that young people may not be best served by the situations they face but we are somewhat powerless to affect changes. These broad ethical considerations – the 'everyday' ethics – require us to use sound professional judgement and reflective practice with others to help us to think how best to respond. Our judgements are also supported by ethical codes of conduct.

Ethical codes of conduct

Ethical codes are statements written or expressed by organisations or professional bodies that seek to safeguard service users and the reputation of the profession, and to guide the work of practitioners. They are used by all of the main educational, health and social professional groups including those in medicine, social work, teaching and youth work. Professional bodies, such as the British Sociological Association or the British Society of Criminology also use ethical statements to inform and guide ethical research practice. Banks (2004: 108–9) identified a number of common features found in contemporary ethical codes:

- statements about the core purpose or service ideal of the profession;
- statements about the character/attributes of the professional;
- ethical principles – general statements such as 'respect for autonomy';
- ethical rules – general 'do's and don'ts';
- principles of professional practice – general statements about how to achieve what is intended for the good of the service user;
- rules of professional practice – very specific guidance on what is good professional practice.

In the United Kingdom, a code of conduct for youth work was first introduced in 2000 that set out ethical and professional principles. Banks's distinction between ethical content, 'attitudes, rights and duties about human welfare, such as respecting human dignity' (Banks 2004: 109) and professional content (the rules of engagement) was captured in the statement, though there was a rejection of setting out specific rules (the 'do's and don'ts'). The code contains eight statements, four of which are 'ethical principles' and four of which are 'professional principles' (see Box 4.1).

The code is interesting on two accounts. It was written at a time when there was no recognised professional membership body for youth workers, so does not hold the same enforcement capability of other professional organisations. For example, if a doctor breaches the ethical code of the General Medical Council, that person may face a suspension of their licence or a similar sanction. Theoretically at least, a youth worker could treat young people with disrespect, fail to promote the welfare of young people and engage in other activities contrary to these principles and not face formal sanctions beyond their own employer's decision to discipline or not. This is changing somewhat in England with the introduction of an Institute for Youth Work (discussed below). The second interesting observation is acknowledged in the code:

> While there have been some calls for a longer, more detailed and rule-based code of conduct, this would be difficult to apply to all types of youth workers working in different settings and agencies. It might also be so prescriptive as to curtail the professional freedom and responsibility of the youth worker.
>
> (NYA 2004: 2)

Box 4.1: The National Youth Agency Statement of Ethical Conduct in Youth Work

Ethical principles

Youth workers have a commitment to:

1   Treat young people with respect, valuing each individual and avoiding negative discrimination.
2   Respect and promote young people's rights to make their own decisions and choices, unless the welfare or legitimate interests of themselves or others are seriously threatened.
3   Promote and ensure the welfare and safety of young people, while permitting them to learn through undertaking challenging educational activities.
4   Contribute towards the promotion of social justice for young people and in society generally, through encouraging respect for difference and diversity and challenging discrimination.

Professional principles

Youth workers have a commitment to:

5   Recognise the boundaries between personal and professional life and be aware of the need to balance a caring and supportive relationship with young people with appropriate professional distance.
6   Recognise the need to be accountable to young people, their parents or guardians, colleagues, funders, wider society and others with a relevant interest in the work, and that these accountabilities may be in conflict.
7   Develop and maintain the required skills and competence to do the job.
8   Work for conditions in employing agencies where these principles are discussed, evaluated and upheld.

(National Youth Agency 2004: 6)

The code itself recognises the diversity of youth work practice, which is commendable but could be somewhat unhelpful in arguing the professional status of youth workers. For example, the lack of explicit references to what might constitute inappropriate 'professional distance' (Statement 5) may open up an appealing debate about how, when and on what terms youth workers engage with young people. Statement 2 would offer us an interesting discussion point when thinking about the case example of young people and the disturbances identified in the earlier part of this chapter.

In avoiding explicit rules, the code instead seeks to serve as a learning tool to aid ethical reflection: 'Its aim is primarily to develop ethical awareness and to encourage reflection as the basis for ethical conduct rather than to tell youth workers exactly how to act in particular cases' (NYA 2000: 2). It is this ethical awareness and reflection that we consider to be vital to being an ethical practitioner, and the final section of this chapter deals with this point.

In September 2013, the first membership body for youth workers in England was launched. The Institute for Youth Work was set up with the goal of

> providing a voice for their views and supporting members to reach the highest professional standards. It will aim to engage all those in the youth sector who work to enable young people to develop holistically and to reach their full potential.[1]

The Institute introduced a register of qualified youth workers, access to approved and accredited continuing professional development opportunities and an ethical framework, embodied in a new code of ethics. Here, the code recognises the diversity of youth work practice but seeks to provide:

> A concise entry point for the IYW so that practitioners from diverse backgrounds can identify whether it is right for them to join the IYW. All members will be asked to sign up to this Code of Ethics when they register to join the IYW. The Code also provides some guidelines for external audiences on what the members of the IYW believe in and stand for.[2]

Currently in draft form, the code sets out twelve statements (reproduced in Box 4.2).

The code reflects the sentiments of the original statements published over a decade earlier. It seeks to provide practitioners with a set of statements that outline the aims and scope of youth work. However, the link to a membership body and the inclusion of more specific examples edges towards a greater emphasis on 'rules'. On its own however it does not provide sufficient guidance to enable workers to make moral judgements nor does it provide the mechanisms by which to act when a worker breaches the code. As the Institute acknowledges, 'more work needs to be done', and plans for developing accompanying commentary and case studies are underway.

Both codes of conduct provide a valuable tool for youth workers to reflect upon how their practice might be construed as ethical. Although they lack prescription in most cases, they do provide reference points for what can be deemed morally acceptable practice. However, as with all statements, words alone are ineffective. Dialogue and reflection are necessary to bring ethical thought and practice to life.

Promoting ethical reflection and dialogue

The day-to-day demands of a busy workplace can sometimes limit the opportunities for reflection and discussion on ethical issues. This chapter started with the proposition that all youth work is ethical by its nature. We went on to explore how ethical codes of

Box 4.2: Institute for Youth Work Ethical Code of Conduct (Draft – September 2013)

The Institute for Youth Work recognises the diversity of the youth work sector, which includes those that work unpaid and paid in local authority, voluntary, faith-based and community groups. Members, whatever their background and setting, make judgements in their work on the following ethical principles:

1 In the youth work relationship, the interests of young people have priority. Youth workers do not act against the interests of young people.
2 Youth workers do not seek to advance ourselves, our organisations, or others – personally, politically or professionally – at the expense of young people.
3 Youth workers' relationship with young people is an ethical one, intentionally limited to protect the young person and the purpose of the work. These limits will be clarified, established and maintained. The relationship is not for sexual engagement.
4 Youth workers seek to enhance young people's capability for positive action by:
   • enabling them to clarify and pursue their choices;
   • helping them to make considered decisions;
   • supporting them to hold people with power over them to account;
   • helping young people to move on when the time is right.
5 Youth workers promote the welfare and safety of young people. We avoid exposing young people to the likelihood of serious harm and injury.
6 When collecting information about young people we make them aware of who will see that information and what it will be used for. Further knowledge acquired from conversations with a young person is not used against them and is treated confidentially (except when necessary to ensure 5 above).
7 Youth workers' engagement with young people, and the resulting relationship, is open and truthful. We declare any potential conflict of interest.
8 Youth workers respect others concerned with the welfare and well-being of young people and will collaborate with them to secure the best outcomes for those young people.
9 Youth workers encourage ethical debate with colleagues, managers, employers and young people.
10 Youth workers work in a fair and inclusive way, promoting justice and equality of opportunity.
11 Youth workers equip ourselves with the resources necessary to work effectively with young people and work in a reflexive way to monitor our work and develop our abilities. We take account of the impact of our work on ourselves.
12 Youth workers maintain consciousness of our own values and interests and approach difference respectfully.

conduct help to uphold certain standards of behaviour and values that we would argue are necessary to ensure the professional practice of youth work. However, codes on their own can fail to take account of the need to continuously think about, share and discuss the ethical nature of our work – especially in the context of the diverse views that we encounter in our work. As Philippart (2003: 70–1) argues:

> Today we live in a 'postmodern', pluralistic, differentiated and multi-cultural society. Many conflicting interests, interpretations of reality, moral and ethical standards, visions and hopes for the future exist next to each other . . . Working in the social professions becomes increasingly complicated as society itself becomes more complex.

This point is worth reflecting on both in the context of how we establish common 'rules of engagement' agreed with our colleagues and also in how we think about our role in working with young people. In the discussion above, we talked about ethical dilemmas posing a number of possible resolutions and that, often, practitioners might not immediately agree the best way forward. We would argue that this reflects everyday life: dilemmas by their nature sometimes invite competing perspectives. Similarly, if one of our main roles as educators is to promote young people's engagement with their own 'moral philosophy' (Young 1999), then we need to acknowledge the diversity of views and experiences that they themselves will bring to bear on any situations we or they choose to discuss.

Responding to this complexity might invite us to take a path of least resistance. We might succumb to the view that all moral and ethical positions, no matter how seemingly disconnected from others, are valid. Put simply: everything goes. In the face of ethical dilemmas or problems, we might be defeatist and take the view that this is no resolution, so it is not worth thinking about. Neither of these positions is tenable. Youth workers are educators whose primary role is to actively create the conditions to enable such conversations to flourish, especially where difference and diversity come into play. So youth workers, we would argue, need to make two commitments. The first of these, a commitment to continuous reflective practice, is discussed in Chapter 11. The second concerns how we can work with our peers, colleagues and young people to nurture ethical dialogue.

There are many valuable approaches that can be used to support ethical dialogue. Socratic dialogue is one such approach that we have used – and have seen used – to good effect. The method we discussed here is based on work by Philippart (2003), who drew on his experience as a social work educator in the Netherlands. Drawing on the systematic approach used by Socrates to examine core issues that faced society, Philippart argues that 'Socratic dialogue deals with questions . . . [It] helps constitute an awareness that is focused on finding consensus on principles, values and ideas' (2003: 71). In the short space we have available here, we can only provide a brief summary of the approach and highly recommend Philippart's chapter as the key reading to develop your practice.

The Socratic dialogue follows what might be called 'regressive abstraction' and Philippart uses an hourglass procedure comprising a number of steps that can guide the dialogue (see 2003: 72–4). The steps in this process are set out in Table 4.1.

Table 4.1 Philippart's hourglass procedure

1)	Setting a question	A well-formulated question or statement enables the dialogue to have a focus. It should be a general question that needs discussion and thought, as opposed to something that can be answered with reference to data or facts. So, an example might be 'When should a young person be removed from a youth club setting?' or 'What is good youth work?'
2)	Collect concrete examples and choose one to focus on	Participants in the dialogue will be asked to provide real examples that fit with the topic. The conditions are that they have experienced or directly witnessed the example they talk about, not that it has been drawn from a third-party reading or similar. A number of valuable examples may be offered but at this stage, one should be chosen. The example then becomes the focus, with the person who volunteered it offering to respond to questions from other participants. So, in the case of 'good youth work', the participant might have shared an example that they felt was evidence of this.
3)	Formulate a key assertion	During this stage, participants will ask the presenter several questions to deepen understanding of the example offered. In doing so, they will work towards a common understanding, or what Philippart calls 'a provisional answer' to the question set at the start. Crucially, the 'assertion' will be agreed by participants. So, 'a young person can only be removed from a youth work setting when their behaviour is likely to harm others . . .' might be an example.
4)	Formulating rules and principles	The dialogue up to now has focused on the particular case put forward by one participant. At this stage, the participants should work towards more abstract and general principles. The participants should work towards a series of rules that support the assertion and rules that would indicate a different assertion. Rules applicable to the above example might include certain safeguards – 'a young person can only be removed if they themselves are not at risk of harm' and so on. Inevitably new rules will result in new questions, and participants should be actively encouraged to ask, clarify and expand statements.
5)	Recording key statements	Throughout, the dialogue is openly recorded for all participants to see (e.g. on a flipchart) so that the progress of the dialogue is carefully mapped.

Source: Adapted from Philippart (2003: 72–4)

The dialogue process is helpful in enabling participants to 'arrive at a clear understanding of the general principles and values that underlie our behaviour' (Philippart 2003: 75). It uses the questions and cases relevant to our everyday practice, and through deliberation and the formation of assertions, rules and principles, helps ethical consensus to flourish.

Task 4.4

Download a copy of *Teaching Practical Ethics* at: www.feset.org/feset/wp-content/uploads/2013/02/Teaching_practical_ethics1.pdf and read Chapter 5.

In conversation with your supervisor, consider how you might use either Philippart's approach to Socratic Dialogue (or a similar process) to support ethical dialogue with your colleagues.

Conclusion

This chapter has reviewed the relationship between youth work and ethical practice. In doing so, it has shown that youth work takes place within an ethical context, with daily ethical issues, dilemmas and problems that require us to think about how we respond in the *best interests* of those we work with. Ethical codes of conduct provide us with a professional framework to support this decision making. Alongside these static codes, practitioners need to use reflective practice and ethical dialogue to ensure that we identify our own ethical responses to the challenges we encounter in our work. It is our contention that this dialogue and reflective practice is likely to lead to more responsive, and ultimately more effective, ways of working with young people.

Notes

1   www.nya.org.uk/institute-for-youth-work
2   www.iyw.org.uk/join-iyw/code-of-ethics/

5 | The informal educator

Introduction

As the first chapter of this book identified, learning is central to the youth worker/young person relationship and, in our view, extends to the role of the practitioner working in communities and with institutions. Whilst it is certainly true that youth workers increasingly engage young people in targeted, pre-defined and often welfare-oriented ways that challenge some of the key tenets of youth work principles, it is also true that education remains *the distinctive practice of youth work* (Young 1999: 2).

What separates youth workers from other professionals engaged in welfare work with young people is this distinct commitment to education and learning. This is a central cornerstone of the professional identity of the youth worker and without it the professional contribution will be at best muddied, and at worst, completely lost.

This chapter sets out the principles of informal education and learning before examining the ways in which students can develop educational practice in a range of contexts.

What is informal education?

Youth workers deliver a range of educational programmes designed to promote the personal and social development of young people. Through creative and engaging methods of working, they expand young people's horizons; promote confidence; and help in the acquisition of new skills. Some of this work draws on either their own specialist interests or their access to resources and ideas from the wider profession. However, outside of these activity-based interventions, there is a wider and distinct role that youth workers play – the informal educator: 'What do youth and community workers do? Listen and talk. Make relationships. Enable young people to come to voice . . . Informal educators . . . go to meet people and start where those people are with their own preoccupations and in their own places' (Batsleer 2008: 5).

For many of us, the words 'education' and 'learning' conjure up images of sitting quietly in the lecture theatre or classroom, taking notes on what the teacher is talking about and occasionally, if we are feeling brave, putting our hand up to answer a question. This quite narrow perspective of education ignores the very rich and diverse ways in which other forms of learning occur, and do so in our everyday life. Our daily experiences, our conversations with friends, watching a drama on television or reading a newspaper all provide us with opportunities to at least think and maybe learn. These are processes that take place almost unconsciously. Sometimes they provoke us, often they confirm what we know or believe to be true.

Informal educators start from the possibility that learning can take place in any encounter between the youth worker and the young person. Learning, however, is not left to chance: informal educators are *intentional* and *purposeful*, and create opportunities or join in the everyday activities of young people 'with the aim of fostering learning' (Jeffs and Smith 1999: 13). They use conversation and activities to stimulate questions that require deeper interrogation and reflection, and this work is guided by values. Conversations, encounters, our behaviour and our relationships between practitioners and with young people depend on what 'makes for human flourishing' (Jeffs and Smith 2011). As the introductory chapter established, values are central to youth work and these in turn inform a sound ethical basis for our work (Chapter 4). Education, according to Jeffs and Smith, embraces a set of values that inform our encounters. 'These values should inform both the content of conversations and encounters, as well as our behaviour and relationships as educators' (Jeffs and Smith 1999: 15).

Education therefore embraces:

- respect for persons
- the promotion of well-being
- truth
- democracy
- fairness and equality.

(Jeffs and Smith 1999: 15)

Informal educators emphasise *process-* over *product*-driven approaches to learning and this poses one of the biggest challenges for student youth and community workers. Our experience has often brought us into contact with practitioners who will say something along these lines: 'I'm designing a drug awareness programme to make young people aware about the dangers of drugs . . . I'll informally educate them about the risks and dangers . . .' When we ask the person to describe why they believe this is informal education, they will say that because the drug education programme is delivered using games or other fun activities, it is therefore not the same as, say, how a teacher would deliver a maths lesson in formal education settings. In the example, the student is right to claim that adopting a creative approach to drugs education may be more engaging for young people and there is certainly a place in youth work for this activity. However, like a pre-determined maths lesson, it relies on the 'product': 'something we build before the educational encounter' (Jeffs and Smith 1999: 61). The practitioner has already determined that drugs are an issue faced by young people and wishes to teach about the 'risks and dangers'. The work does not arise from young people's concerns about drugs, nor does it really respond to their intended direction of learning.

Product approaches to learning are undoubtedly comforting. You 'test' whether someone has acquired the 'knowledge' you have imparted, and in the case above, this would be measured by the extent to which young people understand the risks of using drugs. Process approaches, on the other hand, may be somewhat unsettling! There is often a great deal of uncertainty since the process approach requires the educator to *start from where young people are 'at' and builds from this*: '[The process approach] looks to the qualities of interaction that occur in an educational situation. Rather than having objectives about what people should learn, as in a product curriculum, it has a general aim of intention' (Jeffs and Smith 1999: 63). Informal educators therefore require a great deal of skill in using conversation, observation and constant reflection on the thinking and action of themselves and the young people they work with. The starting point is the conversations that the youth worker has with the young people: 'In conversation everything is so unpredictable. Talk can lead anywhere. In this sense it is difficult to be specific about outcome or aim. Content certainly cannot be sequenced in any meaningful way beforehand' (Jeffs and Smith 1999: 64). The unpredictability means that the educator is able to be responsive to the learning needs of young people. However, unlike the day-to-day conversations we may have with our friends, our engagement with young people is *intentional* and is therefore *planned*. We become part of the lives of young people in order to support, guide and influence, and to provide an educational dimension to their interactions with one another. Our reasons for engaging with young people (often in their spaces and territories) will therefore differ from those of their peers, and will be characterised by deliberate attempts to enlarge the thinking and experiences of the young people we work with.

The online *Encyclopaedia of Informal Education* offers a useful set of characteristics that underpin the approaches used by informal educators. These are as follows:

- *Conversation is at the centre of their activities.* The use of conversation underpins all engagement with young people whether in the facilitation of sports, arts or other activities, or in the encounter the worker has with a young person whilst under-taking outreach sessions in the neighbourhood.
- *Informal education operates in a wide range of settings.* It is not bound to a school or other fixed place. Rather, it can take place in a youth club, at home, the local shop or at a residential trip. It flourishes best in the settings where young people *choose* to go but can also be delivered within the constraints of compulsory settings (such as a school or prison).
- *Informal education looks to explore and enlarge experience.* Whilst informal educators start where young people are at, the educator is always looking for ways to stimulate new ideas and experiences, and to support young people to think and act in ways that enlarge their perspectives on the worlds they occupy.
- *Informal educators put a special emphasis on building just and democratic relation-ships and organisations.* Dialogue is seen to be a central component of democratic thinking and in turn, democratic behavior and thinking is a powerful antidote to oppression and power imbalances (see Chapter 14). By enabling people to engage in conversations that offer difference, new perspectives are brought to bear.

- *Informal educators use a variety of methods.* They work with established or new groups, with individuals or in the wider community. They use play, sports, arts and other engaging approaches to stimulate conversation.

(Adapted from Smith 2011: online[1])

Using informal education

As youth workers, we have many opportunities open to us that enable us to engage with young people in conversation. Often, 'chat and everyday contact provide the point of engagement for later, purposeful conversations' (Batsleer 2008: 70) but equally, running set sports, arts or other activities can create the conditions for powerful interactions between young people and workers. Here, we offer some starter suggestions for thinking about how to use conversation effectively to stimulate informal education in practice. This is by no means the most creative list but may provide some inspiration for thinking about using everyday encounters as learning opportunities, and we encourage you to test them for yourself. In each case, consider the different communication skills you need to draw on in order to make the most effective use of your encounters (see Chapter 13). You will also see that the three examples are on a continuum: from spontaneous responses to planned or contrived activities.

Catching the moment

Catching the moment is self-explanatory, it means being attuned to what young people say and responding to it to further the conversation. Owen Jones, in his recent book looking at the demonisation of the working class, provided an example of a classic 'moment' that needed to be caught. It was, he argued, an

> experience we've all had. You're among a group of friends or acquaintances when suddenly someone says something that shocks you: an aside or a flippant comment made in poor taste. But the most disquieting part isn't the remark itself. It's the fact that no one else seems the slightest bit taken aback. You look around in vain, hoping for even a flicker or concern or the hint of a cringe.

(Jones 2011: 1)

In this case, Jones was at a dinner party in a 'gentrified part of East London' when a friend made a joke based on prejudices around class. You may have found yourself in similar situations where the light-hearted humour of friends is used as a cover for extolling unpleasant derogatory comments. In those situations, how have you reacted?

Moments can come from general conversations such as this one, but they can also be triggered by external stimuli. A classic moment for youth workers is using media to provoke a discussion. For example, a heated encounter about a social issue between two characters on TV or the coverage of a particular story in a magazine can trigger a conversation in which feelings, attitudes and alternative views are discussed.

Informal educators do not let these moments pass: they catch them and engage people in conversation using the most common question, 'Why?' They use these questions and invite viewpoints to encourage people to go beyond and investigate their immediate responses. Through questioning, educators begin to ask for alternatives: 'How *else* would you explain this? What else might be going on? What do you think causes this situation?' Educators avoid hectoring, attempting to win an argument or using the opportunity to indoctrinate: they strive to get people to reflect on the reasons for their thinking and to consider alternatives. This in turn creates the climate where critical thinking can flourish (Young 2006). There may be no consensus at the end of such discussions, but the opportunity for different perspectives to be heard is more important: it provides a 'forked road' moment for the learner to consider which way they wish to go in terms of their own thinking and action (Dewey 1933).

A conversation steer

When one of the authors of this book was starting out in youth work, the supervisor set a task to move a conversation from one relatively light and everyday topic (a pop group that was in fashion at the time) to another, more heavy and challenging topic (female genital mutilation). This is called the conversation 'steer', a directive approach that enables the converser to take an issue and explore dimensions that may not be part of everyday conversation. The case here was relatively straightforward since the pop group, used to start the conversation, embodied what the popular press called 'girl power'. By looking at girl power, the worker was able to talk with young people about what constituted it and under what circumstances women were less powerful. This led the worker to explore issues where women are oppressed and ultimately to introduce the topic of mutilation. Many of the young women in the group had not come across this before, but this would be far from the case for others.

Task 5.1

Try a conversation steer exercise with one of your peers. Each person should take an everyday talking point (Point A) and find a more challenging, seemingly unconnected topic (Point B) without telling the other person. Try to progress the conversation with the other person from Point A to Point B.

What happens at Point B is crucial to fostering learning. The educator should encourage the exchange of views, knowledge and, where it is possible, personal experience. The educator will pass on any knowledge but invite those engaged in the conversation to investigate the topic further. The steer may face similar criticisms to those we identified above – we do start with some pre-conceived idea of where we want our educational encounter to go. That said, as an approach for building confidence in using conversations in a more purposeful way, it is useful indeed.

Creating a talking point

This is perhaps the most contrived of the three approaches, where the educator deliberately sets out to create a talking point by doing or saying something that provokes discussion in contrast to sometimes 'settled' group norms or seemingly entrenched group norms. Here is an example of how this can work in practice:

> A male youth worker had been working at a youth club for a number of months and had built up a friendly and trusting relationship with the young people. During his sessions, he became aware of the dominant sexist and homophobic conversations that young men had with each other, and realised that no other perspectives were given the space to be heard. Young men would support each other's views through homophobic and sexist jokes and stories. Since nobody challenged these views, the young men routinely said 'there are no gay people here, it doesn't matter' and 'the girls don't mind'.
>
> In response, the youth worker arrived at the next session wearing a homemade T-shirt bearing the slogan: Why do you assume I'm heterosexual?

The worker had judged that the norms of the group he was working with enabled collusion around homophobic and sexist views. Having built up a relationship over some period of time, he decided to test the boundaries of this by introducing a 'question' as one way to get people talking about their views and to consider that there may in fact be people who were uncomfortable with the group norms either on account of their own sexuality or their desire to hear alternative perspectives.

The challenge of context

Most writers on informal education acknowledge the importance of two factors that can support this form of learning: the *environment* we work in; and the idea that young people *choose* to participate (see, e.g. Batsleer and Davies 2010; Jeffs and Smith 1999; Smith 1994). However, youth workers engage with young people in environments where young people and youth workers have little say on their surroundings. Similarly, much more youth work is now done in contexts that rely on compulsory engagement. To add to these two challenges, youth workers increasingly take on a number of other roles that fall outside their primary (informal) educational purpose.

Reflection 5.1

Consider the most recent youth work experience you have had or your current placement. What type of work do they do with young people? To what extent would you identify this work as 'informal education'?

In our experience, youth work students have undertaken roles as diverse as classroom learning assistants to personal advisers working with individuals on a range of personal and social issues. By their very nature, these placements do not always allow for the flexibility and openness required to nurture opportunities for informal education in the way that a youth club might, for example. This is not to say that this work is not important and youth workers are often exceptionally skilled at undertaking these roles on account of their capacity to relate to young people in ways that other professionals do not always manage. However, it is *not* informal education and too often, the potential value of using the methods and approaches described above are lost primarily because students do not recognise where they can 'fit' this approach within the organisational context.

To illustrate, we can use the example of two placement students who worked in a school mentoring unit designed to support young people at risk of being excluded from mainstream education:

> *Gerry and Steph worked as mentors with young people who had been referred to the exclusion unit by teachers concerned about learning progression, behaviour or classroom disruption. The 'mentor' would then offer individual and group support in order to identify and address any concerns that the young person was having and help them to understand how their behaviour impacted upon the wider school. Sometimes they would provide advice and information or referral; at other times they might help young people with their school work. It was also common for them to advocate on behalf of young people by challenging teachers where it was felt certain accommodations for young people needed to be made. Many young people returned to normal school activities as a result of spending time with the mentors. The mentors attributed the success to the relationships they built with young people and the intensive contact time afforded to them – factors they saw as different from the teacher/pupil relationship found elsewhere in the school.*

The tutor visiting their placement asked the students to reflect on their interventions with young people, to consider how they would define the work and, in particular, whether they thought what they were doing could constitute informal education. The students could readily identify some of the attributes that would be expected of a good youth worker including the respect shown to young people, the emphasis on the positive relationship and the readiness to challenge teachers as well as students where it was required. In turn, they recognised that whilst this work was valuable, almost none of the principles of informal education were evident in what they were doing. How might their contribution differ if they were to act as informal educators in what appears to be a rather constrained and pre-determined environment? Is it possible to 'do' informal education in these situations? The students were tasked with reflecting on both of these questions.

These are challenging questions and situations that any professional practitioner is likely to encounter, especially when working in an organisation that has a primary purpose other than youth work. The difficulties of contributing a distinctive youth work role are compounded where the placement supervisor does not come from a youth work background (as was the case in the example above) and may not necessarily understand what youth work can contribute. In many organisations, funding or other resource constraints may also mean that youth workers are often called upon to provide extra hands in the day-to-day business of the organisation. This pressure further reduces the opportunities to develop the distinctive informal education practice.

Despite these and other challenges, it was perfectly possible to introduce different methods of working with young people within the constraints of the school exclusion service, as it would be in a youth justice team or with a group of young people encountered on the street during a detached youth work session. How might informal education contribute? Some steps that will help you to reflect on your role are described below.

Step 1: Understand informal education

Take the time to read, test, discuss and understand the principles and methods of informal education. This chapter has provided an overview of some of the basics but further reading is required to develop a more comprehensive understanding of the history and development of this distinct educational practice. Discussion with your peers, supervisors and with tutors will also help bring informal education to life. Above all, be prepared for the uncertainty that comes with a practice that favours processes and openness over pre-determined outcomes. You will need to be clear about the value of this approach when working with people who are often used to the opposite!

Step 2: Observation and reflection

Alongside the general frameworks of planning, delivering and evaluating practice (see Chapter 9), understanding the work of your organisation is vital. In Chapter 7, the importance of the organisational context is explored with some suggestions on how you or students can gain an insight into:

- who the agency works with;
- why the agency works with young people;
- who works with young people;
- what it hopes to achieve; and
- what methods it uses.

In the case of Gerry and Steph above, the purpose of the unit was to challenge and improve the behaviour of young people who had been identified as problematic by teachers. The aim of this work was to reintegrate particular young people back into mainstream education to reduce the risk of permanent exclusion. The methods used included mentoring and learning support delivered through intensive work with individuals. The aims and approaches of this work were further pre-determined by the large number of national and local policies that governed work with young people at risk of exclusion.

Whilst undertaking this task, it is important to reflect on how the practice observed differs from that which is defined as youth work. This will enable you to define the expectations the organisation has of your role and consider how youth work can 'add value' to this.

Step 3: Identify opportunities and set the direction

Having gained a comprehensive understanding of both the principles of informal education and the agency context, it is now time to identify ways in which the two can potentially co-exist. Sometimes this is relatively straightforward, particularly in settings that rely less on structured and pre-defined programmes such as a youth club. It is more difficult in cases such as that described above, where Gerry and Steph were expected to primarily adopt a mentoring role. Nonetheless, some questions can help you to assess the extent to which it is possible to nurture the conditions for informal education:

- Is there sufficient time to build a relationship with the young people you intend to engage with?
- Is there an opportunity to work with young people outside or alongside pre-programmed or pre-determined sessions?
- Is there an opportunity to develop activities or experiences that differ from those already offered by the organisation?
- In what ways can young people set the agenda of your work?

Step 4: Educate and inform others

A common criticism of youth work is that it fails to define itself in a convincing way for others to understand what *it is*. This is an issue compounded by seemingly endless academic and practitioner debates about the purpose of youth work. It is absolutely critical for practitioners to be in a position where they can talk to other professionals about their work and its contribution to young people's lives. Gerry and Steph used a staff meeting at the school to provide colleagues with an overview of youth work, informal education and, in drawing on evaluations of work in schools, how these approaches could complement what was already undertaken by teachers, mentors and other staff. This work was valuable for challenging misconceptions about the role of the youth worker and for securing support for their work.

Step 5: Do!

Two strategies were used by Gerry and Steph to broaden the work that they did with the young people. First, they worked increasingly with young people in groups. Alongside the individual mentoring, they invited young people to participate in group-work activity that was centred solely on conversations. Second, they identified a space (the centre) and different time (after school) where young people could attend on a voluntary basis to meet informally.

Step 6: Reflect . . . and tell the story

The importance of continuous reflection on these steps is central to a healthy professional engagement. Reflective practice enables us to develop our knowledge, skills, confidence and perspective (see Chapter 11). In the scenario described above, Gerry and Steph supported each other to develop 'peer reflection', thinking through and talking about their interventions, linking this to theory and considering the impact of their work. They also sought support from their supervisor and from the visiting tutor. In this particular case, reflection meant moving beyond the day-to-day interventions to broader questions about the nature and purpose of youth work. To do this successfully, Gerry and Steph needed to consider, weigh up and evaluate the interplay between youth work theory and their practice on the ground. When they felt they had a clearer sense of the contribution of youth work in their particular environment, they felt confident enough to 'tell the story'. Articulating the process and impact of youth work is important, especially in contexts where other professionals take 'lead' roles. As Chapter 9 suggests, youth workers have not always been very good at demonstrating how the work they do makes a difference. We would suggest that a deep appreciation of the values, principles and methods of youth work combined with a good account of how it makes a difference in different contexts are the essentials required for telling others, both within and outside of the organisation, about the positive work you have done.

Conclusion: towards a blended approach

Imagine a teacher who is approached at lunchtime by a child who is upset because her pet died at the weekend. Does it seem likely that the teacher will simply dismiss the child's concerns because matters of bereavement and emotional development fall outside the purview of her expertise in primary education? At the other end of the scale, it is unlikely that the teacher would deliver regular counselling sessions to help the pupil come to terms with the loss. Somewhere in between these two extremes is the role flexibility that is usually most appreciated when people talk about their contact with public services.

Using a more relevant example, police officers increasingly spend time engaged in conversation with groups of young people on the street rather than simply dispersing them. They often listen to young people's needs and act as a signpost to various welfare and educational services that can address these needs – hardly an example of traditional crime prevention and detection.

Youth workers have always worn multiple hats. They have been quasi-counsellors, welfare advisers, sports coaches, play workers, artists, teenage pregnancy reduction workers and so on. Amongst the myriad of roles they play and the contexts in which they work, youth workers are primarily educators. They use activities and conversations to contribute to the personal and social development of young people. Their core skill is in using informal education, an open approach to starting from where young people are at, and enabling them to move forwards and think laterally.

Gerry and Steph both worked as mentors ensuring that young people gained the best support they could to overcome the challenges they faced with school work, behaviour or conflict with others. To not do this work would be a disservice to the young people. However, Gerry and Steph contributed to the development of the work of the school by offering a unique youth work service for young people. This approach embodies a commitment to youth work but recognises that practitioners will 'blend' this role with other, pre-prescribed approaches to working with young people. The challenge for youth workers is to identify the opportunities for using informal education in the work both as a philosophy and as a method. To do so, however, requires a comprehensive understanding of *what* informal education is, *who* benefits from it and *how* it can contribute to the overall work of the organisation.

Note

1   Smith, M.K. (2011) 'Introducing informal education', *The Encyclopaedia of Informal Education*, available at www.infed.org/i-intro.htm (last accessed 24/01/12).

Part II

Contexts

Youth work practice does not take place in a vacuum. It is underpinned by the contexts that determine why we intervene in young people's lives, what we seek to achieve and how we work with them. The context of our work is inevitably shaped by forces that we have no control over. Global economic crises can have a significant effect both on the prospects of young people and the extent to which governments are willing and able to resource services that work with young people. Local contexts can be as important as we demonstrate in Chapter 6. For most young people, their own identities and experiences are shaped by where they live: they are essentially 'local'. Along with the local institutions (such as schools or youth clubs), the community plays a significant role, and for many young people, it can be a site of tensions. Chapter 6 reviews the significance of community for youth work practice and outlines some practical steps that can be used to understand and respond more meaningfully to community needs.

Like all other public services, the why, what and how of youth work practice are very much determined by social policy priorities. Social policy analysis is therefore very important for youth work practitioners, and Chapter 7 sets out some of the issues involved in seeking to understand how social policy shapes our work. In Chapter 8, we return to the local context by examining how working with others, in a partnership context, can shape our work. In turn, we explore how youth workers can make a distinctive contribution to the work of other agencies.

The uniting theme in each of the three contexts we explore is the need to have confidence in our practice as youth workers. Having a clear sense of why we do the work we do (Part I) and the techniques we use to engage (Part III) enable us not only to understand the contexts but, we would hope, seek to shape them.

6 The community context

Introduction

The importance of understanding local communities cannot be overstated. Young people, by default of their limited access to resources and mobility, usually spend their time locally and occupy public spaces. They interact with other community members in both positive and negative ways. We come to work with them in these settings, with interventions that are shaped both by the needs of the local community and the wider social policy context of our work.

This chapter explores the role of the youth worker in relation to the local community. It briefly establishes some key theoretical and policy definitions of community and in doing so, establishes why community engagement is central to effective youth work practice. The chapter then offers a series of steps to embed community engagement into your youth work placement and practice more generally.

What is a community?

Task 6.1

What does the word 'community' mean to you? Are you part of one or more communities and if so, which ones? Of each of these communities, in what ways do they make you feel like you belong to them? Share your reflections with a peer.

Community can mean different things to different people. As a starting point, it is often understood in three ways: communities of place (where we live or where we are from), identity (aspects of our cultural or religious identity we share with others) and interest (shared or common goals we share with individuals with similar interests – students, for example). Perhaps the most common use of the word community is as a synonym for a whole host of words that describe the territory we occupy. Words such as neighbour-hood, street, estate and village are often used interchangeably with community, and the term can be applied to describe territories as large as the 'European community' and even 'the international community'. However, when used in this way, community implies only a neutral description of 'place'.

Policy makers, politicians and practitioners tend to think of community as more than mere territory and beyond simple interactions and encounters. Local residents will share this view when they describe their *feelings* about community. These perspectives identify community as a social and political 'space' characterised by sharing: 'shared fate, shared social identities, shared practices (language, religion, culture), shared values' with '*attachments* not simple interactions' (Frazer 1999: 43). Communities are seen to provide connections that ensure individuals are '*enlarged* as a result of social experience and [. . .] sustained by *rootedness*' (Selznick 1998: 16). Thus, community becomes a political and practice preconception: 'crudely, how to get it, and how to secure it once it has been got' (Frazer 1999: 42). All together, this introduces an important word: *meaning*. The meaning we give to something helps us in developing a sense of belonging and connection to our surroundings (Crow and Allan 1994).

To illustrate this point, we can look at the work of the De Montfort University Square Mile community engagement project in Leicester (see www.dmu.ac.uk/mile2). The university worked with a local urban area characterised by rapid social change in terms of declining industry and a seemingly continuous flux in the population demographics. A social capital survey of residents found that people valued positive attributes of 'community' but that the area was characterised by low levels of neighbourliness, a lack of community facilities where people could meet and talk, and a sense of disconnection felt between different groups within the neighbourhood (Wood 2012). These findings are not unique and reflect experiences and perceptions commonly found in urban communities (Power *et al.* 2011). What the findings do help us to do is distinguish between the concept of *neutral territory* (the place where residents live and share resources, etc.) and the *meaning* given to community (the expectations individuals have of their local neighbourhood and the contributions they make to it). In social policy, politics and community work practice, the meaning of community becomes all-important (discussed further below).

In addition to thinking about locality, communities are often used to describe collective identities and interests. For example, much of the literature around community work talks of identity communities, individuals bound to one another most commonly on account of their race, culture or religion and sexuality. These are political and social categories used to identify collective needs (Hoggett 1997). Identity communities can share much in common with communities of place, and often overlap. For instance, the majority of Leicester's Hindu population, of Indian nationality, has historically con-centrated in the East of the city, forming a distinct geographical community. The shared characteristics of racial, cultural and national identity are bound closely to their religious identity, symbolised by the large number of temples in the area. Shared cultural practices are evident through various restaurants offering vegetarian cuisine and rows of shops selling gold and traditional Indian dress. These visible and historical markers of cultural, racial, religious and geographical heritage amount to an identity community that is strong but, like the community of place described above, is not necessarily all-enduring and static. Second- and third-generation migrants may move out of the area of the city and, for some, form new relationships that cross racial and religious traditions.

Communities can also be used to describe groups of people with shared interests. We speculate that you are reading this book because of your professional interests, the requirement to fulfil your course obligations and in order to help develop your work. Naturally, we hope that all of your peers are also reading this book for these reasons! Together, you form communities of interest: students and youth workers in training or practice. Although these labels form part of your identity (see Chapter 3), the connection you have with your peers is not necessarily based primarily on shared cultural, racial or religious aspects, for instance. It is based on your shared occupational and educational interests in youth and community work.

Focusing on communities of place

Other chapters in this book attend to issues of understanding identity (Chapter 3) and how to embed an anti-oppressive approach to practice, in the context of diversity and difference (Chapter 14). Therefore, this chapter considers the relationship between young people and the wider community of place in which they live, work and/or spend their leisure time. We have established that community is a concept used to articulate a range of emotions, concerns, aspirations and hopes connected to our relationships with others who occupy and share our territories. In common political constructions of communities, they are argued to offer people 'what neither society nor the state can offer, namely a sense of belonging in an insecure world' (Delanty 2003: 192) and in doing so they become an important 'moral realm, which is neither one of random individual choice nor of government control' (Etzioni 1993: 254).

The potential contribution that local communities can make to the enrichment of individuals is usually argued most strongly in a body of work called 'communitarianism'. Elements of what we now call communitarianism are not new ones. In mainstream political thought, it was in the 1970s and the 1980s that a 'general theory of communitarianism gradually emerged' (Avineri and de-Shalit 1992: 2). One strand of this general theory is called political communitarianism, which takes the ideal of community and offers 'prescriptions about the political and social institutions that could realise this ideal' (Frazer 1999: 11). There are key shared themes in each of the varieties of political communitarianism, notably an emphasis on 'civic spirit, responsibility for self and for the community, mutuality', the emphasis on participation and that the 'strength of families and the strength of communities are mutually reinforcing' (see Frazer 1999: 35–8). There is also a consensus on what threatens the community ideal including 'selfishness on the part of individuals, ineptitude and betrayal on the part of bureaucratic government, [and] crime' (Frazer 1999: 38). In policy terms, this has included a number of measures designed to strengthen the capacity of communities as sites for 'the realisation of common values in support of social goods, including public safety, norms of civility and trust, efficacious voluntary associations, and collective socialisation of the young' (Sampson 1999: 247).

Communities are sites where levels of inclusion and exclusion affect those living in the local area. Consider for example the De Montfort project survey referred to above. Many residents who had lived in the area for considerable periods of time expressed concern at the rapidly changing (migrant) population that they felt were changing the character of the area and, to some degree, were responsible for feelings of 'not knowing our neighbours'. Similarly, people who had only recently moved into the local area felt that a sense of community did not exist and therefore felt unable or unwilling to contribute to collective local activities. These tensions also applied to relationships between older residents and young people who congregated around public spaces and street corners (explored in more detail below). At the most basic level, these tensions may result in feelings of insecurity or distrust leading to an idea that the 'community was not what it once used to be'. Communities can therefore lead to divisions. For instance, they can become places where people are divided according to age differences, how long they have lived in the area, where they have immigrated from and so on.

Young people and their communities

Young people are, by the nature of their restricted mobility and resources, essentially 'local': 'Locality . . . remains an important site in shaping young sense of place in the world' (France 2007: 157–8). Young people develop their social relationships in communities and the process of 'hanging around' is often undoubtedly *pro*-social. What we know from research is that hanging around in local settings is a critical part of young people's social identity formation (Holland *et al.* 2007). The process of 'asserting' and 'testing' identities is usually conducted in these groups (Hall *et al.* 1999), where a strong attachment to the local neighbourhood is usually in evidence (Weller 2007). At the heart of this idea is that of 'belonging', an essential, inclusionary component of citizenship (Lister *et al.* 2002) particularly in relation to young people and their local 'community life' (France 1996). Young people *belong* within their friendship and other social networks, and have this belonging endorsed by their peers. Where communities exclude, belonging and integration inevitably weaken.

Weller (2007) examined the linkage between young people's sense of citizenship and their activity of 'hanging around' in local communities. In a survey of young people 'hanging out in rural communities' (Weller 2007: 100), the majority of those who responded indicated that they most often met friends or socialised in 'public spaces' such as the beaches, parks/greens, woods, recreational grounds, skate parks and 'claimed spaces' such as streets, benches, bus shelters and graveyards (Weller 2007: 101).

Weller's assessment of public spaces and claimed spaces provided illuminating insights into the uses that young people make of them. They served as 'meeting points' in 'favourite or regular' spaces (Weller 2007: 104). Most of these were sites where they would socialise with other friends and there was a general frustration that there were not more 'affordable and accessible' activities available for young people: 'as teenagers, with greater spatial freedoms, many stated the need for more facilities when away from the home' (Weller 2007: 137). In a context where the majority of young people liked living in their community but only '34 per cent felt a sense of belonging' (Weller 2007:

133), young people hanging around was deemed by others as not 'a legitimate use of space' (Weller 2007: 135). Public space ultimately becomes what Reay and Lucey (2000) termed 'child-hostile social landscapes'.

Much of the discourse around young people and communities focuses on the problems that young people can cause and the desire to control or regulate young people's engagement with their neighbourhoods. Initiatives such as citizenship education, volunteering projects and detached youth work have long been seen as strategies for instilling a greater sense of responsibility in young people towards their local community. Though not exclusively focused at young people, civil powers, such as anti-social behaviour measures or curfew orders, are often targeted at young people on the 'margins' (Yates, J. 2009). As Hughes and Follett (2006: 157) argue: 'The seemingly newly "discovered" problem of anti-social behaviour appears to be increasingly recoded as a problem of young people in deprived and marginalised communities and neighbourhoods'.

The discussion in Chapter 7 on young people's relative position in society reminds us that much media coverage about young people is negative. In neighbourhoods, this media coverage helps to reinforce feelings of fear and anxiety about a seemingly 'visible' threat of young people. In hanging around on street corners, they wear clothes, use language and engage in behaviours that are seen by other residents as a threat. Young people become 'the universal symbol of disorder' (Burney 2002: 473).

A combination of lower levels of public tolerance for incivility together with an increase in the fear of young people (Young and Matthews 2003) serves to disguise the reality of a general decline in youth-related criminal activity (Armstrong 2004; Furlong and Cartmel 2007). Such fear reproduction effectively stigmatises young people further, resulting in yet more surveillance and regulation (Kelly 2003; McKenzie 2005), and a perverse consequence is a vicious circle: 'Society [. . .] becomes increasingly fearful, suspicious of youths, which in turn means they are more closely supervised by the police than any other age group' (McKenzie 2005: 194). The result is that communities, over the past few decades, have at their disposal a range of strategies to police groups that are seen as causing problems. It is little surprise then that much of this is targeted at young people. Muncie (2004) illustrates how communities, individuals and the family are all now held responsible for managing problems of youth crime and anti-social behaviour with a series of 'programmes which seek either to remove young people from the street or to provide them and their parents with coercive "retraining"' (Muncie 2004: 139).

In contrast to this rather negative review of young people's relationship with their communities, there has also been a growth in research in the recent past that has examined the positive contributions that young people make to their neighbourhoods. Lister et al. (2002) found that young people engaged routinely in a range of socially constructive practices that included formal voluntary work, 'neighbourliness, informal political action, and other forms of social participation' (2002: 10). Work by Roker et al. (1999) also found that young people involved in their studies were engaged in a wide range of social participation activities, ranging from informal volunteering through to structured participation. Young people in Wood's study (2009b) offered a range of social participation practices that many of us would be familiar with (see Table 6.1).

Table 6.1 Specific experiences of general social participation and voluntary work

General social participation	Voluntary and charity work
• Helping a lady who couldn't speak English when visiting the housing office. • Babysitting for, or helping, neighbours. • Using the police to help with tackling a particular problem in the community. • Taking part in activities through the local youth club. • Reporting someone who had stolen money from the youth club.	• Helped clean up the local park or helped with a litter collection. • Volunteered at local projects such as the local playscheme or the day centre for older people. • Undertook responsibilities at the local youth club, including planning activities, managing the tuckshop and being on the committee. • Raising funds for charity; helping out with fundraising events.

Source: Wood (2009b: 249)

This brief review has enabled us to think about the relationship between young people and their communities. It can be too common that this relationship is discussed in negative terms and much policy emphasis has been focused on changing young people's behaviour in their local neighbourhood. However, alternative evidence suggests that young people often do play more 'positive' roles within their neighbourhoods.

Reflection 6.1

How are young people represented within your local community? Is there evidence of them being marginalised? Is there evidence that they engage in social participation?

Understanding and working with the community

Whether you are based in a local youth club, working as a detached youth worker or based in a national charity's local office, becoming *familiar* with the surrounding community is vital. As the chapter has so far argued, young people are essentially 'local', bound by resources and mobility to their neighbourhoods. The extent to which you engage with the wider community will inevitably be affected by the remit of your role, but knowing the surrounding area will provide you with valuable insights into the daily life and experiences of young people and the wider community. In this section of the chapter, we consider some common steps to understanding your local neighbourhood. As we discuss each step, it would be helpful to relate this to the neighbourhood in which you work or live, to test the applicability of each approach in your day-to-day practice.

Step 1: Orientation

Orientation involves 'knowing the "patch" or the "ground" – where things are and what is going on' (Smith 1994: 15) and commences with systematic observation of the local community. When people consider moving into an area, some of this observation is undertaken naturally but it is also true that you can walk past something for years and not really notice it there. This is why deliberate observation activity can help illuminate aspects of community life that may have hitherto been unknown to the practitioner.

Orientation involves using very traditional methods and approaches. It starts from the assumption that to understand the spaces we occupy, we need to take stock of what is around us. This means getting out and about in the local community we are based in, making notes about what we see (or are told) and who we talk to in order to develop some insights into the local area.

Reflection 6.2

You are about to set off to undertake a systematic observation of your local neighbourhood. Make a list of the things that you might look out for. How would you document what you see?

Your list may well cover a number of things to look for. It may be useful to develop a list of categories, some of which are set out in Table 6.2 overleaf.

The list in Table 6.2 is deliberately not exhaustive and will undoubtedly develop as you undertake your own orientation work. Some of what you collect will be factual (for example, the number of shops); other things may depend on your own interpretive judgements or impressions about the area. For instance, when looking at the different types of litter you observe, you might begin to form impressions about what particular challenges the neighbourhood faces. The prevalence of cigarette packets or lager cans often may indicate a need to investigate the health profile of a neighbourhood. You might also begin to form impressions about how people relate to one another in the neighbourhood. For instance, do you see different groups interacting? How do people engage with one another in local shops? Who uses the local parks and other public spaces? Do people rush around or do they move at a leisurely pace?

The exercise will also give you insights into the resources and facilities available to a local community. We refer to these as 'assets' and they are often overlooked in thinking about the needs of a local neighbourhood. Our focus is often on the aspects of a community that are not working as well as we might hope. This focus on 'deficits' inevitably leads us to ignoring what potentially might be very good about living in an area and what may be harnessed to make things even better.

During the exercise you may also have the opportunity to strike up conversations with people you encounter. These conversations provide important contextual data –

Table 6.2 Indicators to observe during orientation

Community 'assets'	• Schools and colleges • Local shops • Local businesses/employers • Parks and green spaces • Community centres • Libraries • Social clubs • Pubs, cafes and restaurants • Availability of public transport
Meeting points	• Where are the main social meeting points for people? • What spaces do young people 'claim' (e.g. street corners) and at what times?
Environment	• What observations can you make about the quality of the living environment? • Is there litter in the area? • What type of litter is there? • Is there evidence of graffiti? What does it say? • What is the quality of housing in the area?
Heritage	• What points of historical interest can you find in the local area? • What particular places are valued, in a historical sense, by residents?
Others	• What other indicators might you look for?

they reveal more than relying on observation alone. Conversations at the stage of orientation will be informal, designed just to ascertain how people feel about living or working in the area. We might ask general questions about what is good, what is bad and how this has changed over time.

On one recent community walkabout, we engaged in a number of useful conversations with:

• a group of dog walkers using a local park;
• a park warden responsible for cleaning the park;
• a shopkeeper running an independent off-licence;
• a group of young men congregating around an abandoned house;
• a group of older people queuing in the post office;
• the local neighbourhood police officer; and
• a community worker.

Task 6.2

Step 1 – Orientation

1   Work out a walking route through your neighbourhood to undertake an initial orientation exercise.
2   Using a table or similar recording tool, capture your observations of the categories listed above (and any further categories you can add).
3   Try to repeat the walkabout at a different time of day to see if things are different.
4   Make a record of any conversations you had with people.
5   Share you observations with someone else connected to the community. How much is shared? Did you identify things that the person had not observed before?

Step 2: Developing a community profile

Having undertaken some of your own observations, it is now worth beginning to look at the community in more detail. As Smith (1994: 15) notes, practitioners:

> are there not simply to learn about the area but to intervene . . . to do that effectively over a period of time entails knowing more about the area than where the streets lead and what facilities there are. It involves gaining an active appreciation of local networks and relationships; of how things work; of the norms and values of different groups within the area; of power relationships and 'important' people; and so on.

This requires you to undertake both primary and secondary 'practitioner research', contributing to what is often called a 'community profile' (Hawtin and Percy-Smith 2007). Developing a community profile enables you to understand the range of needs and resources that are specific to an area, and how these compare with other areas. A community profile should set out to address:

* *the area as a place to live* – including the quality of the physical environment and people's attitudes to living there; the extent to which needs are matched with resources; and the extent to which local facilities meet people's goals and aspirations;
* *the area as a social community* – including residents' involvement in the social life of the community; the extent to which the community is supportive; formal and informal networks;
* *the area as an economic community* – including income levels and employment prospects of local residents; the prosperity and viability of local shops;

- *the area as a political community* – including systems and structures of political representation and local area management; the extent to which local people can influence decisions that affect them; the degree of involvement in local decision making; participation in community organizations;
- *the area as a personal space* – the degree of attachment that people have to the local area; memories and life experiences of local people;
- *the area as part of its city* – infrastructural, economic and social linkages between the local area and the city or district of which it is a part; the specific local identity that differentiates the community from the rest of the area/district.

(Hawtin and Percy-Smith 2007: 6)

Doing a community profile takes time. It is important to identify the methods that are available to you in the time and resource given to your role and on a busy placement; these can be very constrained. The suggested approach set out below is designed to support you in undertaking a 'comprehensive [assessment] of the *needs* of a population that is defined, or defines itself, as a *community*, and the *resources* that exist within that community' (Hawtin and Percy-Smith 2007: 5).

Task 6.3

Step 2 – Developing a community profile

Discuss Table 6.3 with your supervisor and set about planning a community profile.

- Which of the elements can you reasonably undertake in the time and resource constraints of your role?
- What other data sources or approaches could you adopt to strengthen your community profile?
- Will the data you capture be used in helping to plan how the local organisation works? If so, how?

Step 3: Situating concerns in a multi-perspective context

The approaches that we use in developing our knowledge about a community will bring us into contact with a wide variety of views, some in agreement, some in conflict. These rich perspectives provide the 'meaning' given to a community and enable us to work more effectively as reflective and critical practitioners. Practitioners need to be open and willing to hear a variety of different views, and this requires special attention when the views expressed conflict with the worker's own values or perspectives. Let us take the example of the following case study to illustrate this point:

Table 6.3 Developing a community profile

Question	Possible approaches
What secondary data is available that tells me about the neighbourhood I work in?	Much of this work can be undertaken at your desk, reviewing a number of online sources that provide useful insights into the statistical picture of the neighbourhood. For useful neighbourhood summaries, try these two websites (using a postcode from the area to bring up the profiles): • Office for National Statistics (www.neighbourhood. statistics.gov.uk) – provides a very useful neighbourhood summary and comparisons in terms of deprivation index data, and is drawn from a range of statistical data sources. • Upmystreet (www.upmystreet.com) – provides an overview of house prices, schools, political representatives, council performance, population numbers, employment data and so on. Other statistical data sources include information held by the local authority, the police and voluntary sector organisations. Use a search engine to find local area 'plans' and 'strategies' for a variety of local government departments. It would also be worth seeing what 'ward level data' is available for your local neighbourhood.
What does my agency know about the neighbourhood? What other organisations might know about this neighbourhood?	Your placement organisation may also hold valuable information about the local neighbourhood, so it is worth checking this prior to undertaking your own primary research. If available, data and analysis of the local area might be found in: • an organisation's community profile or work plan; • funding bids previously submitted; • local surveys or other consultation exercises. Organisations will vary in the extent to which they can successfully claim to have data that is up to date and reliable about their local neighbourhood. It is worth getting in touch with other community organisations in the area to see if they have engaged in any community consultation activities.
Is there a way to systematically collect data on resident perceptions of their neighbourhood?	Undertaking your own survey of residents who live in the neighbourhood can help you to understand how people feel about living in their community. You can use a survey to ask a number of different questions related to perceptions of need and of the quality of public services, and 'visioning' questions focused on what might need to change. As we discussed above, communities are more than neutral territories. They are places where people give 'meaning' to the encounters with each other. They can be places of conflict and tension. Work around social capital (e.g. Boeck 2009) is a useful starting point – questions here tend to focus on feelings of belonging, trust and security in neighbourhoods.

Table 6.3 Continued

Question	Possible approaches
	In one community project, we used a series of statements and invited people to express their level of agreement (from low to high) with each statement. This enabled people to comment on aspects of how they felt about their community. Some example statements are offered below: • This neighbourhood is a close, tight-knit community • This neighbourhood is a friendly place to live • This neighbourhood is a place where people look after each other • I feel safe walking around this neighbourhood in the daytime • I feel safe walking around this neighbourhood at night • I feel I can influence decisions made about my local neighbourhood We also asked about their satisfaction with local services and asked them to rate what they felt were the most pressing issues facing their local neighbourhood. Some examples we offered included: • Crime and anti-social behaviour • Housing • Transport • Education and schools • The local environment • Local jobs The survey concluded with an invitation to participants to imagine one thing that could be different to improve life in the community.
How can I capture the views of those on the margins?	A survey of residents is a useful tool for generating an overall picture of the local neighbourhood's needs. However, the views of those on the margins of the community may be excluded if relying solely on this data collection method. For instance, if the survey is conducted door to door, it may miss valuable insights from younger residents living in the neighbourhood. Similarly, if the survey is conducted only in one language, people with different languages may not be able to participate fully. Some approaches that we have used to capture the views of those who might otherwise be marginalised included running detached youth work sessions themed around the survey questions to gather young people's views. We also attended legal advice centres and services that were tailored towards marginalised groups (such as young parents, carers and asylum seekers). The most important step we took though was to simply 'be around', connecting with people in local shops, libraries and other meeting points to initiate conversations.

During their period of orientation and profiling, a community project team undertook a comprehensive doorstep survey. For many residents, young people hanging around were seen as a major problem that engendered fear and contributed to their feelings of insecurity. As a result, many residents said they did not go out at night, and expressed a reluctance to engage with young people for fear of reprisals. Despite these fears, evidence of criminal or intimidating behaviour by young people towards other residents was limited.

What are your reactions to this case study? As a youth worker, how would you explain the responses?

This case is by no means unique and you may have come across similar situations yourself. Findings from the British Crime Survey exploring the perspectives and experiences of anti-social behaviour identified 'young people hanging around' as the biggest issue with 'being a general nuisance' cited as the most common behaviour of concern (Upson 2006). This sits within the context of media coverage that commonly portrays young people in a negative light, with some 75 per cent of reports focusing on problem behaviour by young people (NYA 2004). Government's preoccupation with anti-social behaviour has also been identified as a contributory factor in increasing fear of young people (Stephen and Squires 2004). In the context of the case study described above, the area had seen the introduction of regular policing to engage with young people, the provision of targeted detached youth workers allocated on the basis of the area being an anti-social behaviour 'hotspot' (Yates, J. 2009) and the introduction of a controversial 'Mosquito' device that emitted a high-pitch frequency only detectable by young people.

Given this context, there might have been a strong temptation to dismiss the resident concerns about anti-social behaviour and young people set out in the case study above. Youth workers might reasonably react by standing up for young people and attempting to tip 'balances of power in young people's favour' (Davies 2005: 7). However, by dismissing what may be legitimate concerns, we might end up failing to address wider problems.

Dispersing young people or actively standing up for them represents two ends of a pole and using either strategy fails to deal with both the fears expressed by residents and the need to enable both groups to engage with one another. A youth worker may be present for just two hours per week with a group of young people on a street whereas the local residents have to live with their unaddressed fears every day. We are also in danger of ignoring the other contextual factors that explain resident concerns. For example, in the case study area described above, numerous other concerns about the lack of collective meeting spaces and community facilities, and the decline of the local environment were seen as important factors in why residents felt negatively about the area in which they lived. Young people congregating on street corners can become the visible manifestation of a whole host of insecurities and concerns that may have been ignored and seem too difficult to challenge.

We also need to recognise that it is highly probable that some residents *have* been intimidated by other people, including young people. Experiences of intimation, no matter how isolated, can quickly become communal anxieties that are reinforced through 'social currency': the conversations that we have with our neighbours, at the school gates or down the pub (Hughes *et al.* 2006: 262). As communicative strategies and interactive media continue to expand through, for example, the internet, yet more information and debates are in the public domain, and these in turn help shape our social currency.

Thus, whilst it may be easy to dismiss resident concerns about young people as unfounded, they are both perceived and in some cases experienced as real phenomena. The youth worker in the community context needs to consider how best to address division and contests within the local area by showing that they can work to bring people together to work through *difference*.

Task 6.4

Step 3 – Considering multiple perspectives

Reflect on the data you have collected so far.

- To what extent are the different groups in your community profile 'united' on the issues facing the community?
- Have different groups in the community prioritised problems in different ways?
- What is the relationship between the perceptions of need and the secondary data in the area?
- Are there any obvious (or less obvious) conflicts in this neighbourhood? How might you explain them?

Step 4: Bringing together

We have so far described a process that enables the youth worker to become more familiar with the local community in which they are working. This chapter has deliberately not focused on interventions, favouring instead an approach that deepens our understanding of the neighbourhoods we work in as important sites for young people (France 2007). This can have a number of benefits. It sharpens our focus on what might be the difference between community 'needs' and 'wants' and gives us an appreciation of the assets already present within a community. It also enables us to understand the experiences of individuals in *depth* and in *context*. Finally, it can help us in thinking through the first steps of how a community might take action about issues affecting the area, with our support. Yet, there is nothing in the approach taken so far that explores how we might bring different groups together to explore common issues or areas where difference might occur.

The final step then is focused on bringing together the different actors within a community. No matter how homogeneous a community appears to be, all contain within them degrees of difference and diversity, whether this is hidden or visible. Sometimes these differences can lead to tensions or conflict, resulting in what Staeheli (2008) terms 'contests'. Communities are by their nature inclusionary or exclusionary (Staeheli 2008) with those who are visibly outside of the 'norm' often excluded. In the common example of anti-social behaviour above, we saw an obvious tension between the needs of one group of residents and the needs of another. Where young people are dispersed or subjected to other criminalising measures, there is the likelihood that they will feel further excluded (Burney 2002). Equally, if concerns about anti-social behaviour are not treated with any seriousness, other groups (in particular, older people) might feel isolated and unable to tackle what may be some deep-rooted fears. Taking one side or the other narrows our understanding of how different groups interact and exchange their perspectives on issues. Since symbols of disorder can mask the real challenges a community might face, there is much to be gained from bringing people together to work towards a consensus understanding of their neighbourhoods. We therefore now focus our attention on the contribution that informal education can make to building *dialogue* in a community context.

In Chapter 5, we explored the principles of informal education and recognised that nurturing dialogue was likely to provide us with valuable learning moments. Dialogue can be a powerful tool for fostering democracy, bringing together people with different perspectives and challenging received wisdom. In a community context, we use dialogue to bridge perspectives, often working with people who have not previously engaged with one another. This practice takes a variety of forms, ranging from truth and reconciliation work where communities have been at war through to the day-to-day intergenerational practice designed to improve relationships between young and older residents in neighbourhoods. Structured approaches to encouraging dialogue invite people to pause, consider other views and contribute their own insights. Most importantly, as Tiffany (2009) found in his study of using community philosophy, people have the opportunity to *listen*:

> [It gave] us a process to talk to and listen to each other. One of the great things is the listening. Now we will listen to each other. And there's turn-taking; it made us be quiet and listen to each other.
>
> (Participant, quoted in Tiffany 2009: 16)

In practical terms, what approaches might we adopt to encourage the space and time for people to listen and talk to each other? There is probably an endless list of creative approaches that may promote more engaging discussion than that found at many community meetings. We offer two particular practical approaches here to be considered.

Listening, and then encouraging others to listen

We draw here on a process used by Nottingham Citizens, an alliance of organisations that uses the tools of community organising to identify and take action on needs. In this model, community organisers make contact with individuals through their member organisations or community groups and engage in listening activities designed to explore personal stories, any problems or issues, and ideas on how things might be different. They then encourage, support and train these individuals to listen to others, initially within their own communities and then beyond. Finally, they encourage individuals to work together to construct plans for action. The results have been very positive for those engaged in the process. In one example, black young men worried about stop-and-search were invited to listen to the police, and vice versa. This built a common understanding of the problem before enabling the different groups to work together on possible solutions. Sometimes, solutions are not the focus and one quite moving example shows how listening in itself can offer value. Following the very public murder of a British Army soldier named Lee Rigby in 2013 in what was termed an Islamic terrorist attack, there was much public outcry and calls from far-right groups such as the English Defence League to mount anti-Islam demonstrations in various cities. The Citizens movement in Nottingham responded very differently. In the week of the attack, the group facilitated a meeting where individuals, from Islam and other faiths or none, came together to engage in one-to-one listening. The focus was on enabling people to hear from each other at a time of particular anxiety, and some 300 people took part. Listening therefore provided an important counterblast to condemnation or misunderstanding. It also enabled people from different walks of life to develop an appreciation of difference.

Community resolution circles

A similar approach has been adopted in local communities where the principles of Restorative Justice have been used to enable residents to share their stories with one another in order to build a common understanding of issues facing neighbourhoods. Restorative Justice is an approach that enables victims to tell offenders about the impact of the crime, get answers to questions and receive an apology for what has happened (Restorative Justice Council 2012). An extension of this is community resolution, designed to enable people to share their anxieties with each other so that a better understanding of the impact of certain behaviours or issues is better understood. However, the focus here is not on blame or on enabling victims to be heard: it is on building reconciliation and common understanding. One approach described to us by a police officer involved meeting first with young people in a circle to enable them to speak and be heard about a range of issues they faced in the neighbourhood. The next circle was with older residents who were invited to do the same. The final circle brought both groups together to share their stories with each other. The role of the facilitator was vital to the success of the groups and their tasks included:

- Investing the time in recruiting people to join each group, providing an honest overview of what would be expected from the process and supporting people to positively opt in.
- Carefully moderating discussions so that as many people were heard within their own individual circles and within the cross-group circle. This was aided by using an object to signify turn-taking, i.e. when you hold the object it is your turn to speak.

- Keeping an accurate record of the progress of the discussion so that participants could see the issues that they had covered.
- Providing support for participants including spotting when breaks were needed and providing individual follow-up on any particular issues that were raised during the discussion.

As in the above example, the value of listening could not be overstated in this process but an added benefit can often be found in communities identifying issues that they can collectively act on. In one example of a circles exercise, the intergenerational group decided to tackle a particularly unsightly park so that it could become a more user-friendly public space for all age groups.

These are just two of many different approaches that might be used to bring people together to continue our process of gaining an understanding of the daily life and experience of the different people living within a neighbourhood.

Task 6.5

Step 4 – Bringing together

Reflect on the above examples and the task you undertook in Step 3, and discuss the following questions with your supervisor:

- Who do you think needs to come together in your community?
- How would you describe the differences between them?
- What methods could you adopt to encourage people to listen to others who may have different views from their own?
- What practical steps and resources do you need in order to make this happen?
- What will be the outcome of this process?

Conclusion

This chapter has explored our role as youth workers working within a community context. We have focused on communities of place, the geography where young people form, assert and test their identities. In order to engage effectively with communities, youth workers need to develop a rich understanding of the neighbourhoods in which they work. This understanding is built from our reading of secondary data and is enriched through observation and conversation: knowing the patch is what helps us to be both accepted by communities and more responsive in our work.

However, it is important that we recognise that communities are not neutral territories; they are often sites of conflict or tension between different groups. If we are committed to a meaningful engagement with those whom we work with, it is unwise to ignore or downplay such tensions. In this chapter, we have only briefly introduced some of the approaches we might adopt to enable people to listen to one another as a first step to resolving any tensions. Whether we are visitors or active members of the communities with which we work, our lasting legacy should be one of communities working together and where possible, of a consensus assessment of what is good (and less good) about their communal environment.

7 The policy and organisational context

Introduction

As students and practitioners in youth work, we find ourselves in diverse agencies that seek to address different policy priorities. Whereas traditionally youth workers would mainly engage in a voluntary, learning relationship with young people in youth centres and through detached youth work, increasingly practitioners will work in schools, youth justice teams, health services and other settings. In addition, practitioners may find that even so-called voluntary engagement is underpinned by targeted approaches to work and the pursuit of accredited outcomes for young people.

This chapter seeks to locate the work of different organisations within a broader social policy context. It is our contention that youth workers can and do make contributions to a whole range of organisations where priorities or aims may be different from those of the principles and values of youth work. However, in order to make informed decisions about whether we can, as youth workers, complement the work of these agencies, we need to consider the policy context of the organisations we find ourselves working with. This requires us to consider not only *what* the organisation seeks to do but also a series of deeper questions related to *why* it works with young people.

Why social policy matters

All organisations that employ youth workers do so within a social policy context that can determine why and how we work with young people and what outcomes are expected from our work. Some outcomes will be explicit and somewhat easy to measure (the award of qualifications, for example). Others might be more difficult to demonstrate, but are certainly worthy – 'raising confidence', for example. The point is that most of these desired endpoints are often prescribed through various policy initiatives. Youth work is by no means unique in this respect. Over a period of nearly three decades, public services in the United Kingdom have undergone significant transformation with increased targeting and measurement of outputs and outcomes (Banks 2004). The trend in the recent past has been towards 'evidence-based' policy and practice realised through interventions that are underpinned by research or good practice. However, 'there is no simple top down linear relationship of . . . [evidence] to policy and practice' (Hine and Wood 2009: 253) since the evidence chosen can be selective and misrepresented to shape existing policy agendas. In order to understand what is required in terms of the outcomes of our work, or the desired ends, we must investigate the social policy context within which organisations and our roles are shaped. Davies (2010) is right when he refers to social policy analysis as a 'first and vital skill' of youth workers, since youth work policy

> lays out boundaries within which practice 'on the ground' will – perhaps *must* – operate. These may be drawn broadly or narrowly, loosely or tightly. They may allow practitioners more or less room for manoeuvre. This space may expand or narrow according to whether the economy is doing well or badly; whether people generally, or influential groups, feel secure or threatened; whether young people are more respected than feared.
>
> (Davies 2010: 7)

Understanding social policy is therefore not an academic or abstract question. Reflecting on the wider influences on our organisation's work can help us to understand the *how*, *what* and *why* questions: How does the organisation deliver its work? What aims does it set? Who does it work with, specifically? These are *methodological* questions that consider the approaches used by an organisation, the techniques it values and uses. Deeper questions are concerned with *why*: What has led to this particular form of work with young people and what does the work hope to achieve? In order to think this through, we need to examine a series of components in the relationship between policy and practice.

Figure 7.1, below, presents a linear process that helps us to explore the relationship between *drivers* (those things that influence or shape organisational practice), the organisation's *aims and methods* (the ways in which it responds to these drivers) and the *outcomes* that are expected as a result.

We start at the end of the process with a discussion about *outcomes*.

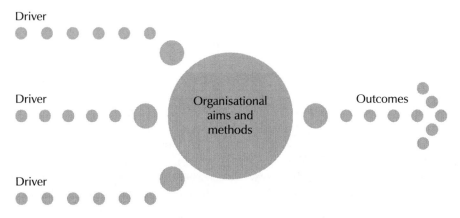

Figure 7.1 Policy drivers, practice and outcomes

Outcomes: what will happen to young people as a result of our work?

It may seem strange to start at the end of a process model but determining the anticipated outcomes of our work is useful in thinking about why an organisation uses particular aims and methods in its approach to work with young people. The fundamental question here is: *What do we expect young people to gain as a result of our interventions in their lives?* Sometimes, this question has had plenty of time to be developed and thought through. For example, we know why a health visitor intervenes in the life of a child. Early advice and intervention on health issues can help the development of personal, behavioural and social milestones in children. Obtaining these milestones is the outcome of the work. Similarly, a teacher working within a set curriculum is obligated to meet a number of prescribed outcomes for young people, not least in terms of standards of literacy and numeracy.

Youth workers will find themselves in different organisations that will claim to work towards particular outcomes. Sometimes these will be outcomes that are shared by a number of different organisations. For example, numerous organisations with very different working practices in different contexts might claim 'raising young people's confidence' as a key outcome of the work. Other times, there will be clear differences and distinctions. Task 7.1 is designed to begin to enable you to think about both distinctive and shared outcomes.

Outcomes then are anticipated to occur as a result of the work. From your cursory review of the different organisations listed above, you may find many different types of outcome, some of which include:

- Short-term and instrumental outcomes, linked to particular interventions or sessions. For example, as a result of attending a particular sex education session, young people might be able to describe how different contraceptives work.
- Longer-term outcomes that build desired physical, emotional or social attributes that can contribute to a 'successful' transition to adulthood. These may be cumulatively built as a result of sustained engagement with young people.
- Those that address particular social policy 'problems', such as an outcome to reduce reoffending or reduce the likelihood of teenage pregnancy.
- Those that are more positively focused, such as those that are 'strengths based', usually 'building on' what skills, knowledge or experiences young people are deemed to already have.

Chapter 9 discusses the successes and challenges that youth workers have faced in capturing, evaluating and describing outcomes. The connection between the outcomes we seek to achieve and the things that lead us to be concerned about them (the *drivers* discussed below) is very strong.

Task 7.1

Using a search engine or similar resource, locate an example of each of the organisations listed in the table below.

- How do they describe their outcomes?
- Which of these do you think are specific to the organisation?
- Which of these might be more generic (i.e. outcomes that may be achieved by other organisations)?
- Discuss your table with a line manager or supervisor and explore what outcomes your own organisation claims to achieve in its work with young people.

Organisation	What does it hope to achieve (specific to its organisation)?	What does it hope to achieve (that might be shared with others)?
Local authority detached youth work team		
Youth offending team		
Teenage Pregnancy Project		
National Citizens Service		
School Mentoring and Behaviour Support Team		

Drivers: why are we concerned?

As we suggest above, starting with the organisational aims and methods should present you with very few challenges. For example, if you are undertaking youth work in a school exclusion unit, the aims might be very explicit. They might include a statement such as this one: to provide young people with advice, support and activities that will support their reintegration into full-time education. Their methods may include a range of interventions that support this aim (structured sessions outside of normal classroom activity, lunchtime clubs, advice sessions, youth council membership and so on). The desired outcome in this case stems quite naturally from the aims – the reintegration of young people into full-time education. When we come to look at the drivers for this particular work, we might begin to see a number of key things that have led to this type of intervention. For one, the school itself might wish to see greater levels of participation amongst young people at risk of leaving their school. You might rightfully conclude that this is a driver. However, why would schools be interested in retaining students who may present particular challenges in terms of behaviour and attendance? Put more crudely, what is in it for the school to invest the time and resources to achieve this outcome?

This is where more detailed analysis of drivers is important. We might ask questions such as:

- How does the school's approach reflect national or local government approaches to dealing with exclusions?
- Is the school operating within a particular legal or policy framework?
- Why is this particular outcome seen as important in policy frameworks?
- What would happen if the outcomes were not met? For the young people? For wider society?
- What research or other evidence is used by policy makers to justify the approach taken?

As we begin to research these questions, we can locate our own practice and the work of our organisations within *proximate drivers* and *wider drivers*.

The word 'proximate' implies something that is close by and in thinking about drivers, we refer here to those localised or immediate circumstances, events or issues that often shape practice responses. For instance, a voluntary youth club may come about as a result of local pressure to respond to anti-social behaviour or because it is perceived that young people need activities to occupy their time. Proximate drivers might take the form of the concerns of residents or a ward councillor, the profile of a neighbourhood, a local authority's particular plans for children and young people, or the local problems or challenges facing young people in a geographically defined area. A strong proximate driver might be the views of young people themselves, campaigning to secure better facilities for their peers. Youth workers often consider a variety of perspectives in assessing the needs that underpin their work. Many of these are proximate drivers.

Proximate drivers are therefore, by their nature, local. Wider drivers on the other hand might be decisions or situations that take place some distance from the day-to-day experience of where we work. For example, decisions to change laws or social policy priorities are often made by central government responding to a wide range of social, technological and economic factors.

Wider drivers can take the form of *direct* influences on our work, i.e. where our practice is guided from a distance but in *explicit* ways. Social workers, teachers, police officers and other professionals are used to operating at a local level but within strong national legal and policy frameworks. The level of resource and explicitness of their duties are set out in statutory guidance and are shaped very deliberately by central government, their professional bodies and other major influences.

Task 7.2

Return to the list of organisations that you searched for earlier.

- Can you find any national guidance that sets out explicitly what is expected of the organisations?
- Can you find any examples of laws or policies that underpin these expectations?

Organisation	Examples of explicit expectations of government or other national bodies	Examples of laws that underpin these expectations
Local authority detached youth work team		
Youth offending team		
Teenage Pregnancy Project		
National Citizens Service		
School Mentoring and Behaviour Support Team		

In some cases, it will be relatively straightforward to link government expectations, the law and the practice of different organisations. Taking youth offending teams as an example:

- Youth offending teams are required by law, having been introduced by section 39(1) of the Crime and Disorder Act 1998, which set out the duty of every 'local authority acting in co-operation with partner agencies (who are under a duty to co-operate with the local authority), to establish for their area one or more youth offending teams (YOT)'.
- The government gives very specific guidance on what is expected from youth offending teams including the responsibilities of the different agencies involved, the specific requirements for what should be delivered and how the team should be governed (Youth Justice Board for England and Wales 2013).

- This guidance builds on previous instruments that told local areas how to set up the teams, who was legally required to be involved and what structures needed to be in place when they first came into force (Home Office 1998).
- Practitioners are mandated to use a standard structured assessment tool on all young offenders who come into contact with the criminal justice system: the ASSET tool (see www.justice.gov.uk/youth-justice/assessment/asset-young-offender-assessment-profile).
- An 'effective practice library' offers a central repository of 'evidence' to inform good practice (see www.justice.gov.uk/youth-justice/effective-practice-library).

This plethora of guidance is just at the surface level of how youth offending teams are delivered within a very direct and explicit set of wider drivers. In other cases, such as the detached youth work team, relationships between law, central government policy and practice on the ground may be more tenuous. For instance, the most recent and relevant law that underpins the provision of local youth services is section 507B of the Education and Inspections Act (2006), which imposed

> a duty on local education authorities to promote the well-being of persons aged 13–19 (and of persons aged up to 25 with learning difficulties) by securing access for them to sufficient educational and recreational leisure-time activities and facilities, so far as is reasonably practicable. The section provides that an authority can fulfil this duty by providing activities and facilities, assisting others to do so, or by making other arrangements to facilitate access, which can include the provision of transport, financial assistance or information. Furthermore, local education authorities are required to supply and keep up to date information regarding those leisure-time activities and facilities that are available locally.
> (Education and Inspections Act, Explanatory Notes 2006: para 34)

In reading this statement we might see why there is plenty of flexibility in how local authorities might design and provide youth services. Of particular note is the phrase 'so far as is reasonably practicable', which implies that local authorities have scope to determine how much they prioritise these forms of services for young people. The consequences of this ambiguity might include:

- greater variation in practice from one local authority to another;
- significant differences in interpreting the law (e.g. what constitutes a 'leisure-time activity');
- variation in the extent to which local authorities act as 'providers' or 'buyers' of services for young people;
- possible threats to services with greater flexibility for local authorities to impose cuts due to limited guidance on minimum standards.

Whether laws are prescriptive or ambiguous, all governments will set particular priorities for work with young people and these priorities are underpinned by a number of systems of thought about what is in the best interests of society. These systems of thought are themselves subject to wider drivers and these we might term as the policy context.

Drivers: understanding the wider policy context

Social policy responds to identified social problems and social groups that are shaped and understood within a broader context (Alcock 2008). Thoughtful study of this context must ask some critical questions:

- How is the social policy problem defined, and by whom?
- What is the evidence base for the presenting problem?
- What is the proposed solution?
- How will it address the problem, and in whose benefit?
- What is the relationship between the social policy and the broader social construction, or even the lived experiences of young people?

Asking these questions enables us to consider how the social policy context influences the direct drivers we discussed above. A number of important contextual factors influence social policy development, some of which include:

- the ideological context
- the position of young people in society
- the economic context.

Each are now discussed in turn.

Ideology and political drivers

Every social policy proposal or action is underpinned by a set of beliefs or values about what constitutes a 'good society'. Understanding these beliefs in essential to deepening our understanding of how social policy constructs and attempts to deal with social issues, problems and social groups. Ideology is the coupling of *ideas* (beliefs or values systems) with *power* (the capacity to act upon them). Thompson (2000: 56 in 2001: 27) discusses the importance of ideology in maintaining 'existing structures and social relations':

> For example, patriarchal ideology (. . . the law of the father) serves to maintain existing power relations between men and women . . . it is largely through the role of ideology that power is exercised . . . Subtle and unquestioned, workings of ideology can be more effective in maintaining power than the overt and explicit use of power

Thompson draws the distinction between overt controls (for example, the use of the military to enforce particular beliefs) and the subtlety and all pervasiveness of ideology:

'norms' that we come to accept, often collectively, as a society. Obvious examples are the norms of work, family life, common aspirations for property ownership and a whole host of other constructions that help to shape the order of society. We can also point to a whole range of behaviours that we commonly subscribe to that we might argue are 'natural' when in fact they are merely so entrenched that we do not think to question them. How odd would it be to see a colleague arrive at work naked? How do we feel when people tell lies? Why is it best not to solve a dispute with physical violence? We might think such questions are somewhat ridiculous, but they are the essence of a society operating within agreed collective norms. It is often argued that political parties will operate on different ideological lines, and this is certainly true, but even these differences can pale into insignificance when situated within the context of a set of dominant ideologies about society.

Ideology therefore functions on the basis of the successful transmission, acceptance and reproduction of dominant ideas about what is 'normal'. In order for something to become accepted, it requires a number of different actors and structures to be involved in the transmission of ideas (see Figure 7.2).

Some of the more obvious influences on norms perhaps need little discussion. The role of religion in shaping society ranges from overt religious governments, known as theocracies, to so-called secular democratic states, such as the United States or the United Kingdom, where Judeo-Christian values exercise powerful influence over political debate on an almost daily basis. For example, the debate about the rights and wrongs of abortion in the United States focuses as much on science as it does on

Figure 7.2 Ideological structures and actors

religious beliefs. Education systems are reflective of the economic models they serve and the political parties that set the laws that govern the curriculum. For instance, you would be hard-pressed to find any recent political speech on education that fails to reference the need for the United Kingdom to be competitive in a global economy. In the institution of the family, the role of primary socialisation is also important for transmitting values from one generation to the next. The norms of society are imparted through seemingly uncontroversial lessons on developing language, manners and relationships within family and peer groups. The function of the media in reproducing dominant values is also worthy of extensive study beyond this brief reference, particularly in terms of the changing nature of media consumption as a result of the technological revolution. The ways in which we use Facebook, Twitter and other forms of social media have enabled us to better contribute to the 'social currency' of particular issues or dominant ideas (Hughes *et al.* 2006).

The success of the dominant ideology can be measured in how effectively each of these actors and structures helps to reinforce the 'status-quo' with very little difficulty and in an almost invisible way. Davies (2009), in his book on media power, captures the contrast of 'overt control' with the more subtle role that the media plays in a 'free society':

> In a totalitarian state, media lies stand up proud and insult their readers direct to their faces. In the free society, the lies rest quietly and in comfort inside clichés – of language, of fact and of value – and slip past their reader's defences with the ease of a familiar friend on the doorstep.
>
> (Davies 2009: 152)

We can conclude from Davies' quote that ideological transmission is most successful when we do not even realise that we are being instructed. As Berger and Luckmann (1966: 49–50) famously said:

> Social order is not part of the 'nature of things' and it cannot be derived from the 'laws of nature'. Social order exists only as a product of human activity . . . Any action that is repeated frequently becomes cast into a pattern, which can then be reproduced with an economy of effort and which, ipso facto, is apprehended by its performer as that pattern.

How then does ideology shape and influence work with young people? We would argue that it is significant in two ways. First, it shapes young people's relative position in society, and second, it determines economic decisions about welfare.

Young people's relative position in society

Young people occupy a curious position in society. A former colleague once noted that young people are the 'repositories of all our hopes and fears'. At any one time, we can be both extremely positive about the elixir of youth and very worried about the state of growing up in today's society. We wish to protect young people from danger, and are frightened of them. We want them to be individually successful and prosperous, but seek to restrain choices that fall outside of our own parameters of success. As we become older, our perceptions of youth are clouded by nostalgic views of our own childhoods. We fantasise that things were always better, cheaper, happier and safer when we were young. In some senses, the policy responses to young people reflect these views. In the United Kingdom at least, we tend to base our policies around enabling young people to pass through a 'transition phase' in preparation for adulthood.

Spence (2005: 47) suggests that youth is often defined as an 'unstable period of life between childhood and adulthood' where various physiological, psychological, social, cultural and structural elements impact upon the period. Obvious physical and behavioural changes have long been used to act as signifiers of adolescence and these changes impact upon the individual's self-identity, awareness and personality. However, this period in the life course that we define as 'youth' is as much a social construction as it is a period of individual change: Mizen (2004: 5) defines 'youth' as a 'socially determined category', and in this respect, it is little use to rely solely on the individual biological markers as a frame for understanding youth. Instead, the cultural, social and political contexts into which young people grow invariably shape how we define childhood, adolescence and adulthood. There are general and universal policy responses to this period. For instance, all children have access to universal education and health provision designed to support their development. In addition to these general interventions, there are targeted policy responses when problems occur in the transition phase. Here, young people are framed as individual sites of concern.

Whether in health policy (the number of teenage conceptions; risky sexual behaviour; misuse of substances), in criminal justice (re-offending rates) or in education (rates of attrition from GCSE to A-Level), a unifying theme is one of policy that positions young people as 'problems' to be managed or solved. Hine (2009) argues that policy not only categorises young people but deals with them as dichotomous categories. For example they are either offenders or victims, educationally active or NEETs (Not in Education, Employment or Training), economically viable or disadvantaged. The difficulty is that dichotomies are rarely helpful. It is, for instance, both possible to be an offender *and* a victim. Similarly, the focus on such neat categories ignores the complexities of our everyday lives. We are more than the sum total of a policy label. Indeed Hine (2009) suggests that most policy understandings of the lives of young people are based upon adult perceptions and interpretations which often have little cognisance of the lived experience of young people.

Policy responses to young people growing up today reflect a curious mix of anxiety and hope. In considering the relative position of young people in society, it is useful to consider how problems facing young people are defined – both in terms of their manifestation and in the causes.

By way of a recent example, there has been much media and political attention focused on youth unemployment. Young people are one of the demographic groups who are disproportionately affected by economic downturns and are, at the time of writing, experiencing what the Institute for Public Policy Research called a 'jobless recovery' (Grice 2013). As *The Independent* reported: 'More than 950,000 young people are now unemployed and almost a third (30 per cent) of them have been looking for work for more than a year' (Grice 2013). In this case, we have *evidence* of the nature and extent of a problem faced by young people. The cause, at face value, is the economic downturn, with its impact felt more heavily by young people than by other groups in society. However, different responses invite us to consider the extent to which young people themselves are *blamed* for the social problem they face. For instance, in reaction to youth unemployment figures, a government minister was widely reported as saying that young people lacked the skills required to enter the workplace, which included 'confidence, grit [and] self-control' (Hurd, cited in Carter 2013). Critics were quick to offer alternative explanations. For example, Tracy McVeigh (2013) suggested in *The Observer* that:

> it was yet another wave of blame toppling on a group with little political voice and an easily sullied reputation ... As public sector jobs decline and the age of retirement rises, the younger part of the job market is bed-blocked by parents and grandparents clinging to their work ... No teenager aspires to be a Neet [Not in Education, Employment or Training]. This government needs to tackle the "grit" being kicked in their eyes.

The contrasting positions of McVeigh and Hurd reflect long-standing debates on the relationship between social problems and 'blame'. The discussion about welfare and economy (below) explores this further, but to conclude this example we can see that the relative position of young people in society is ultimately influenced both by how we describe the problems they face and the extent to which interventions are focused on addressing their own individual deficits or wider structural problems in society.

In McVeigh's quote, we also see reference to the idea of young people having 'little political voice'. We can further understand young people's relative position by understanding their 'democratic power'. Democratic power could be argued to be the influence that individuals have on those who govern them. Furlong and Cartmel (2011: 15) argue that: 'While young people in the UK become eligible to vote at the age of 18, relatively few do so and even fewer belong to a political party or closely identify with a party' and engagement tends 'to be lowest among the working classes and those with limited education'. Low levels of youth engagement contrast with the democratic power of older people: 'fewer than one in two 18–25 year olds claimed to have voted, compared with more than eight in ten over 66 year olds' (Furlong and Cartmel 2011: 15). It is often argued as a result that young people are effectively 'silent' when it comes to political issues that impact negatively on them whereas any change to policies that affect the 'grey vote' are met with powerful resistance. Politicians will court the vote of those who turn out. Issues of young people's engagement in civil society are discussed in Chapter 15.

Also of note in McVeigh's report is the statement that young people suffer from an 'easily sullied reputation'. Much evidence now confirms what many practitioners anecdotally report: in the United Kingdom, young people's well-being is significantly lower than in other comparable countries. The United Kingdom ranks bottom of the 21 richest countries across a range of indicators related to childhood: material well-being, educational well-being, family and peer relationships, risks and behaviours and subjective well-being (UNICEF 2007). British children are less likely to participate in active and creative pursuits than those in other countries and families are 'pushed to find the time their children want, something exacerbated by the uncertainty about the rules and roles operating within the family household' (Ipsos MORI 2011: 2). The Children's Society found that low well-being increases with age – doubling from the age of 10 (7 per cent) to the age of 15 (14 per cent) – and that children who have low levels of happiness are much less likely to enjoy being at home with their family, feel safe when with their friends, like the way they look and feel positive about their future (Children's Society 2012). Why might this be so? We would argue that young people today are victims of excessive 'regulation, over testing, incarceration and exclusion' resulting in a lack of trust in young people's 'capacity to grow up independently of intensive surveillance and support' (Wood 2010b: 50–1). The negative framing of much youth policy is coupled with an intensive media focus on young people as problems. Wider, the increased evidence of generalised fear and insecurity in society (with fears about hitherto seemingly remote threats) has intensified our efforts to 'protect' children. Conversely, as fewer children take positive risks, build relationships and play outside, the more their well-being suffers.

Reflection 7.1

Reflect on your studies around youth issues. What do you think are the major challenges facing young people as they grow up in today's society? What is good about growing up today? How is this different from the past? How would you describe the 'relative position' of young people in today's society?

The economy and welfare

The state of the economy will ultimately have the biggest impact upon the priority given to the type of social policy interventions a government chooses to support and the expectations it has of these. Decisions about the economy are as much ideological as they are pragmatic. Welfare systems in most industrialised nations are under constant review about their effectiveness at addressing social problems. Youth workers work within the welfare system, often in one of the following four groups:

- direct employees of the state welfare system (e.g. through local government youth service provision);
- employees of voluntary and community organisations that receive state assistance (e.g. a voluntary organisation that receives a grant to undertake particular work);
- employees working for private or social enterprise (e.g. an organisation that delivers programmes of work for the government); or

- employees working for charities or groups that respond to problems emanating from government welfare 'gaps' (e.g. a charity that provides assistance to people in poverty).

The welfare state that operates in the United Kingdom owes its heritage to major reforms in the provision of health services, universal education and social security that occurred at the end of the Second World War. Spicker (1995: 29–30) suggests that 'part of the aim of "welfare states" has been to invest citizens equally with a status entitling them to draw on the resources of society'. In this respect, universal welfare was seen as guarding 'equality of status' (Marshall 1992) and avoided what Titmuss defined as 'any humiliating loss of status, dignity or self-respect' (1968: 129). Governments of all political hues maintained support for the welfare state for over two decades before fractures in the 'welfare consensus' began to emerge in the 1970s.

The most significant challenge to this postwar welfare enthusiasm came with the growth of 'neo-liberalism', most advanced in the United Kingdom with what we now term 'Thatcherism' or the 'New Right', seeing the 'reduction of the state's welfare role [as] both positive and progressive' (Dwyer 2004a: 61). It was argued by politicians, policy makers, the mainstream media and supportive academics that welfare needs must be addressed by individual and familial responsibility, with only conditional and residual provision by the state (Dwyer 2000, 2004a, 2004b). As a consequence, there was increasing evidence of hostility to social welfare as a tool for social justice (George and Wilding 1994). Thus, the welfare state was recast as:

- inefficient and ineffective: serving the interests of bureaucrats and professionals over the needs of clients;
- economically damaging: reducing the ability of the free market, and increasing taxation;
- socially and morally damaging: reproducing a 'dependent underclass';
- politically damaging: where government deals with self-interested rights claims as opposed to pursuing the 'common good'.

(George and Wilding 1994; Dwyer 2004a)

Critics of welfare argued that extensive, state-funded welfare entitlements or rights created and reproduced an 'underclass' of welfare dependents, and that dysfunctional behaviour, rather than economic inequality, is what distinguished this underclass. As a result: 'Policies sought to diminish the state's welfare role, reduce or at least contain public welfare expenditure, challenge the power of the welfare state professions [and] promote a residual welfare state' (Dwyer 2004a: 65).

The ideological reframing of welfare took force with the election of the Conservative government in 1979, though as Hill (2003: 36) notes, 'changes had been gradually emerging before that date'. Some notable changes throughout this period included:

- a reduction in the value of contributory benefits, with greater emphasis on employer coverage of sickness benefits;
- pension reform to encourage rapid private pension growth;
- the increase of means-testing, replacing more 'universal' policies;

- a weakening of benefits for the unemployed, including support for under-18s being conditional on training;
- the renaming of unemployment benefit to 'Jobseekers Allowance' to emphasise required behaviour;
- reduction in state-support for single-parent families.

(Hill 2003; Dwyer 2004a)

After nearly two decades of uninterrupted right-wing government, New Labour came to power in 1997 with a different approach to discussing welfare than was previously associated with left-wing governments. New Labour had accepted the new consensus that without serious reform, welfare would fail to make an impact on the social problems it claimed to address. Public services began to undergo continuous reform, leading to new ways of managing public services. It was increasingly clear that welfare assistance was designed to 'activate' a labour market and was dependent on recipients fulfilling compulsory duties or patterns of behaviour (Deacon 1994). The language of 'conditional entitlement' became commonplace and whilst 'notions of "genuine need" and of the "deserving" and "undeserving" poor are not new' (Kemshall 2002: 27), there was a growing sense of *responsibilities* before *rights* (Dwyer 2004b).

In reaction to the global economic crisis of 2008, a newly elected coalition government of Conservatives and Liberal Democrats in 2010 was explicit in its commitment to reducing the role of the state and embarked upon a programme of significant reductions in public sector spending. The rationale put forward was based on the economic case to reduce a deficit in public finances but most commentators recognised an ideological basis for the coalition's programme of work. Over the past few years, the government's public spending cuts programme has resulted in the reduction of a number of welfare interventions, not least youth work. Between 2010 and 2012, for instance, cuts to youth services were averaged at 27 per cent, with some local authorities cutting their youth service budget altogether (Butler 2013). Why might such cuts be possible? Well, youth services suffer from not having a strong basis in law so it is easier for a local authority to cut youth services than other forms of welfare provision (schools and social work, for instance). The absence of a statutory commitment also suggests that governments throughout history have made a decision to not value this particular form of welfare when compared with others.

From our cursory review of welfare and economy, there are some conclusions we can draw:

- Welfare is as much an ideological issue as it is an economic one. The purpose of welfare, its contribution to well-being and whether or not a government chooses to strengthen or weaken it are linked to ideological views on what constitutes a 'good society'.
- There has been an increasing focus on using welfare (in which we would include services that work with young people) as a mechanism to shape more people as 'active' and 'productive' members of society.
- Spending priorities by a government will determine how and what aspects of welfare are funded. Some services may be more prone to cuts if they do not have a

strong statutory or legal framework underpinning their operation, though this is not always the case.

- In order to understand debates about welfare and economy, we need to be mindful of our earlier discussions about the relative position of young people and the ideological context within which our work occurs.

Reflection 7.2

In what ways do you think the current economic climate is impacting upon work with young people? Were things 'better' or 'worse' for youth workers in previous times? What is the evidence for this?

Aims and methods: how does the organisation respond?

We have so far addressed some big themes, focusing our attention on the outcomes and drivers that shape our work. The middle section of our process diagram concerns how an organisation responds to these bigger influences in the context of day-to-day practice. We stated before that understanding the aims and methods of the organisations we work with may be a reasonably straightforward process. However, it is important to also see how these aims and methods are not necessarily neutral – the organisation's work both reflects and responds to a combination of the proximate and wider drivers we discussed.

In addition to any national policies that influence its work, the organisation may also have its own local policy instruments that you will be required to become familiar with. In considering these different elements, we can begin to think carefully and critically about the role of the youth worker in contributing to the work of the organisation.

This final task is designed to assist you in mapping the aims and methods of the organisation.

Task 7.3

This task is designed to assist you in developing a portrait of your organisation's aims and methods and how these relate to wider drivers. The table below offers some headings and possible questions, and you could investigate these using a combination of desk-based research and conversations with your supervisor/line manager and colleagues. You may also discover more information and more questions of interest.

Gather as much information as you can find and discuss the results with your supervisor/line manager to check your understanding.

Category	Some possible questions
Name and type of organisation	• What is the name of the organisation? • How would you classify it? E.g. a youth club, a community centre, a youth offending team, a school mentoring project and so on.
Stated aims and outcomes	• What are the aims of this organisation and how clear are these? • What outcomes are expected? • Who are the beneficiaries of this work? E.g. are the outcomes for *all* young people or *particular* young people? Are there outcomes for *other groups* of people? • How are the outcomes demonstrated? • Does the organisation use any particular sources of evidence to underpin its work? E.g. research, government policy, theories of working with people and so on.
Main methods	• What approaches does the organisation use to work with young people? E.g. informal education, mentoring, issue-based education, outdoor education and so on. • Does the organisation use any other methods? • How does the organisation know that its methods are the most effective or appropriate?
Environment	• Where does the work take place? • Why does it take place in this setting?
Staffing	• What 'professional roles' work for the organisation? How many of the staff are youth workers? How many occupy other professional posts?
Proximate drivers	• What proximate drivers led to this organisation being set up? • Where does the funding for this work come from? • What local policies underpin the work? • Does the organisation deliver all of the work or is it done in partnership with others? If so, who does it work in partnership with?
Wider drivers	• Is this one of many organisations doing this kind of work? • Is the work of this organisation underpinned by law? If so, which one(s)? • What national guidance guides the work of this organisation?

Our mapping exercise should help us to identify the primary aims and methods of an organisation, and in doing so we can begin to think carefully about the role of youth workers in fulfilling these aims. As we discussed in Chapter 5, the role of the youth worker is primarily as an educator, but the contexts within which we work can either support or hinder the distinct contribution of youth work. When reflecting on the drivers, aims, methods and outcomes of the policy context that shape our organisation, we need to be mindful of how and to what extent the work of the organisation aligns with the values, aims and methods of youth work. In weighing up all of the evidence that this chapter will help to generate, a reflective and critically minded practitioner will be able to judge whether they will be afforded the opportunity to make a distinctive youth work contribution to their placement agency.

Conclusion

Contexts matter. They shape our thinking and our practice. This chapter has discussed the significance of understanding social policy and in particular how it influences, either directly or indirectly, the work we do with young people. The study of social policy is not an abstract or academic set of questions. Thoughtful analysis of social policy is necessary to understand why and how organisations work with young people, what they seek to achieve and whether and how we as youth workers can make a contribution to these goals. As with the discussion on informal education (Chapter 5), youth workers can and do make important contributions to the work of other organisations where youth work is not the primary focus. However, if this is to be successful and meaningful work, youth workers need a clear sense of their own professional identity. This means making informed judgements about the possibilities or limits to youth work practice in a range of settings and, ultimately, knowing how our own distinctive contribution can make a difference to young people's lives.

8 The partnership context

Introduction

In the previous chapter, we explored how the policy context can shape much of the aims, methods and outcomes of the work you do as a youth worker. During these discussions, we invited you to think carefully about how a youth worker maintains their own professional identity (and attendant skills, knowledge and so on) in a climate where some organisations may value different approaches to working with young people. Without compromising, we would argue that it is both possible to be a youth worker who makes a distinctive educational contribution in the placement or agency they find themselves working in *and* to assist the organisation in achieving its desired outcomes.

The professional identity of youth workers is further called to challenge when working in partnership with others, yet partnership working is now commonplace. In this chapter, we explore the different types of partnerships that youth workers engage with. We identify three key areas for successful engagement with a partnership: knowledge, attitudes and skills. Finally, we encourage you to consider the ways in which you can evaluate the effectiveness of a partnership that you are involved in.

Understanding partnerships

The word partnership comes from the Latin *partitionem*, meaning 'portion' or 'division'. It is a term that often conjures up the idea of 'sharing', whether that is in terms of responsibilities and duties or in the fruits of labour. Partnership often suggests 'equality', two or more actors coming together to commit equal levels of resource or activity in the pursuit of shared aims. If we consider for a moment the personal partnerships we form in our own lives, we might expect these to be mutually rewarding and dependent on each partner contributing equally or fairly. Sometimes one partner might feel less valued or less important than the other, and this can result in feelings of inadequacy or powerlessness. The best partnerships are those where partners feel valued, and are able to work through tensions and difficulties in pursuit of a bigger or more important goal.

In this chapter we focus mostly on interagency partnerships, in recognition that many types of partnership exist. The core elements that characterise interagency partnerships are:

- the structure or way of working involves at least two organisations;
- the partner organisations retain their own separate identity;
- there is some form of agreement between partners to work in pursuit of an agreed aim or goal;
- the aim is unlikely to be achieved by any one organisation working alone; and
- the partner relationships are formalised within an organisational structure and involve planning, implementation and review of an agreed programme of work.

(Percy-Smith, 2006: 316)

Partnerships have perhaps always been a feature of public services. However, in the United Kingdom at least, there was an increased emphasis on 'joined up' working from 1997 onwards when New Labour came to power. The context of developing partnerships was influenced by a number of drivers. In social and health services for example, the single agency approach was heavily criticised when agencies failed to share information of particular child protection cases. An example of this was in the tragic case of Victoria Climbié, where it was determined that at 12 key points, her death might have been prevented. Closer collaboration between social and health care agencies was deemed critical to spotting – and acting upon – early signs of neglect. In criminal justice, the emergence of Multi-Agency Public Protection Arrangements (MAPPA) was in direct response to the need for a more co-ordinated response to assessing and managing the risks posed by sexual and violent offenders upon their release from custody. Whilst it is true that police and probation continue to take the lead in managing these risky offenders, the development of MAPPA has ensured that other key services have what is known as a 'duty to co-operate' (Wood and Kemshall 2008).

Central to the development of initiatives such as MAPPA is the recognition that people's problems are rarely, if ever, isolated from other issues. This relates to a second key driver behind the development of partnerships: the recognition that problems are multi-faceted, complex and inform one another. In social policy, this approach was best captured in the establishment of the government's Social Exclusion Unit (SEU), set up by Prime Minister Tony Blair in 1997. The unit aimed to 'Improve government action to reduce social exclusion by producing "joined-up solutions to joined-up problems" . . . issues facing teenage parents, rough sleepers, deprived neighbourhoods and young people at risk of social exclusion are complex and interconnected' (Office of the Deputy Prime Minister 2004: 2–3[1]).

Nearly two decades later, it is now deemed commonsensical to approach problems in a much more holistic way than was previously the case. For example, we know that young parents are more likely to also experience disadvantage in their neighbourhoods, access poorer health services and be on the receiving end of inadequate educational opportunities. It was the laudable goal of the SEU to enable agencies to think beyond their 'silos' and work together to tackle the interconnected web of difficulties facing individuals. So, in the case of young parents, we might now see a number of different agencies offering interventions that seek to respond to a range of difficulties rather than simply focusing on one issue.

Youth workers can often be found as active contributors to partnerships. They work with local community partners, sit on national strategic boards, undertake joint needs assessments and serve as advocates for young people's needs. Space restricts us from discussing these many and varied types of partnership but we focus here on three examples to illustrate the ways in which we commonly work with others.

Providing youth work in different settings

Youth workers may work in a number of settings where youth work is not the primary purpose. Perhaps the most obvious example of this is school-based youth work, where the primary function of the school is the delivery of formal education. Youth workers may complement this primary aim by providing youth work interventions and activities during or after school hours. We might argue that the partnership between the school and the youth work service provider means that both entities share a goal of ensuring that young people flourish; we might also argue that youth work is used here as a means to ensure behavioural standards are met through diversionary activity. Youth workers might be considered the 'minor' partner in this context, delivering services within a fairly constrained context.

Responding jointly to concern

The 'integrated' teams that flourished in response to the child protection failings discussed earlier often feature youth workers working alongside other child, youth and family professionals. Here, youth work encounters are seen to offer important opportunities for early detection and intervention, referral to other services and information sharing where appropriate. For example, youth workers may provide part of an integrated response to those children identified as presenting particular risks or problems through the Common Assessment Framework (CAF). The CAF is used when:

a practitioner is worried about how well a child or young person is progressing (e.g. concerns about their health, development, welfare, behaviour, progress in learning or any other aspect of their wellbeing);

a child or young person, or their parent/carer, raises a concern with a practitioner;

a child's or young person's needs are unclear, or broader than the practitioner's service can address.

(Department for Education 2012: online[2])

The practitioner who conducts the CAF will seek consent from the family to share information about the child in order to identify which services might be best placed to respond to the various needs identified. A multi-disciplinary 'Team Around the Child' (TAC) co-ordinated by a Lead Professional (who may be a youth worker) is established to jointly identify need (through the CAF), provide interventions and meet regularly with the child, young person or family.

Youth offending teams (YOTs) are another example where youth workers jointly work with other professionals, such as the police, social workers and probation officers, to support and challenge young people who have either committed or are at risk of committing criminal offences. YOTs support an individual young person through community sentence supervision, deterrence programmes, educational interventions and custody work. At the preventative end, they work with community groups to help reduce the likelihood of young people entering the criminal justice system. Youth workers will often be instrumental in helping to run and improve such interventions, and are often found supporting young people at point of arrest (as 'appropriate adults') or through visiting them in custody.

Critics have argued that much of this work falls outside of the aims and methods used by youth workers. The absence of a 'voluntary principle' for young people in custody is obvious and in the case of working as part of a TAC, the focus is often on reducing problems rather than working with young people on a positive basis. However, it is our contention that youth workers can – and should – support such work, but only on the basis of being clear about how their contribution can be distinctive in enabling young people to flourish. It is difficult to accept that youth workers would not want to see a reduction in crime as a positive outcome of their work. Nor would we support any idea that youth workers have no role to play in child protection. We discuss some of these issues further below.

Enhancing informal education and activities-based work

Perhaps the most common form of partnership work is that which occurs at an informal level, where youth workers work alongside others to deliver activities or projects with young people that involve the active engagement of other professionals. An example might be a project focused on self-esteem and confidence building that draws in professionals involved in creative or performing arts education. This type of work is the opposite of the situation described above, where the youth worker engages in another practitioner's 'territory'. In situations such as schools or prisons, youth workers need to adapt to different environmental conditions that will affect their work. The same is true for those who come to work in youth work environments under the conditions of youth work principles. A common duty for the youth worker in this situation is captured by a practitioner who described their role:

> When we work with the police or other agencies to deliver a joint crime reduction programme at the youth club, it takes a while for them to adjust to how we work. I remember a tricky situation where some young lads were being quite rowdy and the copper was saying 'Why don't you just tell them to shut up and listen?'. I explained that in this situation young people had to choose whether to engage with

our session or not and perhaps we should try adapting our approach to capture their interest. I see this as part of my role when working with others: helping them to think differently about how they engage young people, using youth work approaches.

Partnerships are therefore commonplace. What we can determine from the three types we have set out above (and there are many more we could draw on) is that the nature, type and structure of our working relationship with other organisations will vary considerably depending on what we are seeking to achieve and the methods we use. The next section of the chapter enables you to reflect on and map the different types of partnerships you might be engaged in.

Mapping partnerships

Task 8.1

In discussion with your supervisor or line manager, make a list of the key partnerships that your organisation holds:

- How many separate partnerships is your organisation a part of?
- Does each partnership 'fit' within one of the three types above? If not, how would you describe it?
- Who are the partners involved in each?
- What are they seeking to achieve? What is the overall goal?

As a result of your discussions, you may have identified a number of different partnerships that your organisation is – or was – a part of. They might vary considerably in a number of ways, and some useful themes for exploring partnerships are set out below.

Context of the partnership

The first dimension to explore is the context of the partnership, by asking the question: How and why did this partnership come about? Working in partnership implies that a single-agency approach cannot respond to the needs or aims of a particular intervention. Sometimes the partnership is formed on the basis of recognition from a youth work organisation that it needs particular expertise to enhance its work (see the example above about involving specialist workers) and vice versa: police or other organisations may value the particular skills and approaches used by youth workers. We might term these informal partnerships, usually established between key individuals from two or more agencies who wish to enhance their work. Increasingly many of our partnerships will be directed by central or local government policies that require us to co-operate with others. These statutory partnerships set out clearly who is to co-operate and how. So in the case of the TACs described above, social workers cannot *choose* to opt out of working with others. Legislation is important here as it sets out the expectations and duties of those involved in the partnership.

Collaborative aims

A linked point concerns the aims of the partnership and the extent to which these are driven by dominant agencies within the group or reflect broader, collective aims. Often partnerships are brought together to address pre-determined goals linked to their statutory basis or the aims of a particular organisation that has driven the partnership. For example, the police may be the lead in a community safety partnership that aims primarily to tackle crime and anti-social behaviour. Youth workers may thus play a part in helping to meet this pre-defined goal. Other partnerships may have more fluid or open goals where the aim might be to generally improve the well-being of children and young people. This could encompass practically any intervention or action across a range of health, social, criminal justice and educational aims and outcomes. The extent to which the partnership goals are in line with each participating organisation is also important: this we might refer to as congruence of aims. So, for example, it may be perfectly reasonable for a youth worker to be a partner in a crime reduction group so that they might advocate for young people and ensure their voices are represented at the table. This would seem highly congruent. However, should that youth worker be asked to attend the partnership with the sole aim of reporting on young people's behaviour and providing intelligence on where young people congregate, we might suggest there would be an incongruence between the values and principles of youth work and the surveillance role they are required to undertake.

Levels of co-operation

Partnerships will vary in terms of the extent to which they co-operate and collaborate. A whole array of things helps us to judge this, from the resources that each partner commits to the partnership through to levels of integration between different services. So, some partnerships will involve a number of different agencies who merely communicate with one another around some common goals (usually through sharing information). Others may involve different agencies being co-located in the same building, joint working on different issues and being accountable to the same line manager. Liddle and Gelsthorpe (1994) provide a useful way for classifying different levels of co-operation:

- Communicating partnership – agencies recognise that they have a role to play in relation to each other but do not take this beyond communicating.
- Co-operating partnership – agencies agree to work on a mutually defined problem, but maintain separate boundaries and identities.

- Co-ordinating partnership – agencies work together in a systematic way and may pool resources to tackle mutually agreed problems.
- Federation – agencies operate integrated services, sharing some central focus.
- Merger – agencies become indistinguishable from each other working on a mutually defined problem and they form a collective resource pool.

In the final section of this chapter, we explore some of questions that can help us to judge the effectiveness of a partnership, but in doing so, aspects of what we have discussed here are important.

Task 8.2

Return to the list of partnerships you generated in discussion with your supervisor and consider:

- How many of these might be classified as 'informal' or 'statutory' partnerships?
- To what extent do you think there is 'congruence' between the aims of the partnership and the expectations of a youth worker?
- Using Liddle and Gelsthorpe's (1994) list as a guide, at what levels do the partnerships co-operate?

Being a good partner

Working in partnership can be challenging. Different agencies are represented by different individuals, all of whom bring to the table their own personal and professional values, personality traits and prejudices in terms of working with others. Often the time taken to build trust between partners can impact upon communication, clarity of roles and the overall effectiveness of a partnership (Hudson 1999). Conflicts can also arise when the boundaries between different agency responsibilities or roles become blurred (Secker and Hill 2001).

Reflecting on these issues is important as it helps us to think about how effectively *we* and *others* contribute to partnerships. In doing so, it is important to understand our own values and prejudices (Chapter 3), our approach to developing relationships (Chapter 5) and how we contribute to groups (Chapter 12). We would suggest that there are three areas that potential partners should consider as part of their engagement with partnerships: knowledge, attitudes and skills.

Knowledge

In the section above, we explored the types of partnership that are common in youth work practice and illustrated how they can vary in terms of their structure, the drivers that bring them together and the extent to which their aims are prescribed by policy or other contextual factors. Having a sound knowledge of the structure of your partnership, how it works and what it seeks to achieve is essential. Some questions that aid this process include the reflective tasks you undertook above, together with some further and more specific questions (see Table 8.1).

Many of these questions serve to help us understand the partnership, but it is also true that youth workers need to understand the *partners*: the groups who are represented at the table. Sometimes these are statutory or voluntary sector agencies that we may believe we are familiar with. In many cases, partnerships might include representatives from local neighbourhoods or faith groups for instance. In the previous chapter, we explored how an organisational context can 'shape' youth work practice and we argued that understanding these organisations would enable youth workers to

Table 8.1 Further questions to aid analysis of effective partnership working

Origins	How did the partnership come about? Who (or what) was instrumental in setting it up?
Policy context	Is your partnership underpinned by any legal or policy developments? Have these frameworks resulted from a central or local government initiative? To what extent do organisations have a 'duty' to work together?
Funding and other resources	How is your partnership funded? By partner organisations or through external funding? What are the expectations of funders? What other resource commitments, other than funding, are partners putting into the partnership?
Your contribution	How would you define your youth work contribution to the partnership? What do you seek to achieve? To what extent is this congruent with the aims of other representatives?
Their contribution	Who are the different partners? What do these organisations 'do' outside of the partnership? What methods do they use in their work? How would you define and assess the contribution of others? What are they seeking to achieve?
Defining progress	What successes can be attributed to this partnership to date? What difficulties or challenges has the partnership encountered?

better articulate their own contribution and distinctiveness. This issue is more acute in partnerships. If we are to work effectively with others, we need a good knowledge base of what the various partners do outside of their contribution to our collective work. This means having a sound understanding of their aims, values, methods and approaches to work and the expectations placed upon the partners by appropriate governing bodies. As important as knowledge is, attitudes also shape how we work with others.

Attitudes

Often, the working context of a partnership is determined by the attitudes and approaches that individual practitioners bring to collaborative working arrangements. It is perhaps little surprise that where individuals have good interpersonal relationships with their colleagues or demonstrate high trust in other practitioners, there is often evidence of good work. Many of the partnerships that we start ourselves come from a desire to work with particular individuals because we value their skills or other contributions. However, what about those partnerships where we might find ourselves encountering barriers to working effectively?

Our attitudes towards partnership working may be shaped by a number of different factors that we need to reflect upon. Some of these may reflect how we perceive our fellow partners. For example, many youth workers express distrust towards other professional groups, sometimes based on their own personal experiences of being on the receiving end of less-than-satisfactory experiences. Similarly, youth workers may have witnessed young people receiving a poor service from other professional groups. It is common for youth workers to express distrust or other negative feelings towards police officers and teachers, for example. These experiences form our pre-judgements about what we expect from other professionals, in terms of their approaches to their work and their behaviour. This is distinct from the point above about *knowledge*. We may well *know* about the ways in which another agency works but still feel *antipathy* towards them. Linked to this issue is one that concerns professional expectations or values. As we have encountered in the previous chapters, our own principles and values can sometimes clash with those of our professional body. Similarly, our professional values might sometimes clash with those of other groups.

We might also struggle with methodological approaches. Whereas youth workers may favour approaches that emphasise participation and empowerment, it may be more common for other organisations to adopt different styles of working that challenge our own methods. Sometimes, educating others about the benefits of a youth work methodological approach is crucial, particularly if we feel that young people's voices and opinions are missing from strategies to intervene. However, we must also recognise that in order to be an effective partner, we should consider the value of other approaches to working with young people.

All of these issues, and many more besides, suggest that one good attitude to hold in approaching partnership working is that of *openness*. It is certainly true that practitioners from all of the various agencies we encounter in our work have let young people down (not least, many youth workers) but it cannot be true that this is always the case. Being open to different aims, values and methods is the first step to building an effective partnership. This sometimes means listening to voices that counter your own opinions or assessments of a situation. In Chapter 6, on working with communities, we show how 'tipping the balance in favour of young people' is important but should not be done at the expense of taking into account the views of other people living in the community. The same can be said of working in partnership with others, as this example illustrates:

> *I was asked to join a crime reduction partnership in a local community. I was quite reluctant as I've had loads of problems with the police in the past. There were loads of organisations involved but I had a real problem with how the police approached the issue. As usual, it was all young people this, young people that. I spent most of the time arguing with the police about why they were wrong to judge young people so harshly. Then I met an older resident who came along to one of the meetings. She was representing a group who had been victims of anti-social behaviour for about a year. They were at their wits' end and I began to see why the police were under so much pressure to do something.*

The example given here is quite a common one. The youth worker started out with pre-conceived expectations of working with the police, which, it was felt, were confirmed by the tone of the discussions about young people. The youth worker then describes engaging in conflict with the police representative, a situation that was likely to make working together a difficult process. Finally, upon hearing from an older resident, the youth worker's own views on the situation are challenged. The question is what might be a good resolution to these tensions? At the very least, it may have been more helpful if the youth worker had approached the partnership with more of an open mind. Equally, we might suggest that the police probably approached the issue by stating their view of the problem before taking into account the various perspectives that might exist in the community. As views were challenged by the older resident, this spurred the youth worker to consult more effectively and meaningfully with young people in the neighbourhood and, ultimately, to ensure they were represented on the partnership. The rationale for doing this was twofold. First, the youth worker felt that it would be good for other partners to hear from young people. Second, by including young people, it was felt that they would be challenged to think about their own behaviour.

Openness requires us to 'suspend judgement' and to take into account the very many different perspectives of the issue we are trying to address. This does not mean that we expect youth workers to always agree with other professionals and we are certainly not implying that the judgement of a youth worker is less valid. There are ways in which youth workers, confident in their identity and their approach, can constructively challenge partners for the good. In the case above, the move to include young people in the partnership group was welcomed by the police and other agencies as they recognised that this was a distinctive contribution to what they were trying to achieve.

Skills

Our knowledge and attitudes help us in understanding and contributing to partnerships. So too do the skills that we bring to working with others. There are perhaps no distinctive skillsets required to work in a partnership that depart radically from effective work with individuals and with groups. We would expect partners to be able to use techniques to listen effectively (Chapter 13); foster relationships that are mutually beneficial and build trust (Chapter 5); plan, deliver and evaluate work in a thorough way (Chapter 9); and work effectively with groups (Chapter 12). If these skills are well developed and coupled with a positive attitude to partnership working, then effectiveness is likely to follow.

We might also emphasise the importance of some common skills used in partnerships. We discussed the various roles that youth workers might play in the first part of this chapter, amongst which was the 'advocacy' role. Advocacy 'has become established as a way of promoting children's participation, voice and resistance' (Boylan and Dalrymple 2009: 60). In order to do this with any degree of effectiveness, we need to be aware of how systems interact, shape and in some cases oppress young people. This requires us to develop skills that strengthen our understanding of these systems. Advocates, therefore, develop and prioritise:

- listening skills
- research skills
- good questioning strategies
- assertiveness skills
- negotiation skills
- goal-setting skills, including action planning.

Evaluating a partnership

Having considered the various types of partnership we might be involved in and thought about some of the attributes we need to consider, this section of the chapter invites us to question how we judge the effectiveness of a partnership. How do we know whether it is functioning effectively? How do we know whether it is achieving what it has set out to achieve? How might we judge its overall effectiveness as an organising unit? As you progress from thinking about partnerships, being involved with and ultimately convening them, evaluation becomes an increasingly important component.

Although partnerships are indeed commonplace, it is also true that there has been limited substantial research that supports them as a model of working (Berry *et al.* 2011). Evaluations of partnerships have tended to focus on processes, structures and systems of agencies working together rather than whether a partnership, in place of alternative arrangements, is the most effective way of addressing problems (see for example the evaluation of MAPPA by Kemshall *et al.* 2005). As a result any evaluation of a partnership starts from us trying to understand what might be the significant contributions that a partnership makes which cannot be achieved by a single agency.

Table 8.2 Questions in evaluating partnerships

Roles and contributions	Does the partnership have clearly defined roles? Is there evidence of effective leadership and chairing? Do partners feel that their contributions are effective and valued? Are the right people and organisations included?
Outputs and outcomes	To what extent does the partnership deliver what it intends to deliver? What are the measures of the partnership's success?
Relationships and collective responsibility	To what extent do partners take 'collective responsibility' for their work? Is there evidence of good levels of trust between partners?
Sustainability of the partnership	Can the partnership continue in the absence of key individuals? What strategies are there in place to ensure the 'legacy' of its work?
Accountability	Who is the partnership accountable to? How does it demonstrate its accountability? Do partners demonstrate accountability to the partnership? How does the partnership hold people to account?

We then seek to determine how effectively partners work together to achieve these collaborative aims. Table 8.2 offers some questions that might help to address these two evaluative themes.

Conclusion

The policy interest in partnership approaches to addressing social groups, issues and problems has seen a plethora of different initiatives develop in the recent past. Youth workers are increasingly called on to contribute to partnerships and to build relationships with other organisations that, in principle at least, can make a better contribution to young people's lives. Partnership work requires us to have a clear professional identity so that we are aware of the distinctiveness of what we can contribute. We also need to have a good understanding of the 'others' that we are working with so as to determine how they work with young people and to what end. As is so often the case with approaches to effective working, youth workers therefore need to understand themselves, other organisations and the work and effectiveness of a partnership as a whole. In doing so, practitioners are more likely to be able to act as advocates for young people to promote their voice where it may otherwise be absent.

Notes

1   Office of the Deputy Prime Minister (2004) *The Social Exclusion Unit*, London: Office of the Deputy Prime Minister.
2   Department for Education (2012) 'The CAF Process', available at www.education.gov.uk/childrenandyoungpeople/strategy/integratedworking/caf/a0068957/the-caf-process (last accessed 23/07/13).

Part III

Skills for practice

Writing a series of chapters that attempt to capture the practice of youth work presents a number of challenges, not least in our inability to document the many varied skills that practitioners bring to their work. Alongside the core and common skills used in everyday conversations with young people, practitioners will use their own added skills to enthuse young people: workshops on website design, music, performing arts, outdoor pursuits, sports and even circus skills are common valuable additions to practice. The second point to make is that this whole book is concerned with practice: we have consciously sought to apply often abstract discussions around theoretical and policy debates to everyday practice concepts. Thus, the chapters that precede this section contain within them some helpful strategies for strengthening practice skills.

That said, the remainder of this book is concerned with enhancing some core and common aspects of practice that we would argue are essential to enabling meaningful youth work to flourish. This starts with developing our approaches to assessment, planning, intervention and evaluation both in terms of useful methods but also in thinking about the benefits of using such frameworks for practice (Chapter 9). Our own practice learning and development is supported by attending to two important elements: a commitment to supervision (Chapter 10) and reflective practice (Chapter 11). Both provide us with the individual space to think about our practice, articulate our own learning and think of how we might develop our work. They are also opportunities for collective learning with our peers, managers and young people.

We recognise that much youth work is now delivered with individuals, often in what might be called 'case-work' relationships. However, a virtue of youth work practice is its commitment to working with young people in groups, since this provides a number of important learning opportunities for young people (Chapter 12). Whatever methods of engagement we use, we cannot overestimate the importance of using good communication, and Chapter 13 revisits two key skills: listening and questioning.

Finally, the book concludes with two chapters that remind us of the youth work contribution to empowering young people and challenging injustice. Chapter 14 looks at the principles and practice of anti-oppressive youth work, providing the reader with practical strategies for supporting young people to think critically about prejudice, discrimination and oppression, whilst Chapter 15 explores how practitioners can strengthen the voice of young people through participatory practice.

9 Frameworks for practice

Introduction

When compared to how other professionals engage with young people, youth work interventions can sometimes appear on the surface to be less structured and, by extension, less planned. School teachers, for example, use tightly structured time slots to teach students, drawing on lesson plans that are informed by a national curriculum. Ultimately, the success (or otherwise) of their educational interventions can be measured through student performance in tests and exams. Youth workers by contrast often meet young people in settings or contexts that are governed by looser structures. They may encounter young people on the streets and seize upon conversations to introduce learning in response to what young people are saying (see Chapter 5). Despite these obvious differences, there are very few examples where youth work is unplanned. The more obvious challenge is identifying how planning, implementation, review and evaluation occur in different ways across the diversity of modern youth work practice. This practice takes place in an increasingly wide range of settings, over the short and longer term, through projects and through informal encounters.

In whatever context youth workers operate, practice is usually more positive where it is accompanied by the effective assessment of needs, good planning strategies, effective implementation and the evidence to show whether and how what they have done has made an impact. This chapter briefly reviews some of the approaches that you can adopt as a youth worker to assess, plan, deliver and evaluate your work. In doing so, you are encouraged to test some of these approaches in the context of your placement or workplace using an example of one planning framework: the ASPIRE model.

Involving young people in the process

Participatory practice is a cornerstone of youth work practice. Chapter 15 demonstrates how the active engagement of young people fulfils a number of important legal and moral conceptions of young people's rights and it is important that you consider how to engage young people in the processes described below. Fleming and Hudson (2009) argue that good participatory practice is where young people 'collaborate' or 'lead' in the design, delivery and evaluation of activities. In the context of this chapter, your aim should be to engage young people at the outset as 'co-producers' in the development of a framework for practice. In each of the tasks within this chapter, we encourage you to reflect on how young people have helped to shape your thinking and vice versa. The additional and very practical value of engaging young people throughout is the probability that they will acquire or enhance skills in planning, delivering and evaluating work – all of which are likely to be worthwhile learning outcomes for young people.

Introducing the ASPIRE model

Youth workers, like many other professionals, have access to a vast array of planning tools that can assist in the process of developing a thoughtful and considered approach to practice. Planning tools will vary but the main message always seems to be one of assessing, planning, doing and reviewing. In this chapter, we will deploy Sutton's (1999) interpretation of the ASPIRE model which has been used to work with children, young people and families. ASPIRE stands for:

AS – Assessment
P – Planning
I – Implementing
RE – Review and Evaluation

We shall now focus on each element.

Assessment

The word 'assessment' can have connotations that we do not usually associate with youth work. We may think of doctors who assess a patient coming into the emergency ward or of a probation officer assessing the risk of an offender engaging in further criminal activity. Usually, types of assessment form part of all of our daily experiences, both personally and professionally. We continuously think about the situations we find ourselves in, weigh evidence and arrive at judgements. The same is true in our youth work practice: we seek to understand what is going on to 'enhance understanding of the [young person's] situation, helping [us] to identify areas for potential change that will assist the development of a rationale for future intervention' (Parker and Bradley 2010: 9). Assessment strategies sit across a wide continuum ranging from informal, unplanned conversations with young people through to structured assessments designed to record progress against a range of measures in education, and personal and social development. It follows that the approaches we use to assess need to reflect the type of work we seek to do with young people, and the outcomes we hope to achieve.

The first task is to determine what assessments are used in your placement or work-place.

Task 9.1

- What is the purpose of assessment in your organisation? What does the organisation seek to learn from assessing?
- How is assessment carried out? What sources of information inform an assessment?
- How is assessment information recorded?
- Is the assessment concentrated on individuals or groups of young people?
- To what extent are young people included in informing the assessment processes?

Discuss your findings with your supervisor or line manager.

How we assess and to what end will vary significantly from one agency to the next. If you work in a youth club following a fairly unstructured programme of informal education, you may find assessment is relatively informal and based largely on your conversations with young people and your colleagues. As the chapter on informal education demonstrated, these conversations are vital to developing our educational response. Your example might have drawn on more formalised, structured and technical assessments, such as the ASSET tool used by youth justice practitioners. This tool focuses on a number of aspects of a young offender's identify, offence profile, and educational and social circumstances in order to identify particular needs and difficulties. Whatever approach is used, the practitioner uses assessment to:

- understand the needs of the young person or young people they are working with and locate these within the context of their everyday lives;
- think about and plan responses to these needs.

There are a number of important points to make about what makes good assessment practice. First, your assessment techniques should be designed to enable you to be a more effective youth worker. In essence, this means working in partnership with young people and others from the outset, trying to investigate issues that you, or others, can respond to. In a practical sense, knowing what your agency seeks to achieve and how this fits with the values and principles of youth work is a crucial first step, as this will guide what assessment approaches you adopt and what information you gather. It is also important to draw on what you have learnt during your studies – how does a particular theoretical framework or research paper help you to make sense of the situation you are presented with? A related point to make here is that although much of the work is often problem oriented (that is, we seek to respond to an issue or need), where possible we should strive to be strengths and solutions focused. When thinking this through, we should continuously reflect on the relative position of young people in society, as discussed in Chapter 7. Assessments should seek to identify the possibilities and positive attributes that can be built upon, rather than the negative deficits that need to be addressed.

Second, practitioners should seek to 'triangulate' their sources of information by drawing on different perspectives to inform their judgements. For example, as a detached youth worker you may be asked to go to work in a neighbourhood as a result of a local councillor expressing concerns about rising anti-social behaviour. The councillor may cite police reports and the views of residents as evidence for the need for a youth work intervention. This is important information but tells only part of the story: for instance, where are young people's perspectives on living and socialising in the neighbourhood? What difficulties or challenges do they face? Do they themselves identify anti-social behaviour in the area? Do they think of themselves as perpetrators? As victims?

Through taking into account a wider range of perspectives on a 'problem', you are in a better position to plan a response. We would argue that central to this is listening to young people themselves, but we would reject any notion that you *only* listen to young people. Figure 9.1 shows some examples of information that can help to inform a rounded assessment of the needs of young people that you work with. What else might you include?

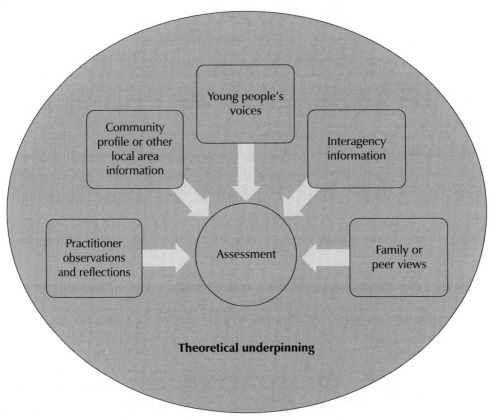

Figure 9.1 Multiple perspectives in assessments

The detached youth work team who responded to the issue of anti-social behaviour described above provides a good example of how multiple perspectives can enhance assessment:

We work for a mobile youth work provision commissioned by the local authority. A local councillor asked us to start working on weekend evenings in a neighbourhood where the police were reporting high levels of anti-social behaviour (interagency information). We took some time to familiarise ourselves with the local area, visiting local shops, services and walking around during the day and night to see what goes on at a street level (practitioner observations; community profile). Before we engaged with the groups of young people, we asked the police who they had built up a relationship with in the local area. They put us in touch with a group of young people and a group of older residents who had complained about young people in the area. We asked the young people to take us around the neighbourhood and tell us what they liked about living in the area and what the problems were (young people's voices; community profile) and had the opportunity to ask their parents and carers about the issues young people faced living there (family or peer views). We then visited older residents to ask them about their concerns and experiences (community profile). Throughout the process we kept a log of our findings, took photos and met as a team (with the group of young people we had met at the start) to discuss the issues. We then took the bus out to meet where groups of young people were congregating and used conversation to explore their experiences and share our observations and intelligence (young people's voices).

The example above shows a range of methods that the team used in order to get an insight into the concerns that the community expressed and the needs of the young people living in the local area. As a result, their work will benefit from multiple perspectives and they are more likely to understand the issue in context, enabling their response to be much more grounded in the reality of those experiencing tensions in the community. They also approached their work with sensitivity to the values of youth work and community development, and adopted approaches to consultation and reflective practice that resonate with sound theoretical underpinnings.

Even in unstructured or fluid situations it is important to ensure that assessments are conducted in a thorough way. As Parker and Bradley (2010: 9) argue, 'When assessments are undertaken without adequate preparation and without a clear sense of purpose and direction they are unlikely to produce good quality material that will help in planning to improve the lot of service users'.

We can all think of examples where we have rushed to judgement or responded to a situation we perceived to be most pressing, only to discover that our interventions did not help or in fact were poorly received. The practitioner not only needs to demonstrate a commitment to breadth of assessment (by drawing on a range of perspectives, as above) but also to depth: what is *really* going on here? Spending time in conversation, collecting other sources of information and using reflective practice techniques (see Chapter 11) can provide you with the space and time to think through the particular needs or challenges. Linking wants and needs is also a good way to identify what might really matter to the young people with whom you work. For example, young people may *want* to have more trips or more exciting facilities on offer at their local youth club. When we ask questions about why these are necessary, young people may identify that they *need* to feel like they have things to do in their spare time and be with their friends in a safe environment. As we get to know the young people through our conversations, we may identify a number of additional needs: some young people may lack confidence, and organising trips or activities may offer the opportunity to build this. We might find that young people spend most of their time in conflict with adults, so one need might be to build better relationships in the community so that people from different backgrounds feel greater levels of generalised safety. Drawing on theoretical and research understanding is crucial here: what we know about communities, about intergenerational relationships, groups and groupwork, moral panics and media and so on, is all helpful in analysing a situation from a number of perspectives.

Task 9.2

- What multiple perspectives can you draw on in developing your assessments on placement/in your workplace?
- Who are the people you need to talk to in order to inform a thorough assessment of needs?
- What other sources of data could you draw on to inform your assessment?

Discuss your findings with your supervisor or line manager.

This brings us to how we prioritise assessments. When working in new contexts, it can seem like there are a number of different and sometimes competing challenges that warrant our attention. A skilled practitioner has to make judgements about what needs are greatest in the minds of those that we seek to work with. Using participatory approaches to assessment is worthwhile here for two reasons. First, we are able to provide a forum for young people (and/or others) to engage in both voicing their views on what matters to them and deliberating with others about which needs may take priority over others. Second, our assessment priorities are more likely to be grounded in the views of those we are working with and they themselves have contributed to the ordering of what matters. A practical example of one way to prioritise needs is set out in Table 9.1.

Task 9.3

- Test out the steps in Table 9.1 with a group of young people.
- What issues came out from the discussions?
- What techniques helped you to facilitate the group discussion?

Discuss your findings with your supervisor or line manager.

Table 9.1 Listing, grouping and prioritising needs

Step 1	Listing	We start by encouraging young people to list their many different issues, needs or concerns on Post-it notes. For this to be most effective, we ask them to do this on their own or in pairs. It is useful to develop a question that can help to frame these issues. For instance, we might ask: 'What are the bad things about living in this neighbourhood?' 'What would you most like to see different at your local school?' More general questions may also help: 'If you could change one thing to make your life a bit better, what would it be?'
		
		Whichever approach you use, the ideal is that you generate as many ideas as possible, each on an individual Post-it note or sticker. The ideas may often seem initially disconnected or young people may write down concerns that they share with others.
		
		`Litter` `Bullying` `Need a skate park` `Park needs cleaning`
		`Nowhere to go` `Hassled by police` `Drug needles on park`

Step 2	Grouping	The next stage involves asking young people to work in small groups to identify commonalities amongst the various Post-it notes. The task here is to find patterns and similarities to 'group' the data gained in Step 1. So, for example, young people might begin to bring together issues that seem similar to one another:
		
		`Litter` `Drug needles on park` `Park needs cleaning`
		
		At this stage, young people might wish to develop categories for the emerging groups – so, we might classify the above three as:
		
		`Cleaning up the park`
		
		It is important at this stage to try to frame things in a more positive way so that we move from listing problems or issues to identifying actions or needs that can be addressed. In this case, 'cleaning up the park' implies something that needs to be done rather than just listing what is wrong with the park.

Step 3	Prioritising	The final step in this process is concerned with prioritising: deciding which of the grouped needs or actions is at the top of the list in the group's mind. Here, the whole group works together to discuss, debate and decide on a 'rank'. For the purposes of this exercise, we have produced a diamond ranking template where the issue of most importance is at the top (number 1) and the least is at the bottom (number 9). Many different needs may fall somewhere in between top and bottom (numbers 2–8). Reaching a group consensus can take time as different individuals may dispute the perspectives of others. The task of the facilitator is to enable the group to have the space and time for discussion until some form of agreement is reached. Diamond ranking: `1` / `2` `3` / `4` `5` `6` / `7` `8` / `9`

As a final point, it is often wrongly assumed that an assessment ends and then the real work begins. Assessment is ongoing; it is fluid, and just as individual lives and circumstances change, so too must our attention to them. For example, a young woman we are working with may present with particular needs that we are working with her to address. Then after some weeks of working together, she might announce that she is pregnant. This news represents a major life change that requires us to think about the new needs she may now face. Good assessment practice recognises that young people are not static: their personal and social worlds change frequently, and whilst not all changes may be as significant as this example, they require us to be constantly aware of how best we are supporting those we work with.

Planning and implementation

Youth workers deliver a range of different activities in partnership with the young people they work with. A quick unscientific survey of some youth workers found that in the week of writing this chapter, they had been engaged in a number of activities that reflect the diversity of youth work practice:

- Delivering the last few sessions of a term-long outdoor education programme for young people at risk of permanent exclusion from school. The sessions this week had featured caving and abseiling.
- Running a support and advice group for young first-time dads, exploring how to be an active parent.
- Engaging with young people in the evenings through a pop-up cafe in the middle of a local park.
- Holding sessions at the local youth club with a wide range of sports and arts activities as well as places for young people to just hang around.

The reason for illustrating the diversity of approaches used by youth workers is to demonstrate that the types and levels of planning they are involved with vary significantly. In the case of the outdoor education programme, a substantial plan was put together to attract external funding for the young people who participated in it. In other situations, such as the youth club session, session planning may have been required for the arts and sports activities, but less structure was needed for the informal engagement with young people who use the space to meet with one another. However, even in these informal encounters the youth worker approaches the young people with purpose; they are entering a meaningful relationship that will stimulate learning, even where this is seemingly unplanned.

Some foundation questions to ask when planning your work are worth stating at this point:

- What am I aiming to do?
- What will happen as a result?
- How will I go about doing it?

- What resources do I need?
- Who needs to be involved?
- What if it doesn't work?

What am I aiming to do?

Through the process of assessment, you will have identified a number of personal, social and collective needs that youth work can make a contribution to addressing. Using different perspectives, prioritising needs and working with those you seek to make a difference with can all help with shaping the aims and objectives of an intervention. Your aims are the overarching ambitions of your project and set out a broad statement of what you hope to achieve. In the example of the outdoor education project, the aim was to reduce the risk of exclusion and increase the educational attainment and attendance in school of Year 9 pupils. The objectives demonstrate the things you will have done by the end of the project to meet this aim. So, again in the case of the outdoor education project, some objectives may have been phrased thus:

- work with 150 referred young people through a programme of 12 weekly sessions;
- use outdoor education challenges to support young people in the development of social and personal skills, knowledge and attitudes;
- work with groups to increase participants' experience of working with others;
- provide pastoral and intensive tutorial support for young people to develop key personal and social skills.

The objectives should always be elements of meeting your overall aim.

Task 9.4

Now apply this to a project you are undertaking for your placement or workplace. What are your overarching aims? What are the objectives you need to set in order to meet your aim? To what extent have you involved young people in setting these?

What will happen as a result?

Thinking carefully about what you expect to be the outcomes of your interventions is an increasingly important feature of youth work practice. Later on in this chapter, we explore approaches to evaluation in practice but desired outcomes should be considered at the planning stage. Outcomes should be specific, measurable and realistic, and directly related to the programme of work that you are about to undertake. When thinking about what outcomes you want to specify, think also about how you might prove that you have met them. Returning to the outdoor activity project, we can see the types of outcomes they sought to demonstrate and how they would evidence these:

Table 9.2 Example outcomes for an outdoor activity project

Type of outcome	Evidence
Increased school attendance at 3 and 6 months after the programme	School attendance records (pre- and post-programme).
Increased school attainment at 3 and 6 months after the programme	School attainment records (pre- and post-programme)
An increase in young people's confidence, self-esteem, decision-making and team-working skills	Young people's self-completion tool using scale measures (1–10) at start and end of the project

The project team were careful to build in some outcome indicators that would enable them to measure change as a result of young people's engagement in the programme. To do this, they identified baseline data (how things are at the start) and end data (how things are at the end). Types of data you might capture are covered in the Evaluation section of this chapter but it is worth identifying what baseline data is currently collected in your organisation, and what further data you might need to collect as part of your project.

How will I go about doing it and what resources do I need?

Given the diversity of youth work practice, it is unsurprising that the methods you might employ to undertake your work will vary from one situation to the next. Thinking about, writing down and consulting on the approaches you intend to use will enable you to determine whether:

- what you propose can be achieved within the constraints of your organisational resources;
- young people are likely to respond to and engage positively with the methods;
- the proposed methods will help you to meet your aims.

As you develop your ideas, it is important to consider a number of different resource questions. Are you considering developing a programme that runs just once, or over a period of weeks? Do you need staff support to deliver the work? What material resources do you need and how will you pay for these? What do young people need in order to take part? One youth worker reflected on their experiences of costing a project:

Thinking about resources is really important. We costed up the programme for staff time, the materials we needed etc. One thing we didn't think about was the cost of being involved for the young people themselves. We asked them to bring along anoraks and boots, and to bring a packed lunch. When we met the group, we hadn't factored in that many of them didn't have the particular clothes they would need and because they were from lower-income families, would be unlikely to get hold of them. They also depended on free school meals so the cost of a lunch each day for five days was also a big hit for families to take on.

It may not be possible to fund all aspects of the programme you want to deliver, so building in these resource questions during your planning will enable you to be flexible and responsive, adding and taking out elements before it is too late.

Who needs to be involved?

The 'who' questions may seem obvious but are worth thinking through carefully at the planning stage. They include questions about staffing (who will run the project) and partners (who needs to refer young people or work with us to deliver the project). Identifying who you will work with will also contribute to successful planning. Is the intervention designed for *all* or *some* young people? If it is targeted at some, how will you reach this group of young people? What additional time and people resources might you need to build in to recruit participants, especially if they are outside of mainstream provision?

Task 9.5

Return to your emerging aims and objectives. What kind of intervention do you propose to deliver? What methods will you use? How long will it take? What will it cost? Who else needs to be involved? To what extent have you involved young people in this process?

What happens if it doesn't work?

The more careful the assessment and planning, the more likely the work will be successful, but as a relative of one of us was fond of saying: 'Always have a Plan B'! This is more commonly known as a risk assessment when you are preparing a funding application for delivering project work. Discuss potential problems and pitfalls with your line manager and peers, and with young people themselves. Some common problems include:

- limited take-up of a project by participants, including those 'targeted' groups who are deemed 'hard to reach';
- lack of access to organisations or potential partner agencies (e.g. schools);

- bad weather conditions affecting outdoor activities;
- late start to project knocks timetable out.

Task 9.6

Discuss your plans with your colleagues and the young people you are planning with, and make a list of potential problems. For each potential problem, can you identify a possible mitigation strategy or solution? Remember, even where there are aspects that you cannot control (bad weather being a common one), you should have an idea of what to do instead.

Review

The final two letters of the ASPIRE mnemonic refer to Review and Evaluation, two distinct but interrelated processes that assure and enhance our work with young people. We turn first to reviewing, which, like assessment, is a continuous process throughout your project and is especially important when interventions take place over a number of sessions. Regular review provides opportunities to:

- identify what is working and what could be improved;
- express and attend to the feelings of the participants and staff;
- keep the project 'on track' in terms of take-up, resource allocation and other factors;
- identify and respond to any difficulties or challenges as early on as possible.

Monitoring is often an essential component of this review process. External funders may require data on the number and nature of young people who are engaged through the programmes that they support. In this case, it is important to establish clear procedures for collecting data and ways in which this can be stored and retrieved when it comes to evaluating the project. Monitoring data can also help to identify any particular trends in engagement where a project runs for a period of time, e.g. over a number of weeks. Monitoring the learning achievements or accredited learning opportunities is often a common feature of youth work, with many local authorities requiring projects to demonstrate tangible evidence that young people have 'achieved' during their engagement with a project.

Task 9.7

What sources of data will you need to collect to monitor your project? Through conversations with your line manager or supervisor, peers and young people, consider what funders require, what your organisation needs and what might help in evaluating the project at the end.

How and when reviews occur will depend on the length of time the project runs for and who is involved. Whether you are delivering the project on your own or with others, it is important to think about the mechanisms you can build in to ensure that you take stock of the progress of a project and attend to your feelings and those of others. Some strategies that might be useful include using supervision, holding post-session team reflective sessions and writing session recordings. Young people's views on the project will also need to be heard through the review points, so thinking about creative and engaging ways to capture these is essential.

Task 9.8

How often will you review your project? What review strategies will you use? Who needs to be involved in the review activities? How will you capture young people's views throughout?

Evaluation

Youth work practitioners face a number of challenges in capturing and demonstrating the impact and effectiveness of the work that they do. A recent review of the relationship between youth work research and practice will perhaps resonate:

> Often, practitioners will talk of the young person they chance upon a decade or so after first meeting them in a youth club. The individual will share stories of how they have changed into a 'responsible adult' and attribute some of their valued experience and knowledge to the youth worker's involvement . . . At present, mostly such evidence remains in the realm of the anecdotal and in contrast to their liveliness in describing these encounters, practitioners will also often share some frustrations at not being able to raise such rich description of what they do to the status of 'evidence'.
>
> (Spence and Wood 2011: 3)

It is often hard to determine the long-term impact we might have on the young people we work with and in the day-to-day experience of our practice, evaluating work can pose particular challenges. There has long been concern that youth work does not adequately articulate the contribution made by practitioners, nor does it effectively demonstrate its impact (House of Commons Education Select Committee 2011). As a result, the sector struggles to 'make the case' for the work it does (The Young Foundation 2012: 5). Often, the pursuit of evidence, outcomes and evaluation can make us suspicious since it can be 'related directly to the desire to undertake cost-benefit analysis of services, and to control and reshape practice according to current political agendas' (Spence and Wood 2011: 4). As a consequence, evaluation is often framed in terms of 'what works' with 'reference to pre-determined aims and objectives' (Spence and Wood 2011: 4). However, as Hawkins and Shohet argue: 'helping professions are best able to facilitate others to learn if they are supported in constantly learning and developing themselves' (2007: 150). This 'learning culture' can be aided by good preparation for practice (Chapter 2), using supervision to grow and develop (Chapter 10) and placing primacy on reflective practice (Chapter 11). Evaluation also plays an important role.

Good evaluation enables us to capture and demonstrate our work, which can benefit young people by improving the services that we offer (Hoggarth *et al.* 2009). Like others in the public sector, we also need to demonstrate public accountability for our work but we do not see this as a weak form of accountability where we merely provide data to offset criticism that we are not doing enough. Rather, accountability can be rich, enabling young people and the wider community to understand and influence the positive impact of our work. Retreating from evaluating work inevitably fuels powerful arguments that youth work fails to demonstrate its worth, and this is particularly problematic in times of funding constraints.

Evaluation is therefore useful in a number of ways, but like all aspects of doing good work, requires careful planning. In thinking about the approach to evaluation, it is worth thinking about the intended audience. For example, an evaluation completed for your practice assessment marked by the university tutor may depend on the continuous interplay between theory and practice, and would draw on lots of academic references (we hope!). On the other hand, preparing an evaluation for politicians requires a different approach since they are often in receipt of numerous reports, briefings and presentations on a very wide range of work that goes on. Colleagues have found brief summaries that highlight key messages to be much more effective with this audience. Whichever audience you are pitching to, it is important to think about your strategies for communicating your evaluation to your core constituent group: young people. Providing young people with copies of an evaluative dissertation you are particularly proud of may seem like a commendable act but may reduce access to the findings of your work. In an era of social networking and the 'online generation', much more creative and interactive ways of communicating evaluation findings are in abundance.

Alongside thinking about your intended audience, you should ask the fundamental question: Who will benefit from evaluating this work, and how? Discussing this with your supervisor, colleagues, partners, funders and young people will help to decide the best approaches to take in gathering, analysing and reporting your evaluation data. Some examples are offered in Table 9.3. In the table, we outline some basic approaches to answering some questions but also offer suggestions for how you might 'go deeper' to understand issues in more detail and in context.

As a final reference back to the assessment section of this chapter, it is worth stating again the importance of using a multi-perspective approach in your evaluation. The diagram on page 122 showed how using a number of different sources within a sound theoretical framework can enhance the quality of assessment. The same is true in evaluations: the views of young people themselves when combined with other per-spectives provide more powerful narratives of change and impact than reliance on single sources of information. In research terms, this is often referred to as triangulation or multi-method designs.

Table 9.3 Approaches to evaluation

What do you want to find out?	What methods might you use?
Did young people respond positively to the programme? Did they enjoy it and get something out of it?	*Basic data:* Ratings of satisfaction after sessions and at the end of the programme. *Go deeper:* Young people to keep a diary of feelings, of things they learnt and enjoyed, and of what they would do as a result. Young people take part in a video room and talk about their experiences at the end of each session and at the end of the programme. Focus group with young people to explore what they have learnt.
Did young people 'change' as a result of the programme?	*Basic data:* Questionnaire at start and end of the project using ratings on aspects that we want to see change (e.g. personal and social development 'goals'). *Go deeper:* Use pre- and post-data as above but combine with creative workshop or focus groups with young people to identify *why* changes occurred. Hold focus groups with staff and partners to identify their perspectives on how young people have changed. Where young people have reported significant changes or very limited change, undertake individual interviews to investigate issues in more depth.
Was the work an example of good practice? Could others learn from and use the approach we took?	*Basic data:* Report on different activities including methods, participation and snapshot of views. *Go deeper:* Use Action Learning Sets (Chapter 11) to identify areas of good practice. Pick particular sessions and invite staff to undertake a 'case-review': what worked, why and how this could be transferred.

Task 9.9

How will you evaluate your project? Who is your intended audience? What format(s) do you need to use to communicate your findings? Discuss your ideas with your supervisor, colleagues and with young people.

Conclusion

Good youth work practice is not haphazard. It depends on using frameworks for practice that enable a comprehensive assessment of needs, effective planning, implementation and attention to review and evaluation. We do not advocate a bureaucratic approach to assessment where emphasis is placed on filling in the correct forms for forms' sake. Rather, assessment is an engaging and dynamic process that can bring you close to the needs of young people and of other groups. Taking into account different perspectives can enrich our understanding of how best to work alongside young people to make a positive difference in their lives. Whilst it is true that much youth work practice is informal and works from the agendas of the young people we work with, the best practice is effectively planned so that hurdles and challenges can be anticipated and mitigated. Finally, this chapter has reminded us of the challenges youth workers face in demonstrating the impact of their work. Criticism has rightly been levelled at the profession that it does not do enough in this regard, so the question of how to evaluate our work should be considered throughout our practice. The ASPIRE model has proved to be a useful tool in bringing these issues together, and as students engaged on placement, we very much hope it can be effectively applied to your own work.

10 Supervision

Introduction

> Supervision can be a place where a living profession breathes and learns.
>
> (Hawkins and Shohet 2006: 205)

Youth and community workers, like other helping professionals, grapple with a range of challenges on a daily basis. Meeting the needs and expectations of young people, managers, the organisation and outside stakeholders together with the practitioner's own expectations of what they are able to achieve can be a potent mix to manage. Schön describes such work as demonstrating 'complexity, uncertainty, instability, uniqueness and value-conflict' (1983: 39). Under these circumstances, the need to effectively reflect on practice in order to not just cope with these demands but also to continually develop and grow as a practitioner is important, not only for the individual practitioner but for the profession as well. Structures to support this are therefore vital; this is why supervision is essential. Supervision provides practitioners with the time and space to share, to reflect and to learn.

This chapter aims to explore the journey of the emerging practitioner with regards to supervision; a journey that progresses from learning about the role of a supervisee in terms of understanding and using supervision to that of an effective and competent supervisor of others. This journey is outlined in Figure 10.1.

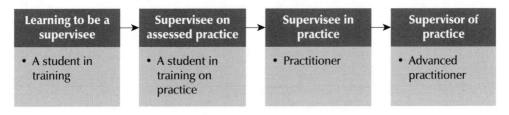

Figure 10.1 Journey from supervisee to supervisor

Students in training or those new to practice are likely to need greater levels of support and guidance, encouragement and reassurance, in short, to be more dependent upon their supervisor. As they become more experienced and skilled, although still needing support, they are likely to prefer a relationship that is more equal, egalitarian and less dependent. There is no doubt that the skills and qualities required for effective supervision are complex and that the process of becoming a competent and capable supervisor takes time, experience and practice to develop. This chapter aims to chart this journey. It will achieve this by exploring what is meant by supervision, its purpose and functions, models, skills and the fundamental importance of the supervisory relationship.

The learning from this chapter aims to serve a dual purpose. First, it can help to develop understanding and expectations about supervision, especially for those new to supervision. Second, it can help the reader to reflect on the steps in the learning process in terms of the supervisor they aspire to be. The intention is to help facilitate the development from supervisee to supervisor by encouraging reflection and the application of best-practice approaches.

What do we mean by supervision?

The concept of supervision is evidently not new; the desire to talk with others about issues that concern us or the wish to seek another's opinion are arguably age-old traits of all humans. Within a work context, the use of supervision varies across professions and it encapsulates a number of allied tasks and relationships. It has been developed within professional disciplines to meet the needs of practitioners and those with whom they work, and is deemed an essential element of practice within the fields of psychology and counselling. Woods (2001) suggests that its introduction into youth and community work followed the practice of using groups for social work. Irrespective of when or why it was first used, supervision is certainly widely practised within all areas of youth and community work today.

Task 10.1

What do you understand by the term 'supervision'? Write a definition that encompasses what it means for you.

Although we may feel that we understand the concept of supervision, it is necessary to define our terms. This is especially important given that within the literature it has many different connotations and often contested meanings (Davys and Beddoe 2010: 9). So what exactly do we mean by 'supervision'? Supervision is made up of two words: super, meaning 'above', and vision, meaning 'sight or seeing', hence overseeing. Indeed, many people still associate it with overseeing, that is, line management and someone with authority ensuring that a job is being done to an acceptable standard. However, within the helping professions, it is seen more as a commitment to continuous personal and professional development. 'There is a continued focus in the literature on supervision as a process of in-depth reflection by practitioners on their work in order that they continue to learn and develop from their experiences' (Davys and Beddoe 2010: 20). This concurs with a definition from within youth and community development work that describes supervision as:

> A process of critical reflection in which youth workers discuss ongoing work and professional development issues with a more experienced youth worker, whether a manager or peer. Professional supervision focuses on the core values of youth work in order to support good practice and learning from experience.
>
> (Sapin 2009: 187)

There are a number of different forms that supervision can take. These include: group, individual, peer group, team, managerial and non-managerial. The focus in this chapter is on individual supervision between a line manager and practitioner because this is by far the most common form of supervision (Hawkins and Shohet 2006). How does this compare with your understanding of supervision? Are there any key differences?

Fundamentally, the process offers the opportunity for a supervisee to:

- examine their practice openly and honestly, acknowledging any limitations as well as elements of good practice;
- consider ethical and professional implications;
- develop new ways of thinking, learning and practising.

The importance of supervision for youth and community practitioners should not be underestimated, given the variability of contexts for practice, the multiple relationships formed and sustained, and the complexity of the work.

There is no single definition of professional supervision that is in use within youth and community work. Arguably, it is not important to accede to one single shared definition, but perhaps it *is* important to agree some key purposes and functions.

Purpose and functions of supervision

The key purpose of supervision is to develop capable professional practitioners. In order to make this broad aim more useful and applicable to practice, it needs to be broken down into subsidiary objectives. These include but are not limited to the following principal goals of supervision:

- providing students/practitioners with the opportunity to reflect on practice;
- supporting and enabling a practitioner to take responsibility for their own personal and professional development;
- developing the practitioner's self awareness (Chapter 3) and emotional intelligence;
- encouraging the development of more effective working practices;

- exploring the relationship between theory and practice;
- facilitating the monitoring, evaluation and enhancement of practice (Chapter 9);
- ensuring safe and ethical practice (Chapter 4).

Our understanding of supervision can be further developed by considering the functions alongside the purpose that it serves. Within the literature, there are many different models and approaches to supervision. Most emphasise the multiple functions of supervision including quality and the focus on transforming practice. Such models have typically identified three core functions or tasks. Although differently labelled, these functions have remained relatively constant over the years. Two functions models have guided much supervision theory and practice within youth and community work:

- Kadushin's (1976) model of supervision within social work; and
- Proctor's (1987) model from within counselling.

Respectively, the three components of effective supervision they propose are:

- *Administrative/normative*: Kadushin uses the term administrative supervision to include assigning cases, monitoring, reviewing and evaluating work, promoting and maintaining good standards of work, and the co-ordination of practice within organisational policies. Similarly, Proctor uses the term normative to describe a function that promotes and complies with organisational policies.
- *Educational/formative*: For Kadushin, this encompasses activities that develop the professional capacity of supervisees, including developing self-awareness and teaching knowledge and skills. Similarly, for Proctor, formative supervision addresses skills and knowledge development.
- *Supportive/restorative*: Kadushin sees this component as the maintenance of harmonious working relationships by providing appropriate praise and encouragement and helping workers to handle job-related stress. Proctor's restorative component is a comparable support function, aiming to help the practitioner understand and manage stress.

Although these models may appear to be similar, there are notable differences in emphasis between them. Specifically, Kadushin's approach gives more control to the supervisor and greater emphasis is placed on the administrative function (Bradley and Hojer 2009). A likely explanation for this is the recent negative publicity resulting from high-profile child protection cases, which is why the importance of quality-assuring the work is seen as paramount. Proctor's model, whilst non-managerial in approach, sees the supervisee as somehow 'in deficit', that is, they need help and direction from the supervisor in order to practise effectively. Therefore, we propose that a third model, by Hawkins and Shohet (2006), which uses the terms resourcing, developmental and qualitative, is more appropriate. Their model is most closely aligned with the supervision of youth and community workers, where the supervisor and supervisee both take responsibility for the effectiveness of the process.

In youth and community work, there is an emphasis on:

- developing skills, understanding and capability through exploration and reflection on practice (*developmental*);
- managing any emotional toll from practice (*resourcing*); and
- quality-controlling and maintaining appropriate standards in the work (*qualitative*).

During the process of supervision each of these functions will need to be addressed; this may be helpful although not imperative within any one supervision session. The balance between the three functions will, however, almost certainly vary according to the different needs and concerns of the supervisee and the different contexts in which the supervision takes place. For example, the balance may lean more towards the qualitative function for a student on placement, where there is a greater need for assessment, but this would not negate the need for working on developmental and resourcing aspects as well. Crucially, the agenda can be set by either the supervisor or the supervisee, but preferably by both, in order to meet all identified needs.

The following task will give you the opportunity to reflect on your role as either a supervisee or supervisor in the workplace.

Task 10.2

Reflect on any supervision you have experienced/undertaken.

- What was the balance between the three functions?
- Who decided on the agenda/the balance?
- Would it have benefited from a change in the balance between the functions?
- How helpful would it be to use such a model? Would it improve/develop your practice?

Content models

These models help us to consider the purpose and functions of supervision. They could also be used as a broad framework for an individual supervision session. Within the literature, such models are often referred to as content models, that is, models that provide a structure for the content of a session. One such model is Hawkins and Shohet's (2006: 61) CLEAR supervision model. This provides an understandable yet comprehensive structure to help in the preparation/planning of sessions and a guide to what might be useful to include within sessions.

- CONTRACT: revisit ground rules; agree agenda, discuss desired outcomes from the session.

- LISTEN: help supervisee develop understanding of the issue through active listening skills, reframing and making new connections to what has been said.
- EXPLORE: through questioning and reflection, develop insight and awareness to allow alternative ways of seeing/resolving the issue.
- ACTION: reflect on possible courses of action. Decide on and practise 'first steps'.
- REVIEW: review actions agreed; encourage constructive feedback on session; agree how planned action will be reviewed.

Task 10.3

For supervisee and supervisor:

- Use this in planning a supervision session. How useful was it?
- How does it link with the functions of supervision discussed earlier?

There are parallels to this model with Egan's (2010) three-stage skilled helper model, comprising of stage 1: the current scenario; stage 2: the preferred scenario; and stage 3: action strategies. This is very much a person-centred approach where the emphasis is on the helper empowering the individual to help them make their own informed decisions. It essentially addresses three main questions:

1 *'What is going on?'*
2 *'What do I want instead?'*
3 *'How might I achieve my aims?'*

This provides a framework for conceptualising the helping process, and has evident similarities with the developmental process within a supervision session.

Selecting from the different models of supervision can provide a much-needed framework for emerging practitioners (supervisors or supervisees), who may feel more confident working within a clear structure on which to scaffold their practice. However, as with all such frameworks, they can also seem overly restrictive and limit flexibility and creativity. Arguably, it is the *way* the model is used that is important; it should not serve as a straitjacket but rather as a recipe to which one can add or take away some of the ingredients.

Task 10.4

For supervisee and supervisor:

- Within your supervision, have any models been used/made explicit?
- Would you find the use of such models helpful?
- If so, how could you incorporate their use into your supervision?

For supervisor:

- If you already use a model(s), how do these compare?
- Would use of the above models enhance your practice further?

Process models

The above models are extremely helpful when considering the content of individual supervision sessions. However, a useful distinction can be made here between these models and holistic models, that is, models that describe the whole supervision process. Arguably, having a structure for individual sessions is not sufficient without having a clear overview of the whole process. Supervision is seldom a 'one-off' event but rather a dynamic process that develops and changes over time. Having a clear framework in which to place the journey through supervision is therefore important. Again, there are many examples of these process models in the literature (see for example Page and Wosket's (2001) Cyclical Model of Counselling Supervision; Feaviour *et al.*'s (2002) five-phase supervision relationship). For the purposes of youth and community work, the process model shown in Figure 10.2 may be helpful. It charts the typical stages of a supervision journey.

- *Creating the relationship*: primarily concerns the preparation for the establishment of the supervision relationship. Decisions need to be made about: how you will work together, the context for supervision, purpose and structure, expectations and understanding of both parties – essentially, the negotiation of how you will work together. The relationship begins to form through this 'getting to know each other' process. At this stage, the supervisee is likely to be more dependent on the supervisor for guidance and direction than at later stages.
- *Developing the relationship*: initial rapport has been established. The focus is now on continuing to develop the relationship between supervisor and supervisee, building the trust and openness, and moving towards a more interdependent relationship, represented by greater equality with more shared power. Essentially, it is the same process as building a relationship with a young person.
- *The working alliance*: this is equivalent to Tuckman's (1965) 'performing' stage, where effective supervision takes place. This is characterised by appropriate levels

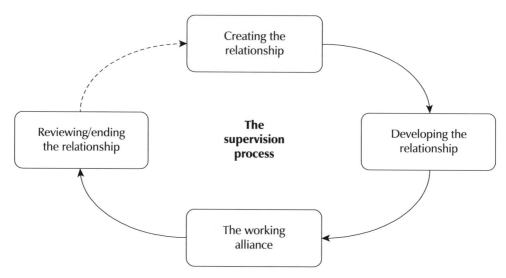

Figure 10.2 The supervision process

of sharing, exploration, reflection and challenge. The quality of the supervision relationship is represented by feelings of mutual respect, genuineness and trust, taking place within a safe and empathic environment. The focus is on the development in skills, competence and experience of the supervisee, and their consequent changing needs. There is a commitment to a shared process of reflection and learning, where the possibility of transformational learning (Mezirow 1997) can take place.

• *Reviewing/ending the relationship*: the opportunity to regularly review the content, process and progress within supervision needs to be built into the initial contract, to ensure that the supervision remains relevant and constructive for both parties. This includes reviewing the supervision relationship and any significant learning. This is particularly important when the supervision relationship ends, for example, when a student finishes their assessed practice. The opportunity for mutual reflections can help to identify best practice, any areas for development and any particular challenges, and to further embed the learning.

This whole process has evident parallels with youth and community development work. All work begins by discussing the aims and objectives, agreeing the ground rules and negotiating the boundaries, building and maintaining relationships, and reflecting on and evaluating practice. It is useful to keep this in mind at all times, to make the process of supervision less intimidating.

Task 10.5

For supervisee and supervisor:

- Incorporate this process model into your supervision practice.
- Where are you in the process?
- What impact does it have? What are the strengths/weaknesses to using it?
- Does such a process model help to develop your practice further?
- How important is it to have an overview of the whole supervision process?

Learning to work together

> Getting the contract right does not of itself in any way guarantee successful supervision, but it does provide a firm foundation for effective work. Without a meaningful contract endorsed by both supervisor and supervisee, supervision is likely to be beset with difficulties and misunderstandings.
>
> (Brown and Bourne 1996: 50)

The significance of the supervisory relationship cannot be overestimated; indeed the quality of the relationship has been identified as one of the most powerful determinants of successful supervision (Davys and Beddows 2010). The first meeting is therefore crucial in laying down the building blocks for an effective relationship. One student reflected on their first assessed practice:

> *Before I went to supervision for the first time, I was feeling really nervous. I had to go as part of the assessed placement but I didn't want to. I had no idea what they would ask me. What if I couldn't answer their questions? What if I came across as not knowing what I was doing; as incompetent? Also, isn't supervision for problems? I had only just started on my placement so I hadn't got any problems as such. I'm dreading it . . .*

It is usual to experience mixed emotions ranging from fear and apprehension to hopeful anticipation and optimism before attending your first supervision session. One way of trying to allay at least some of these anxieties is to be prepared. The first session of any new supervisory relationship usually begins by discussing and forming the contract (Hawkins and Shohet 2006), which is also known as the supervision alliance or working alliance (Proctor 2001); this essentially means agreeing how you will work together. So thinking about what you expect from supervision and how you would like to work with your supervisor prior to the meeting is key.

The value of contracting is recognised within the literature, where the factors that are deemed important are largely consistent. Table 10.1 charts some of the key elements:

Table 10.1 Key features of supervision contracts

From Page and Wosket (2001)	From Hawkins and Shohet (2006)
• ground rules	• practicalities and meeting arrangements
• boundaries	• boundaries
• accountability	• working alliance
• expectations	• session format
• relationship	• organisational and professional context
	• taking notes

Agreeing how you will work together is essential. A clear and agreed contract or working agreement serves to make the purpose and process of supervision explicit by creating a common understanding. It should be jointly owned by the supervisor and supervisee thereby ensuring that the needs of both parties will be met, and should be reviewed regularly to ensure that it remains apposite. Within youth and community work, some of the important factors to discuss include: the boundaries of confidentiality, especially where some form of assessment of the supervisee is involved; the expectations, aims, purpose and functions of supervision within the specific working context; acknowledgement of the power differentials and the possible consequences of this in terms of trust and disclosure; and the practicalities of agenda setting, note taking and meeting arrangements. In this way, the potential opportunities and constraints can be openly discussed and the start of the relationship building can begin.

In summary, contracting:

• aims to demystify what supervision is and provides a clear structure, outlining the purpose and functions;
• is a conversation between both parties where expectations, previous experiences and hopes for this relationship can be negotiated and agreed;
• forms the basis of the working alliance, which should be reviewed regularly when building and maintaining the relationship.

However, even though the importance of contracting is not disputed, worryingly it is an element of practice that is often inadequate (Scaife 2009). Indeed, many students on practice report never having agreed or established a working agreement with their supervisors in their assessed practice placement. This may be due to their reliance on the supervisor to initiate it. However, the reality is that some supervisors may not be as effective as we might hope. The contention here is that even if the supervisor, who is often in a position of power, does not initiate this contracting, the supervisee can and should. Using the elements of an effective contract (see above), it is possible to ask about: practicalities and meeting arrangements, the proposed session format, expectations and boundaries without coming across as demanding, over-assertive or indeed inappropriate in any way. On the contrary, most supervisors are likely to be impressed by the evident preparation undertaken beforehand by the supervisee, as well as their ability to engage in meaningful conversations and their willingness to take responsibility for their own learning and development.

It may be helpful (and perhaps comforting) to draw attention to the clear parallels between the contracting that takes place between a supervisor and supervisee and that of a youth worker and young person. Any work with young people begins with the negotiation of ground rules and boundaries; how we intend to work together. From this, common themes usually transpire that include the core conditions of respect, trust, honesty and consideration, key elements of all positive relationships (Rogers 1980). The outcome of such a process is that there is often a palpable change in the balance of power; the young people recognise that they are being listened to and that their views are respected. This in turn results in relationships that are more open and with a greater sense of mutuality. There are evident similarities here with contracting at the start of a supervision relationship, where the key element is that it is a *shared* endeavour; it is critical that the supervisee as well as the supervisor has their say. So although practitioners are often worried about beginning a new relationship with a supervisor, this recognition that it is no different from a part of their own practice that they would consider the 'bread and butter' of their work may lead to greater confidence.

Reflection 10.1

Reflect on any supervision with which you are/have been involved.

- Did you/do you have a clear and negotiated working agreement established?
- Is it something that you revisit regularly?
- Are there any elements that remain unspoken or not agreed?
- Are there any tensions or difficulties within the supervision relationship/ arrangement?
- How might you address these?
- Does the contract need changing/developing?

The supervision relationship

The ability to build and maintain effective relationships is a key skill within our work practice as well as within supervision: 'It seems that whatever approach or method is used, in the end it is the quality of the relationship between supervisor and [practitioner] that determines whether supervision is effective or not' (Shohet and Wilmot 1991: 87).

A final-year student on their placement reflected on the importance of relationships:

I'm so enjoying my assessed practice. I think I have built up really good relationships with the young people and other staff members, as well as my supervisor, and I'm even leading on a particular project which seems to be progressing well. However, I have been asked to write a report about my work as part of a bid for funding for a residential. The problem is that I have no idea where to start. I have never written a bid before, in fact I haven't even written a report before. I've tried mentioning it in passing to my supervisor but she just says I'll be fine. I don't know what to do. I can't take it to supervision because then she'll know that I'm not as good as she thinks I am and that I'm not working at the right standard.

All supervision takes place within the context of a relationship. It is evident that a positive supervisory relationship is a critical factor in determining the quality and effectiveness of supervision. Unfortunately, the case study above is fairly characteristic of students on assessed practice but we would suspect it is not uncommon in wider practice. There are two key issues here:

- trust
- assessment.

Allowing any element of your practice to be 'scrutinised' is anxiety-provoking enough for most people, but disclosing an area where you are struggling or where you do not know what to do is arguably worse. This is the dilemma facing many supervisees: should we be trusting and take a real issue that we are struggling with to supervision, thus making ourselves potentially vulnerable by exposing our weaknesses; or should we take something less 'exposing' that makes us appear more competent? This is particularly relevant where any formal assessment of practice is involved. This would suggest uncertainty about the nature of the supervision relationship and the likely behaviour of the supervisor. Are they someone who would embrace the concept of the developing practitioner and value honesty and integrity, or are they someone who would simply judge the supervisee as a weak practitioner and make a correspondingly low assessment of them? The quality of the relationship between the supervisor and supervisee is likely to determine the answer to these questions. However, I think it would be true to say that most good supervisors understand that a significant part of their role is to help the practitioner to develop their competence and confidence, and would much rather a supervisee was open and honest, and demonstrated a willingness to learn and develop, than hide behind their anxiety and lack of skill. However, establishing trust is a complex process and can take time, but it requires some movement on our part: 'paradoxically, one of the ways to begin to establish trust is to take risks through the willingness to be open' (Davys and Beddoe 2010: 62).

The supervisor can significantly aid this process by creating an environment where the supervisee feels sufficiently safe to be willing to take risks in the knowledge that the outcome will be the opportunity for further learning. One effective method is to model such behaviour. This would be particularly helpful if practised from the very beginning of the relationship. For example, in the first session, the supervisor could be open and honest about their hopes and fears, their expectations and their experience of supervising during the negotiation of the contract. Again, there is often a parallel process taking place between the supervisor and supervisee during the first meeting. It is one that for both parties is often characterised by feelings of anxiety, and by the need to appear in control and knowledgeable. This is deemed understandable for the supervisee but seldom considered for the supervisor, yet it is imperative that supervisees recognise that supervisors are not all confident experts. Quoted in Hawkins and Shohet (2006:

47), one supervisor new to supervision stated 'I'm anxious – I'm never quite sure whether I'm giving the people I'm supervising exactly what they are wanting . . . I'm really afraid about what they will say about me so I don't ask'.

To be honest about your fears but to demonstrate a willingness and motivation to learn would constitute the start of an open and functional relationship. Such honesty contributes to 'a virtuous cycle of trust building between supervisor and supervisee' (Lizzio *et al.* 2009: 136). Ideally, during the initial contracting, the supervisor will raise the issue of expectations, the balance of power and the potential impact of assessment on the supervisory relationship, but if they don't, the supervisee can and should so that both parties are clear.

Task 10.6

For supervisor and supervisee:

- How would you describe your supervision relationship?
- How open and honest are you? If you find this difficult, why is this? Can you share your reasons?
- How open are you about your strengths, your concerns, your feelings?
- How open are you to giving and receiving feedback?
- Do you fear being judged/assessed? Are you able to discuss these fears? How can you overcome this in order to make the most of the supervision?

Alongside honesty, there are a number of other core skills that are helpful in establishing and maintaining an effective supervision relationship, for both the supervisor and supervisee. These include:

- the core conditions of respect, empathy and genuineness (Rogers 1980);
- knowing yourself, or the willingness to continually develop self-awareness (see Chapter 3);
- the ability to be an effective reflective practitioner (see Chapter 11);
- the willingness to work with and through feelings of confusion and 'not knowing';
- the capability of asking appropriate questions (open, reflective, probing);
- skills in working anti-oppressively (see Chapter 14);
- the ability to work with authority and power constructively and positively;
- using the skills of challenge and assertiveness;
- the ability to engage in potentially difficult conversations, for example, the ability to discuss the supervision relationship openly and honestly;
- the capacity to work with and manage anxiety and stress.

This list is evidently not exhaustive. At each stage of supervision, such skills are fundamental to success. If a positive supervision relationship is developed from the outset and maintained in the manner suggested, the capacity for both parties to flourish is not only enhanced but is also a realistic outcome. Being open to reflect and learn more about ourselves and our working context can lead to a deeper understanding of professional roles and responsibilities, culminating in enhanced practice.

Conclusion

> It is the perpetual exchange of knowledge and experience which brings out the best in people and practice.
>
> (Wilmot in Shohet 2008: 129)

Effective supervision enables individuals to develop all aspects of their practice. A willingness to prepare for and engage with the learning journey referred to at the beginning of the chapter will be rewarded by personal and professional growth. The time and space for meaningful reflections within the supervision process diminishes the likelihood of feeling unable to cope with Schon's aforementioned 'complexity, uncertainty, instability, uniqueness and value-conflict'. It does not mean that practitioners will never again experience such uncertainty or stress within their work but rather that they have access to professional support, a place of safety where this can be worked through. As the supervision process develops, so does the knowledge, competence, self-awareness and reflective skills of the practitioner. However, the unfortunate reality is that there are some supervisors in the field who have little knowledge, lack the necessary skills and/or understanding, or have little interest in the supervision process as explored within this chapter. This can only improve if supervisees better understand supervision, value the support that it can provide and become effective supervisors themselves. This is why the main aim has been to help the emerging practitioner to develop their understanding of what supervision is in terms of its purpose, functions, models and skills. The intention has been to empower them so that they can take an active part in the whole process from the initial contracting to how the sessions are managed; not to passively accept poor or indifferent practice. This learning journey can help them to decide what constitutes best practice and consequently shape the supervisor they aspire to be.

As one student commented:

> Supervision has allowed me to develop new perspectives. I am so much more aware of my personal beliefs and values and the impact they have both on myself and others; this has given me a whole new insight and allowed me to be aware of issues that I wouldn't even have recognised as issues before. But perhaps even more importantly, I now have the confidence and ability to do something about it. So not only have I made significant and positive changes in my own life, but the essential skills I have learnt during the supervision process have enabled me to support young people through difficult transitional periods in theirs.

The process of supervision can at times be challenging and uncomfortable but it can also be enlightening, even inspirational. At best, it has the potential to literally transform lives.

11 Reflective practice

Introduction

> Reflective practice is as much a state of mind as it is a set of activities.
>
> (Vaughan 1990: ix)

What kind of practitioner are you/do you want to be? What are the values and attitudes you bring to your work? Are you content to 'get by'; to just do enough? Or are you someone who constantly strives to develop and improve what you do and how you do it? The answer to these questions may well determine the importance you place on reflective practice and your motivation and ability to develop into an effective reflective practitioner.

Developing the skills of effective reflective practice is one of the primary methods for embedding lifelong learning and continuous improvement in our professional practice. Indeed, reflective practice is widely viewed as one of the key underpinning models for professional formation, competence and effective practice. This is true for many helping professions including nursing, social work and youth and community work (e.g. Johns 2009; Rolfe *et al.* 2011; Thompson 2005). In essence, reflective practice is a process that aims to help the practitioner to achieve a better understanding of themselves, and their skills, competencies and knowledge in order to enhance and develop their professional capability. Effective and critical reflective practice is a skill, and like any other skill, it takes time and practice to become competent. This chapter aims to aid the process of developing this skill. It will help you to navigate the journey from being a novice to an experienced and expert professional. This will be achieved by exploring:

- what reflective practice is;
- relevant underpinning theory;
- when and with whom to practise;
- some of the methods and frameworks that can be used;
- the potential benefits and blocks to effective reflective practice.

Task 11.1

What do you understand by the term 'reflective practice'? Write a definition that encompasses what it means for you.

What is reflective practice?

Arguably, the concept of reflection can be traced back at least 2,500 years to when Socrates advocated learning through questioning and feedback, making the claim that 'the unexamined life is not worth living'. It is perhaps debatable that it is possible not to ponder on our lives given that reflection is very much a human activity that everyone engages in from time to time. However, this 'navel gazing/pausing for thought' form of reflecting, referred to by Moon (2004) as 'common sense reflecting' is not what we are referring to here. What this type of reflection lacks is the element of directed learning from the experience. As Biggs (1996: 6) points out, 'a reflection in a mirror is an exact replica of what is in front of it. Reflection in professional practice however, gives back not what it is, but what *might* be an improvement on the original'. Reflective practice is thus an extension of reflection: while reflection is a mental process that may lead to thinking about an event in great detail, this in itself is not sufficient; a significant element of reflective practice is concerned with helping to develop and enhance practice by extracting the learning from past/present experiences.

Defining reflective practice

There is no one universally accepted definition of what reflective practice is, although the underpinning philosophy is not dissimilar and there is some consensus amid the profusion of definitions. Here are some for you to consider:

- 'Reflection is a form of mental processing – like a form of thinking – that we use to fulfil a purpose or to achieve some anticipated outcome' (based on Moon 2004).

The premise here is that we do not reflect in a vacuum but rather we do it to achieve something, for example, to improve our practice, to evidence our learning or to learn from our mistakes.

- 'A reflective practitioner is a worker who is able to use experience, knowledge and theoretical perspectives to guide and inform practice' (from Thompson 2005).

Thompson adds the use of theory to ensure that our reflections are based not only on our own views but also with some valid and shared underpinning thinking/ideas.

- '[R]eflection enables individuals to make sense of their lived experiences through examining such experiences in context ... reflective practice is the process of turning thoughtful practice into a potential learning situation which may help to modify and change approaches to practice ... it entails the synthesis of self-awareness, reflection and critical thinking' (Brechin *et al.* 2000: 52).

This definition encompasses the key features of reflective practice as espoused within this chapter, specifically:

- learning through and from experience in context;
- gaining new insights into self and/or practice;
- critically evaluating responses to practice situations;
- using new understandings to inform and improve future practice.

Reflection 11.1

How did your explanation/definition of reflection compare with these?
In what ways did it differ?
Would you develop your definition in the light of these?

The aim of reflective practice is to purposefully allow the possibility of learning through experience, during or after it has occurred. This is not an automatic occurrence though; as mentioned earlier, effective reflective practice is a skill that needs developing like any other skill. Indeed, we can go through our lives having experiences but not learning from them. So in terms of reflective practice, we need to consciously consider our experiences in order to draw out our learning. In essence it is a process by which you, as a practitioner:

- stop and think about your practice;
- consciously and critically analyse it;
- draw on theory and relate it to what you do in practice;
- decide how this learning can impact positively on your future practice.

Theoretical underpinnings

The literature on reflective practice is prolific. It offers a range of perspectives, each with a slightly different emphasis, rooted within various fields of professional practice and education. Some of the key perspectives most often used within youth and community development work are presented below.

Timeline of key thinkers

- Dewey (1933): was the first to identify reflection as a specialised form of thinking. He saw the act of reflection as central to human learning and personal development: 'we learn by doing and realising what came from what we did'. Such reflections stem from when we experience doubt, a dilemma, a 'forked road' in our practice which would then lead to purposeful inquiry and problem resolution. Dewey's ideas provided a basis for the concept of reflective practice.
- Schön (1983): believed that reflection is one of the defining characteristics of professional practice. He saw professional practice as complex and unpredictable, so in order to cope, professionals have to be able to do more than follow set procedures. His significant contribution was the notion of:
  - o *reflecting in action* (examining experiences and responses as they occur, what he refers to as the core of 'professional artistry'); and
  - o *reflecting on action* (examining experiences afterwards, allowing for more in-depth reflections, with more time to explore learning opportunities in order to revise, modify and develop future practice.
- Kolb (1984): argued for a clear relationship between thinking and experience. He views experiential learning as a cycle involving action and reflection, theory and practice. To capture this, Kolb developed a four-stage model that can benefit professional development and thus help to develop practice.
- Boud *et al.* (1985/1993): added to the debate that when we reflect on experience, we must also recognise that our feelings and emotions are involved in the process, and that these feelings can impact on the way we perceive an experience and hence what we learn about it. They suggest that the process of reflection involves three elements: returning to the experience, attending to (or connecting with) feelings and evaluating the experience.
- Brookfield (1995): suggests that we need to employ four 'critical lenses' through which to view and reflect upon our practice to ensure appropriate depth and breadth to our reflections. Applied to youth and community work, these might be:
  - o from our own point of view (which Brookfield refers to as *autobiography*);
  - o from the point of view of the young people and communities we work with;
  - o from the point of view of our colleagues/supervisor/tutor (as mirrors/mentors/critical friends); or
  - o from the point of view of various theoretical perspectives and relevant literature.
- Moon (1999, 2004): developed some guiding principles underpinning effective reflective practice and writing. These include: the need to reflect on the same experience but from different viewpoints (different people and social institutions), different time frames (reflections on the same day, a week later and a month later are likely to be very different), taking account of the impact of emotional reactions to events, and the importance of collaborative methods to deepen reflection.

From this timeline of key thinkers, it is possible to derive some key principles that underpin effective reflective practice. These include:

- ensure the focus is upon *learning* with the aim of developing and improving practice;
- impose a structure, however simple; for example, describe context, reflect, analyse, identify learning;
- reflect from different points in time, for example, straight after the experience, a few days later, two weeks later;
- use relevant theory to underpin reflective practice;
- reflect from different perspectives, not simply your own, to ensure greater depth;
- consider aspects that went well, as well as those that need further development;
- include some specific action points that demonstrate what you have learned and what you are going to do differently next time.

In keeping with Schön's notion that professional practice is complex and unpredictable, it is imperative that students and less experienced practitioners quickly come to terms with the fact that the work often involves uncertainty and that answers are seldom clear-cut. Claxton has suggested that 'learning to learn, or the development of learning power, is getting better at knowing when, how and what to do when you don't know what to do' (1999: 18). This links with the concept of metacognition.

Metacognition and reflective practice

Metacognition is increasingly recognised as a crucial component of effective learning and an important aspect to developing skills in lifelong learning and reflective practice. It is often described using phrases such as 'thinking about thinking' or 'learning about learning'. Dunlosky and Metcalfe describe metacognition as 'our ability to think about our thoughts, and our ability to use this thinking to control our thoughts and action' (2009: 37). For the reflective practitioner, the ability to reflect on and regulate thought and action are crucial components of professional development. Focusing specifically on the process of learning may be of particular value to the developing practitioner. Such activity can lead the individual to a deeper understanding of how best they learn and give greater confidence in experimenting with techniques to maximise learning.

Consider the following questions:

- What do I know about the need to manage the environment to best learn from my experience? Are there particular times or places, for example, that are not conducive to effective reflection?
- Is individual reflection most effective or can interactions with colleagues and peers maximise my learning?
- What system do I have for putting what I have learnt into action? For example, do I summarise my reflections into learning points and time-bound action points? How do I transfer these into my practice?
- What model am I using and what others are there that I could benefit from using? Where can I find these? Do any of these complement my learning style? For example, could pictures or diagrams help to more effectively capture thoughts and feelings?

How far do these questions help you to 'learn about your learning'? Are they useful for developing your skills in reflective practice?

Understanding your attitude towards learning and the learning processes you adopt is likely to affect your capacity and motivation for learning and in turn your professional development. Undertake the following exercise to help you consider this.

Task 11.2

- Write down the first eight words you think of that describe 'learning' for you.
- Using your eight words, try to summarise how you feel about learning and the learning process in a sentence or two.
- What strikes you about the summary and keywords? Are they positive, negative or mixed?

For some, the answers may be overwhelmingly positive, for others they may be less so. In reality, whilst learning can lead to all sorts of benefits, the process is often characterised by struggle. It is often our attitudes and beliefs that play an important role in determining the extent to which we engage with the challenges of learning. Kolb and Kolb (2009) describe characteristics they associate with a positive learning identity and its opposite pole, a fixed self-identity. Figure 11.1 captures the two identities. Plot your own identity for each factor on the chart.

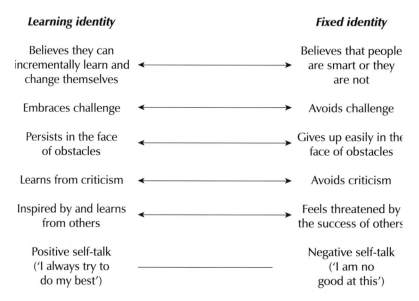

Figure 11.1 Plotting your learning identity

Where you have placed yourself? How would you describe your 'identity'? Thinking about your learner identity together with your answers to Task 11.2, now consider:

- what impact your attitudes and beliefs about learning might have on your readiness to engage with the process as a reflective practitioner;
- what aspects of learning you find difficult or threatening;
- whether you can identify aspects of your attitudes and beliefs that are associated with either pole of the learning identity spectrum.

The extent to which we display characteristics associated with either pole may depend on many context-specific factors, such as the nature of the task we are undertaking. However, reflection on learning and our relationship with it can help us develop useful insights into our strengths and weaknesses as a learner, and in turn, as a reflective practitioner.

So far we have considered some definitions of reflective practice, outlined some key literature most often used within youth and community development work, and explored the importance of attitudes to learning and the metacognitive skills that underpin effective reflective practice. The next two sections focus on the practicalities of how to begin the process of undertaking reflective practice by looking at how and with whom to practise alongside some possible methods and frameworks that can be used.

How and with whom to practise

The term 'reflective practice' carries multiple meanings. These encompass a range of activities which it may be helpful to place on a continuum from superficial to deep reflective practices. On this continuum, these include:

- occasional 'naval gazing';
- adopting a thinking approach to practice;
- sporadic reflective peer discussions;
- individual reflections via the use of, e.g. diaries;
- regular, formal reflections within, e.g. supervision;
- regular formal group reflections, e.g. action learning sets.

Authors such as Schön (1983, 1987) have argued that reflection lies at the centre of nearly all significant learning, but how and with whom it is undertaken to best effect has been less well explored. Certainly, the principal mode of reflective practice is predominantly an individualistic, personal and retrospective exercise (Reynolds and Vince 2004) where the onus is on the individual to reflect upon and evaluate their own practice. A common tool used in youth and community practice is the use of a reflective journal or diary. This often begins in professional education and training, where students are frequently taught how to reflect through the use of a diary or by using one of the many structured models of reflection. The advantage of reflecting alone is that it allows practitioners to maintain confidentiality, and to reflect on issues or situations where they have struggled, or where they lacked confidence and/or competence; experiences they may not choose to divulge to others, especially those in positions of power and who are involved in assessing their practice (Rees 2007). The disadvantage is that we may be unable to take full advantage of the potential for learning due to our own defences (see Chapter 3). There is an argument that 'Working alone does not nurture critical reflection and that we need others to clarify and challenge tacit assumptions, the existence of which we may be unaware' (Findlay 2008: 17).

Possible methods/frameworks

There are no definitive rules about how to reflect and there is no one method for reflection that is universally accepted as right. Indeed there are a profusion of strategies and techniques that can be drawn upon to help us develop critically reflective practice. The difficulty for many practitioners is knowing how to actually start the process. For those at the beginning of their journey, some structure in the form of a methodology may be helpful. One constructive means of helping people to begin to reflect is to provide them with a pre-defined set of questions that prompt and focus their thinking. Such questions can be used in a range of contexts in which reflective practice can take place.

The following is a simple checklist of questions to prompt reflection on practice:

- What do I want to reflect on?
- What was my role?
- What did I do and why?
- How did I feel?
- What are the consequences of what I did?
- What could I have done differently?
- What have I learnt from this?

Task 11.3

- Use the questions above to reflect on a recent practice experience.
- How helpful was this checklist in structuring your reflections?
- Were some questions more useful than others? Can you add any?
- Do you prefer more or less structure? Why?

The importance of questions should not be underestimated as a means of interrogating experience and learning from it. As Remen (2006: 293) writes: 'The most important questions don't seem to have ready answers. An answer is an invitation to stop thinking about something . . . An unanswered question is a fine travelling companion. It sharpens your eye to the road'.

Superficial, unthinking answers are indicative of surface learning and have no place in reflective practice. Questions that provoke effective reflection and deep learning tend to be open questions that start with: 'What?' 'Why?' 'How?' Even where the question may appear straightforward, the answer should not be.

Such questions can be formed into a model for practice. An early example is from the work of Borton (1970), who devised a simple but useful framework. It is based essentially on three cue questions:

- What?
- So what?
- Now what?

In this very basic form, the framework has the advantage of being a model that is easy to remember so practitioners can call upon it at any time as a structure to underpin reflective practice. However, it provides very little detail about actually how to undertake critical reflective practice. Rolfe *et al.* (2011) have remedied this by developing a framework that provides some very useful prompt questions for each stage of Borton's model. This helps to move people on from a purely descriptive level of reflection to one that incorporates all of the necessary areas for critical reflective practice.

- *What?* (What happened?): This is a description of the situation/experience to be reflected upon.
- *So what?* (So what am I to make of this?): Invites reflection and analysis of the event. It moves beyond the description to a personal theory-building stage, developing theory about why what happened did happen and the possible reasons for it.
- *Now what?* (Now what can I do to make the situation better?): This stage helps individuals to plan an active intervention based on their theory.

Task 11.4

Apply Rolfe *et al.*'s (2011) model to the same experience you used for the checklist of questions above. Critically analyse each model:

- Which did you find most helpful and why?
- Did either/both help you to engage in effective reflective practice as defined earlier?
- Would you use either of these in your practice? When and why?

This is one of numerous models/methods that you may or may not find helpful. The choice of method(s) however, is and should be, down to individuals, who can use them creatively and flexibly to suit their circumstances and learning preferences. For example, for some, a staged model provides them with the necessary focus and structure within which they can gain a good overview. For others, such techniques are overly restrictive, denying them the creativity that they need.

Task 11.5

Read Chapter 3 'Models and Frameworks for Critical Reflection' (pp. 31–51) in Rolfe *et al.*'s *Critical Reflection in Practice: generating knowledge for care* (2011), for an overview of a range of models available for use.

- Were you familiar with any of the models presented in the chapter?
- Do any fit particularly well with your learning preferences?
- What works best for you? Why is this?
- What didn't work? What are the reasons for this?

Try using different models within your practice – experiment with different forms of reflection in different contexts. What have you learnt from doing this? Have your preferences changed?

All models of reflection are merely devices to get the novice practitioner to begin the process. As suggested in the exercise above, it is useful for students to practise using different forms of reflection in different contexts: for example, trying to reflect in and on practice; following a prescribed model versus experimenting with your own creative approach; engaging in individual, dyadic or group reflection. This way, students and developing practitioners can learn what works best for them and what is most effective in different contexts. Certainly no model should be used as a prescription that tells you what you must do; rather, they can be used to help inform the process. It is the process that a practitioner works through that it important; the critical dialogue that helps them to interrogate themselves and their practice, hopefully culminating in improved practice. A good reflective practitioner will consider a range of models and choose one or more that suits them best.

Individual and collaborative reflection

Individual and collective reflective practices are not mutually exclusive of each other but rather are part of the same learning process. However, as has been stated above, most of the literature paints a picture of individuals reflecting alone, rather than on working collaboratively with others. This does not take account of the growing literature on and understanding of the wider social and organisational aspects of reflective practice (Thompson and Thompson 2008). Working with others can encourage and enable individuals to engage in the process of critically analysing their practice.

Reflection 11.2

What benefits of collaborative reflective practice can you think of?

There are a number of potential benefits of collaborative reflective practice:

- *Developing knowledge*: through dialogue, group members can share their knowledge base. This can include different theoretical underpinnings to practice and different perspectives from which to assess practice situations. There is the opportunity to explore problems and dilemmas from differing viewpoints, differing theoretical positions and different models of practice.
- *Developing skills*: other group members can demonstrate higher-level practice skills, for example, the use effective reflective questions to promote deep reflection. These individuals can serve as role models for enhanced skills acquisition. Collaborative reflection thus offers the opportunity not only to learn about but also to practise these skills.
- *Developing confidence*: appreciating that others also lack confidence and have anxieties about their practice can put some of our fears into a more realistic perspective.
- *Developing perspective*: through others, alternative perspectives can be created, explored and challenged. Dialogue can be entered into that helps to identify and confront any misguided or habitual practices. Group reflections can encourage breaking out of routine, habitual or preferred ways of working. Acknowledging that yours is not the only way to practise can be enlightening and empowering.

Thus, collaborative reflective practice can be an affirming, reciprocal and shared process. One practice method that can help practitioners to realise the benefits of collaborative reflective practice is working in action learning sets (ALS). ALS provide an organised and structured reflective space for set members to learn about practice and also about themselves. They allow the practitioner to reflect and reconsider past events to make sense of their actions to potentially find new ways of behaving at future events (McGill and Brockbank 2009). This is achieved by set members bringing to the group genuine real-life practice difficulties and dilemmas. The authentic nature of this activity serves to motivate members to take reflection seriously and to view it as a valuable and meaningful learning experience. Through critical reflective questions, ALS can help set members to:

- receive feedback on their understanding and analysis of the issue;
- identify any assumptions and prejudices;
- make connections to prior learning;
- gain a realistic perspective concerning the issue and their handling of it; and
- develop strategies for dealing with the issue.

Feedback from youth and community development students who have undertaken ALS provide testament to the power of the learning achieved:

The most difficult part of this learning was to question and change my own values and norms . . . this learning has aided me in understanding how the capacity to engage in reflective practice becomes one of the means of enhancing the quality of my work, thus promoting my learning and development. In the group I felt supported. Being able to reflect on the questions that had been asked and my answers made me see the issue with a clarity that had previously been missing. I found myself constantly reflecting both during the set and after, something I would not have done had I not been challenged by the members of the set.

Potential barriers to effective reflective practice

Reflective practice is an approach that involves a personal commitment to continuous learning and improvement, and a willingness to take responsibility for our own continual professional development. In order to achieve this we need to adopt a reflective and critical stance towards ourselves and our work. The successful achievement of this is something that most practitioners would aspire to. However, it is not always possible to achieve for various reasons.

Task 11.6

- What are the challenges associated with reflective practice?
- What might or does prevent you from becoming an effective reflective practitioner?
- What are the potential or actual barriers that get in the way?

Make a list of these.
Now consider what you might be able to do to overcome them.

Actual or potential obstacles to reflective practice range from individual factors such as your attitude towards reflective practice or your personal skill level, to organisational factors or workplace expectations. However beneficial reflective practice has the potential to be, there are many factors that can impede and inhibit its practice. Table 11.1 charts some of these:

Table 11.1 Overcoming barriers to reflective practice

Barriers	Possible ways of overcoming the barrier
Fear: for many students and even experienced practitioners, there is a real fear of exposing any potential weaknesses or perceived vulnerabilities, which results in a resistance to revealing themselves and thereby exposing themselves to potential criticism from others. 'The close examination of one's professional performance is personally threatening' Stenhouse (1975: 159). This is an area that some people wrestle with throughout their career (and indeed life).	Such an attitude closes off any opportunities for constructive feedback and support. Learning is not always easy. Workers need to try to adopt the reflective view that every situation, no matter how painful, can be an opportunity for learning and growth; where challenges are opportunities worth exploring rather than threats worth avoiding. Far from showing weakness or incompetence, this is what makes us effective and shows strength. Supervisors/managers have a role to play here in helping workers to feel safe, secure and able to take risks in order to learn.
Power/oppression (linked to fear): most often, those with whom we share our reflections are in positions of power over us, e.g. managers and educational assessors. Here there may be tensions between being honest vs. appearing competent. The result can be superficial, strategic and guarded reflections. As Hobbs (2007: 413) puts it, 'reflection and assessment are simply incompatible'.	The key factor here is the need to establish working relationships where honesty, integrity and above all recognition of the importance of reciprocal learning are key. Students/practitioners and educators/managers need to be aware of the risks and work together to overcome them. The careful establishment of explicit and negotiated boundaries is also important.
Lack of time: most of us experience a continuously hectic pace in our daily professional lives. Such a pace is not conducive to reflection and learning. Often, the dominant culture is one of doing, with seemingly little or no time for reflection and learning. Busy, over-stretched professionals are likely to find reflective practice taxing and difficult. This can lead to the following potential obstacle:	Effective reflective practice saves time by: not repeating ineffective practice; making more informed decisions; knowing what works well in different situations; being able to take more control of your workload; keeping up to date with what works. Viewed in this way, it is a necessary investment of time rather than a waste of time. Arguably, the busier you are, the greater the need for reflective practice.

Table 11.1 Continued

Barriers	Possible ways of overcoming the barrier
Unreflective practice/mindless routine: the antithesis of reflection is mindless routine and unthinkingly following organisational practices i.e. doing it the way it has always been done. Arguably, this is the prevailing practice, especially for many qualified workers. Reflective practice (and evidence of) can become yet another requirement in an already busy workload. This can result in either little or no reflective practice or poor practice, for example a 'tick box' activity which goes against the whole underpinning philosophy; this is then likely to be an ineffective waste of time.	If you perceive reflective practice in this negative way, try discussing it with colleagues who use reflective practice to see whether their experiences change your opinion. Certainly, to achieve any learning that has the potential to impact positively on practice takes time, effort and the right attitude i.e. determination to develop and improve. Reflective practice is as much a state of mind as it is a set of activities (Vaughan 1990: ix). Try to engender such an attitude by practising the skills of in-depth, meaningful reflection for a time to see whether you can identify any positive changes to your practice. This may help you develop a 'state of mind' that understands and experiences the potential of reflective practice.
Lack of knowledge and/or skills: and experience on how to reflect effectively can be a problem. If applied uncritically, reflections can reinforce prejudices and bad practice. The respective abilities of 'novices' and 'experts' are relevant here. Novices may lack 'practical mastery', and are therefore more likely to follow models mechanically to begin with. However, such reliance on models is likely to lessen with experience.	Reflective practice is a skill and therefore needs practice like any other skill. It is likely to be easier to develop the skills and knowledge with the support of other more experienced workers/managers/supervisors, in order to mitigate against uncritical reflections. Helping novices to develop their skills in reflective practice is arguably best achieved through practice experiences. With or without support, you can: try out various models/techniques to see which works best for you; keep up to date with the literature that provides helpful theory; keep a reflective diary; take pertinent issues to supervision.
Organisational cultures or structures: these may hinder effective reflective practice by not providing the infrastructure, methods, practices or processes. The context in which reflection (practice or teaching) takes place has a powerful influence (Findlay 2008). Of crucial importance is the value attached to reflection by an institution or profession.	It is possible to become an effective reflective practitioner without the support of the organisation (although evidently it is easier with it). This can be achieved via individual methods, e.g. use of journals and diaries, via supervision or with a colleague who is willing to be a critical friend. It may also be possible to help the organisation to develop such structures, especially if a worker can show how their practice has improved as a result of reflective practice.

Conclusion

Effective practitioners are by definition reflective practitioners because they constantly strive to improve their own practice. This involves a process of consistently challenging and questioning what they do and how they do it in order to become the best practitioners that they can be. If undertaken effectively, it is an approach that has the potential to:

- develop critical thinking skills;
- identify ways in which practice and professional conduct can be enhanced;
- promote autonomous learning where practitioners take responsibility for their own learning;
- develop understanding of self, others and practice, allowing practitioners to be constructively critical of relationships with colleagues, 'clients' and organisations; and
- help students and less experienced practitioners to gain the resilience and resourcefulness they need to continue to be lifelong learners.

Developing the skills of effective reflective practice can support the journey from a novice to an experienced and expert professional. All practitioners should be encouraged to aspire to such personal mastery; to adopt an inquiring and critical approach that allows for continuous professional growth. However, reflective practice is complex and difficult, with many potential barriers. Its success is dependent upon the motivation and skills of the practitioner. The extent to which the practitioner attempts to critically and honestly reflect upon themselves and their practice, and embrace change and, at times, even transformation, is crucial. All practitioners must avoid bland, perfunctory reflections. Only by developing and maintaining a reflective 'state of mind' can practitioners hope to engage with and manage the inevitable complexity, variability and uncertainty in their work with other people, and in the process, develop into effective reflective lifelong learners.

12

Working
with groups

Introduction

In the introductory chapter, we argued that youth work is a social practice. Youth workers work primarily with groups to nurture association, stimulating the conditions for learning to occur and for democracy to flourish. Despite the growth in case-work related roles that emphasise work with individuals, we would argue that the groupwork role of youth work remains central to our professional contribution.

This chapter explores how we work with young people in groups. It briefly explores the importance of groups before taking us through some practical steps that enable us to think about the efficacy of the groups we are part of and work with. The chapter concludes with some guidance for supporting effective groupwork facilitation.

Why groups?

Imagine we were to take a helicopter view of how our society organises itself. We would see various different units where two or more individuals interact with one another with some sense of common identity or purpose. These are groups, and they can be found in all societies throughout time as mechanisms for exchange and collaboration. Some groups are ones that we self-select (our peers), others are determined for us (our family). Some may be driven by particular interests (being in the local political party) or by our faith or religion (being part of the church choir group) and some we are born into (our ethnicity, our gender). Groups are a central feature of human existence and as such are a normal part of our everyday lives; indeed, one of the harshest punishments that we will have heard of is 'solitary confinement'.

The view above suggests that groups are inevitable, ubiquitous and omnipresent, but in this chapter we want to pay particular attention to the idea of *intentional* groups, where individuals:

- engage in frequent interactions;
- identify with one another;

- are defined by others as a group;
- share beliefs, values, and norms about areas of common interest;
- define themselves as a group;
- come together to work on common tasks and for agreed purposes.

(Benson 2000: 5)

Most people involved in youth work acknowledge that groups and groupwork are central to our practice. Whilst we spend much time working with individuals on a one-to-one basis, it is through groups that the principles and methods of youth and community work are most commonly used and can have the most impact. For young people, groups have particular importance in terms of their potential development benefits. During adolescent development, young people confirm or challenge their identities through their changing relationships with the family, institutions and their peer groups (Coleman *et al.* 2004). Groups, by their nature, are social: they can provide the context through which norms, attitudes, codes of conduct and behaviours develop. Self-selecting groups, such as our close friendships or a church group, can provide refuge for young people seeking to escape isolation or adult control. They can also provide young people with belonging and loyalty through being identified with an 'in-group'. Other groups are mandatory, where young people may find membership difficult but have little option to leave, for example their school or class group.

Since young people's membership of groups is so common, it stands that youth workers will come into contact with many different groups. Youth workers engage with groups in a number of different ways, and in doing so, play different roles. Sometimes they are invited or invite themselves into existing groups to stimulate learning and challenge or extend the experiences of the group's members. They might convene groups for particular purposes, for example forming a group to plan a one-off project. It is also common practice for youth workers to address difficult social or health issues through the medium of groups: convening around a theme of sexual health education or similar. Like the young people we work with, we might assume one of two roles in groups. A *functional role* is pre-determined and stems from the position a person holds, for example a chair, parent, job title, etc. These are easy to recognise and there is usually a shared perception and expectation of the role and its validity. We need also to understand *behavioural roles* within groups. A behavioural role is determined by the nature of the interactions between people, for example the joker or the challenger. These are often less clear and perceptions or expectations may not be shared. Behavioural roles are not fixed and fluctuate for most people depending on the group/setting – being the 'expert' in the bar does not necessarily equate with being the 'expert' at home with the family.

Working with and through groups has the potential to enable our work to be more effective than engaging with individuals. Some benefits include:

- *Groups enable relationships to flourish.* Most young people will self-select their peer groups based on a combination of factors including admiration for their peers, genuine feelings of warmth or friendship, shared interests and the desire to be included or look up to others for role modelling. Even where groups are not self-selected, people may develop meaningful relationships that had not previously existed. When they function at their best, groups provide people with the opportunity to work together, learn about one another and develop a shared identity that is conducive to the development of positive relationships.

- Through this process, *groups can model, confirm and challenge behaviour*. They provide a 'real' experience of learning about how to engage in a pro-social way with others, enabling young people to set, test and develop boundaries. Behaviours that may be accepted in one group may be challenged in another: how you engage with your peer groups may be very different to how you work with your colleagues in groups, for example.
- Groups enable us to *understand and work with dominant and minority views*. As the chapter on anti-oppressive practice sets out (page 194), group behaviours often reflect cultural norms. Working with groups helps practitioners to create the context when these norms can be challenged through dialogue. Views that might be considered a 'minority' perspective can be voiced and explored through effective facilitation. Silence, the use of humour and other verbal and non-verbal cues also give us insights into how topics or issues are 'felt' and experienced by a group.
- Groups provide opportunities to *build 'life skills'* as young people take on functional roles or responsibilities. A group context enables youth workers to develop participatory learning approaches, where the role of the practitioner is as facilitator enabling young people to take the lead. These life skills are developed in a collaborative and collective way. Through working in groups, both individuals and the group as a whole have the potential to develop skills and experience in team work, conflict resolution and, crucially, co-operation.
- Groups can *bridge understanding*. When new groups comprise members with different identities, they often provide the forum through which differences can be explored and better understood. High-profile examples of this model of groupwork include truth and reconciliation commissions, where different parties with long-held conflicts come together in dialogue for the first time. Similar, and perhaps more relevant, examples include interfaith dialogue groups, mixed-gender groups focused on sexism and restorative justice circles.

So far, we've been positive about groups but inevitably there are some downsides/ problems to look out for:

- Groups are *microcosms of the wider society*. They are capable of amplifying and reinforcing oppression as well as challenging it. They can be cliquey and exclusive, and bullying can take place.
- Whilst it is true that groups can nurture a sense of belonging, the reverse is also true. As groups bond, *individuals may find their feelings of not belonging or isolation exacerbated.*
- Linked to this, *group membership might undermine the uniqueness and autonomy of the individual*. This can more consciously appear as peer pressure, where individual behaviour is constrained by fear of what might happen if they do not go

along with the group decision. Or, it can manifest itself in a form of subconscious groupthink – when an individual can lose their sense of identity.

Practitioners need to establish ways of working that avoid, or at least minimise, these risks. In order to understand how we can work effectively with groups, this chapter will now explore our own relationship with the groups around us before setting out some approaches to working with particular groups.

Our groups

Reflecting on our own group membership, the roles we play in each and the effectiveness of these groups can help us to think about how we might transfer this learning to working with groups of young people. In this section of the chapter, you are encouraged to think about your own groups by analysing what they are, why and how they function and the role you play in them. Some questions that will be explored include:

- How many different groups are you a member of?
- How would you classify each of these groups?
- What role do you play in each group?
- How does this role vary?
- What roles do others play?
- How does the group function?
- How do you feel about being part of these groups?

We will investigate these questions in two ways. We first invite you to consider your own personal experiences of being part of groups, which in turn leads to some questions about how you work *with* groups as a practitioner. To do this, the chapter will draw on approaches used in *network theory*.

Network theory has gained increasing popularity in the social sciences in recent times, partly because of the rise of new technologies that have changed how we connect with each other. In essence, network theory is used to explain the organisation and 'representation of societies' (Boltanski and Chiapello 2005) by investigating who we are connected to, what these connections mean and how they enable us to consolidate or change our identities, relationships or circumstances. As Zeldin (1994: 88) puts it: 'every individual is connected to others, loosely or closely', and we investigate these connections to understand what they mean for people.

When people analyse networks, they look at groups as relationships between social entities. This means exploring the relationship between group structure and individual performance (Whyte 1943), the strength of 'ties' in a group (Boeck 2009), how a group engenders belonging or resistance (May 2011) and the perceived or experienced 'value' of the group. To look at this in the context of our relationships with groups, we will follow a four-step process. Each step is designed to both support you in reflecting on your own personal groups and provide you with a mechanism to do the same with young people.

Step 1: Listing

The first step in this process is to identify your own network and the groups that you are part of. Figure 12.1 below is a simple diagram that invites you to consider two starter questions.

Task 12.1

- How many groups do you identify yourself with?
- What name would you give to classify each group?

Using the outer circles you can record the names of each group that you identify with. Given that research suggests we are on average a member of 17 different groups (Carvel 2006), our diagram is purely an illustration: we have created just five outer circles. At this stage of the process, we encourage you to just list groups, not attribute any particular judgements about which might be valued or prioritised in terms of our contributions, for instance.

Figure 12.1
Mapping my
network

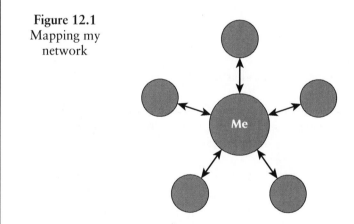

Typical lists might include family groups, close or distant friendships, work, social clubs, religious groups, online groups and so on. Having listed these, we can begin to think about what our relationship to these groups actually entails. The diagram contains two-way *arrows* and these are designed to represent the contributions we make to groups and what we gain from being part of them. Contributions and gains can be described by thinking about both the *function* of the group and the *functional or behavioural roles* that we and others play.

In determining the functions of the groups that you are part of, it may therefore become easier to identify your role within them and how these may differ depending on the context of the group. Groups will inevitably perform different functions and this in turn alters how we think about our role within them and what we hope to achieve by being part of them. Consider your contribution to a recent task-oriented group. You might have been preparing a presentation to deliver to the rest of your class, working with a few other classmates. The function of this group is clear – it is focused on a task that will ultimately be delivered and finished, much like the weekly tasks set for contestants on the popular reality television show, *The Apprentice*. The presentation (product of the group) might be assessed both at an individual contributor and group level. Just like *The Apprentice*, you, as a participant, might have wanted to demonstrate that you are both a team player and that your own individual skills or attributes contributed to the successful outcome of the group. Your functional role within this group might have been to lead on preparing visual materials to accompany the presentation. It might have been to take an active role in calling the group to task and challenging 'poor performance' of particular group members. In a sense, the function of the group in this case might very well determine and constrain the roles required to meet the task. To take an opposite example, your friendship group may have a wholly different set of functions that will vary from person to person, group to group. The characters in the sitcom *Sex and the City* clearly valued their intimate peer group as a source of humour, personal and emotional support, confirmation and challenge of choices as well as a forum in which to relax and revel in the identities that they do not project in the other arenas of their lives. Although an obviously more fluid group than a task-oriented one, careful viewing of that sitcom will reveal that each member of the group plays particular behavioural roles at important moments. Sometimes, one of the group members is required to lift the spirits of the others. At other times, it may be down to one member to organise things so that the group does not fall apart. Each person's individual personality characteristics also help hold the group together as a combination of serious, light-hearted, outrageous and conservative characters ensure that the group feels 'balanced'. Despite the diversity of groups and their function, as we begin to analyse them we come to learn that all groups contain some fundamental elements that ensure they fulfil what they need to.

Double-sided arrows suggest some degree of reciprocity in our relationships with groups, but through reflection, we begin to determine that in some cases, we give more and receive less and vice versa, according to the group we are thinking about.

Step 2: Connecting

In the first step, we talked about groups as isolated from one another, mapping our own relationship to the various groups we are part of. As we move on with our analysis, it is worth thinking about the connections between the different groups (Figure 12.2).

Connections provide insights into the relationships between our different groups and the value these relationships might have. These connections impact in different ways:

The impact of connections on us

We discussed above that groups help to shape our identity and reinforce behaviours, values and norms. In cases where our groups are 'congruent', there may be consistency

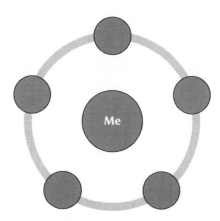

Figure 12.2 Connecting

in how our identity develops. However, in cases where our groups hold obvious differences (e.g. in values), we might find ourselves receiving and giving incongruent messages. For example, one of our groups might be an animal rights charity that we are actively involved in. This involvement may reflect our desire to be active in ending animal testing. Another group might be an employer we work for (other than youth work) that relies on animal testing to undertake its work. Our family and friendship groups may hold different views on this issue also. As we stated above, our own functional or behavioural roles may vary from group to group. We would not necessarily act the same way with our colleagues as we would with a long-established peer group. Equally, we might find ourselves 'role bound' across different groups, being perceived to be a particular kind of functional or behavioural role no matter which group we are part of. Altogether this results in some 'internal' or individual tensions about how the many groups we are part of help us to thrive.

The impact of connections on them

The relationship between the different groups also invites us to consider how they relate to one another. Put simply, does each group value the other? This is often a particularly acute issue for young people, who often experience tensions between family and friendship groups as they begin to naturally challenge and resist authority figures during adolescence. We can perhaps recall our own stories of valuing friendship groups more than our own family groups at one stage or another, even if looking back this was built more on resisting authority than not liking our families! In other examples, we might see very real difficulties in how groups relate to each other. For instance, a conservative church group may take serious issue with a radical left-wing political group, and for a young person it is perfectly possible to be a member of both.

Task 12.2

Think about how your groups connect. Do the groups relate to one another? What is the impact of these connections on your own identity?

Step 3: Ties

The first two tasks have concentrated on describing the number of groups we connect ourselves with and what our roles are in relation to these groups. These exercises are descriptive insofar as you may have focused on drawing together fairly neutral 'lists'. As you reflected on the roles that you play in each group as well as the gains and contributions, you may have begun to form a view about how you *feel* about these groups. Tasks 12.3 and 12.4 are designed to support you in building thoughtful judgements about feelings. Groups can be places where we find and reinforce a sense of belonging and a shared identity. Common purpose, aims or task-oriented missions can also bind a group. However, groups can also be oppressive environments where certain behaviours, norms or attitudes dominate over others, causing discomfort for certain members.

In this stage of our analysis, we encourage you to reflect upon the *strength of ties* you have with a group. Network analysis encourages us to think about the strength or depth of connection we have to our various groups. Some bonds might be strong (or thick), others may be weak (or thin). How might we distinguish between these two polar positions? It depends on what we think constitutes a strong bond. For example, social capital theorists often explore the difference between 'bridging' and 'bonding' social capital (see Boeck 2009 for a good review). Those with bridging networks may use groups to enable them to access new opportunities, increase gains and ultimately help individuals to 'get on' in life. Many people in senior roles will describe their access to a wide range of powerful and ultimately beneficial networks that enable them to increase their gains and consolidate their positions of power. However, they are often described as 'weak ties' because they may only be surface-level relationships. Deeper, bonded ties are more evident in longer-term, more established relationships.

The opposite of 'bridging' networks are those referred to as 'bonding'. These, according to social capital theorists, are those networks that are necessary for providing security, consistency and longer-term support. Bonding networks are often common-place in communities where people are supported by their peers to 'get by' – for example, close-knit communities might provide immediate help in terms of resources to tackle situations of crisis. The use of food banks to combat shortages of food in circum-stances of poverty is an example of this. Bonded networks might also signify reasonably stable groups such as our established friendships or our relationships with close family or carers. It is not often that family members 'churn' over in the way that happens in bridging networks.

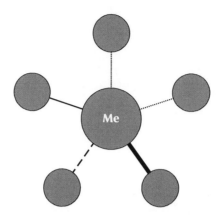

Figure 12.3 Strength of ties

How then do we measure the strength of ties? Using Figure 12.3, we have introduced some different lines that might serve to help us map our ties to our various groups. The thicker and bolder lines in this case indicate the strongest ties; the thin, dashed lines serve to represent the weakest ties.

Social capital and groupwork theorists offer us a number of different questions that help to judge our ties. These include:

- Can we 'get on' or 'get by' without the group?
- To what extent do we *trust* our group? How would we describe this trust?
- Is the group *time-bound*? Are we likely to depart from it at some stage?
- How strong is our *loyalty* to the group?
- Do we think our membership of the group is based on *reciprocity*? Are the gains and contributions in equal balance?
- Is the group *closed* or *open*? Do members come and go?
- Does the group make us feel *valued*?
- Does the group offer *stability, security, a sense of identity*?
- Does membership of this group *boost our self-esteem*?

Reflecting on these questions enables us to begin to identify things we might value about our relationships with groups. In doing so, we might consider how groups make us (and other members) *feel*. Attending to and connecting with feelings is a fundamental part of reflective practice (Boud *et al.* 1985). Our feelings about group membership can sometimes be at odds with the strength of ties. For instance, we may consider ourselves to be tightly bound to our friendship group but when we engage in reflection, may find this group to be a source of frustration or difficulty. Similarly, we might find very positive emotions connected to groups we might have previously considered to be weak.

In Figure 12.4, we have used icons to symbolise how we might ascribe different emotions to groups. For the purpose of illustration, we have used a smiley face (to signify happiness or contentment) and a lightening bolt (to signify conflict or tensions) as well as mathematical symbols where plus ('they do lots for me'), minus ('they do nothing for me') and equals ('we share responsibilities and roles equally') provide a way of illustrating feelings related to gains and contributions.

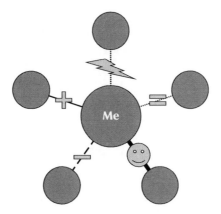

Figure 12.4 Feelings towards groups

Task 12.3

Return to your list of groups.

*   Make a judgement about the strength of ties with each of your groups and record this on your diagram.
*   Reflect on your feelings towards each group using icons that help capture these.

These steps have enabled us to consider the different groups that we are a part of, our contributions and gains from each group and, crucially, how we *feel* about our membership. Taken together, this analysis helps us to begin to make judgements about the effectiveness of the groups both in terms of their function and in terms of how they enrich or inhibit us as individuals and vice versa. The experience can be illuminating. We may often make assumptions about the effectiveness of our various groups because, on the surface, they may achieve certain tasks or goals that they set out. However it is possible for these groups to be effective at tasks and problematic in supporting people. Or it may be the case that we find that particular groups work well in all respects and valuable learning can be drawn from analysing why this might be so.

Good practice in facilitating groups

The discussion so far has acknowledged that we are part of and play roles in numerous different groups and networks, and that these have very different functions. Understanding the roles we play in our own groups is useful but it is critical that we distinguish between these and the role we play when working *with* groups. As an individual, you might think of yourself as the 'group leader' or the best at organising a group. You might demonstrate all the characteristics of being successful at these roles. It is perhaps too easy then to transfer this role to working with young people, where the temptation to take the lead may be strong, especially in task-oriented groups. At the opposite end, you might often take a minor role within groups, preferring to be directed to complete tasks. When translating this to working with a group, you may find that you struggle to offer the level of support it needs to get off the ground. This is why the concept of *facilitation* is helpful and important.

In this final section of the chapter, we wish to focus on those groups that are *intentional*: initiated or facilitated groups that are bound by a purpose and are distinct from those we encounter in less formal ways through our work. Payne (2005) refers to this distinction when he talks about formal groups: 'By formal we do not mean that the group behaves in formal (or conventional) ways, but that the group begins to take on a *form* of its own' (Payne 2005: 125).

In youth work settings, formal groups are most often set up in response to a defined need, as explored in the earlier section of this chapter. We work now from the assumption that as a youth worker you will convene and facilitate groups in a time-bound and task-focused way, either as a practitioner established in practice or currently on placement as part of your training. This section of the chapter therefore encourages you to reflect on some good-practice approaches to being a *facilitator*. Whilst group behaviour very rarely follows a distinctive linear set of stages, the role of the facilitator of a task-focused or time-bound group does contain within it some common traits that might lead to a more successful group process (shown in Figure 12.5).

Underpinning and responding to each stage are three core elements that enable us to be effective and reflective practitioners:

- *Reflection*: using techniques set out in Chapter 11 to reflect upon your engagement with a group. Reflection enables you to step back, to reflect not just on how the group is performing but on learning about your own learning, through which you can explore how your role as a facilitator is developing. For example, in Chapter 11 we state that 'the ability to reflect on and regulate thought and action are crucial components of professional development' (page 153). This will be tested when groups fall into conflict or make limited progress with their tasks. Developing our own responses and role requires us to step outside of the group, to think and consider how we engage, what we might need to change and, as importantly, how this role is making us feel.

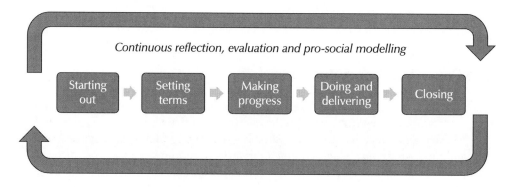

Figure 12.5 A groupwork process

- *Evaluation*: monitoring the group's progress, seeking views and developing ways to assess whether the group has 'functioned'. In some contexts, determining whether a group is functioning is straightforward, at the surface level at least. If a task-oriented group does not function well, there is usually the absence of a product or other outcomes by which to judge its ineffectiveness, albeit often too late in the process. In other situations, groups may find themselves in serious difficulty and will present with very different indicators. Group conflict, tensions, the absence of members or other features may present themselves. More positively, we need also to identify when a group works, how we know this is so and why. Chapter 9 provides useful advice on capturing both 'soft' and 'hard' outcomes, and knowing these will be beneficial to understanding the benefits of groupwork.
- *Pro-social modelling*: If one of the benefits of groupwork is the opportunity to model behaviour then this must start with our own approach to facilitation. We briefly mention above the distinction between our own group role and the role of the facilitator, but this warrants careful thought throughout the groupwork process. We need to reflect on whether we are *enabling* others to flourish in the group, ensure that we not exerting power or *leading* the group and, where possible, use praise to encourage the group to identify their progress points. The simple rule underpinning pro-social modelling is: model the behaviour you want to encourage.

Keeping these principles in mind helps us in bringing together and facilitating groups. Many groupwork writers describe the process of a group as a journey of some sort or another. We follow this by setting out five stages (shown in Figure 12.5). Prior to setting up the group, it is worth thinking seriously about what the group is for (the goals) as this will determine much of the activity that follows. Sometimes the group goal may be focused on a particular structured task (a group to identify possible sports activities for the youth centre), less structured and linked to an identity (a group for young men to meet and discuss any issues) or focused on bridging groups (a group for older and young people to share their experiences and issues). We would suggest that each of these examples might present particular challenges for group performance, collaboration and the types of conflict that might arise. Thinking about group goals is necessary: what is in it for members to be part of this group? Why is it being created? What will happen as a result?

Task 12.4

Discuss your ideas for a groupwork project with your supervisor or line manager.

- What needs or issues have led you to want to establish a group?
- What particular project or task do you have in mind?
- Have you considered what the goals of the group might be?
- How clear are these goals?
- In what ways can you build in strategies to reflect and evaluate during the groupwork process?
- In what ways might you demonstrate pro-social modelling? Give some examples.

Having considered what the goals of the group might be, we now turn briefly to the five steps of facilitating the group.

1) Starting up

As we start out on setting up a new group, we need to consider some important questions relating to its structure. Questions about the membership of the group come first:

- Is the group self-selecting? If not, how are members recruited and by whom?
- What strategies of recruitment does the facilitator need to employ in order to ensure people feel able and supported to join the group?
- Are certain identities missing from the group? Does the group represent the interests and views of the wider diversity of the young people you work with?
- How and when does the group plan to meet for the first time? Is the environment inclusive and supportive?

The composition of the group obviously reflects the goals of the group. Many youth workers will have set up intentional single-gender groups to provide space for issues to be discussed in a supportive environment. For example, a 'men's den' was set up by one of the authors to enable young men to discuss issues related to sex and relationships. In this particular case, the exclusion of young women was intentional and purposeful. However, the facilitator needed to ensure that the group of young men reflected other aspects of diversity in the wider group, particularly in terms of differences on account of 'race' and sexuality (whether known or not). In other situations, exclusion based on gender may be an unthinking action. One worker set up a group to plan a fashion and dance show at the local community centre and recruited only young women to take part. During a supervision session, she disclosed that there had been no desire here to provide space for women to work together – rather she had simply not thought the idea would be relevant to young men. The environment for the group also matters and we think of this both in terms of 'space' and 'time'. A young parent's group that starts first thing in the morning may exclude many members on account of their childcare responsibilities. A group for young women to explore identity issues would perhaps start badly if held in a room usually dominated by young men.

The size of a group also warrants serious consideration. It may seem an obvious point to make, but the size can have a serious impact on the roles, goals and functions of a group. As Smith (2008) points out:

> Size impacts on group communication, for example. In smaller groups a higher proportion of people are likely to participate – there is potentially more time for each, and the smaller number of people involved means that speaking may not be as anxiety-making as in a large group. In addition, large groups are more likely to include people with a range of skills and this can allow for more specialization of labour. In addition, larger groups can also allow us to feel more anonymous.

Task 12.5

In setting up your new group, consider:

- Who could be members of this group, and why?
- Who is included and who may be potentially excluded? What is the justification for this?
- How will members be supported to join? What roles will you have to play to support people in becoming members?
- How big or small should the group be?

In discussion with your supervisor or line manager, reflect on whether these plans fit with the overall goals of your intentional group.

---

2) Setting the terms

We have started these steps on the assumption that you have considered the goals of the group and that you have been instrumental in bringing it together. This means that group members perhaps start from a slightly different position to you. This is why setting the terms of a group needs to be a collaborative and participative process to ensure that members feel that they are contributing to a 'group identity'. The goal here is twofold. We want to help nurture the 'positive feel' of a group where people feel they can contribute to each other's efforts, and we want to ensure that the 'terms' of a group are in place to help the development of its norms.

When starting out, the group may be coming together for the first time as a unit and it is best not to make any assumptions about the existence and quality of any previous relationships between members of the group. Starting from the position that the group needs to learn more about each other in order to work together is a positive way to help people think about their collective identity. Commonly, youth workers will use 'icebreakers' or 'trust-building exercises' to get people engaged with one another. These activities are often fun and engaging, and plenty of examples exist that can be drawn upon. Many groupwork facilitators will use these activities throughout the groupwork process, not just at the start, as they provide an entertaining way of energising the group, particularly at points where interest or commitment may be strained.

We have used the word 'terms' to encompass a number of important structural or functional considerations relating to the group formation. These include but are not limited to: the groundrules (what will be acceptable to the group in terms of commitment, behaviours, attitudes and values); the clarity of goals (do all members of the group understand its purpose?); the clarity of roles (are specific functional roles needed, and if so, who will fill them?); and the logistics (when, where and how the group will meet).

The first session with a group can be a daunting experience but spending time on planning it will pay dividends. How a group initially comes together will help to shape participant views on whether it is worthwhile engaging in it, how they might contribute and what they hope to get out of it. Using a session plan that sets out how you plan to bring the group together is a good step.

Task 12.6

Prepare a session plan for your first encounter with the new group.

- What icebreakers or trust-building exercises can you use to help nurture a 'positive feel' in the group?
- What creative techniques can you use to help people to identify and agree: 1) the groundrules; 2) the goals of the group; 3) the functional roles if needed; and 4) the logistics of the group?

In discussion with your supervisor or line manager, reflect on whether this session plan fits with the overall goals of your intentional group.

---

3) Making progress

Your group is now underway and is ideally engaged in the types of activities you have planned together. Functional roles may be taking shape and people may be adhering to the agreed terms that they set out in the first session. You will now be able to take stock of how the group is progressing both in terms of the development of its identity and cohesion, and in terms of meeting its goals:

- Are things progressing as planned?
- If so, what is working?
- If not, why not?

The role of the facilitator is different from that of a group leader in many ways, not least in terms of trying to enable a group to set its own direction and tackle its own issues. We act as guides, trying to reduce the extent to which we are 'directive'. This means avoiding the temptation to intervene at the first hint that things might not be progressing as we would like. However, we also need to know when intervening will positively assist the group in moving forwards. Thinking about the ways in which the group is progressing, the dynamics of the group and the behavioural roles that people are taking on can help us to consider when to intervene.

It is a good idea to try to anticipate and think about mitigation strategies for some of the most common challenges that groups face as they progress. These might include:

- losing sight of the goals of a group;
- problems with people not performing their functional roles;
- problems with certain behavioural roles impacting in a negative way on the cohesion of a group;
- individuals feeling oppressed or silenced in groups;
- individuals dominating groups;
- other forms of conflict between group members.

We have already established in this chapter that groups can be fertile ground for differences to be experienced, negotiated and disputed. Whether we think of difference in terms of a person's identity or in terms of the expression of viewpoints, groups can either acknowledge and explore differences or suppress and ignore them. We need to keep in mind both the needs of individuals and the needs of a group as a social entity: 'Groups are not merely sets of aggregated, independent individuals; instead they are unified social entities. Groups cannot be reduced down to the level of the individual without losing information about the group unit, as a whole' (Forsyth 2006: 13).

A facilitator will be keen to ensure that the group unit reflects the diversity of voices within it. Some questions that help us to think about whether and how to intervene include:

- What is the nature of the relationships group members have with each other? Are the members strangers or do they know each other? How do they feel about one another?
- What prejudices do the members bring to the table? Have these been challenged before and what was the outcome?
- How does difference manifest itself? How do people exert their own views? What strategies are used to silence or repress differences in opinion?
- Is the environment conducive to enabling difference to flourish?
- Are there any practical strategies that can be deployed to ensure that people listen more effectively to one another?

4) Doing and delivering

We have discussed here some of the challenges that a group faces but we should also acknowledge that this is the stage where we would expect to see some 'doing' and 'delivering'. We signalled above that pro-social modelling is one key characteristic of good group facilitation and this should take the form of offering praise to the group as it progresses through various milestones of activity. These milestones may be seemingly 'small' compared with the overall goal of a group. Take this example:

I was facilitating a group of young people that had decided to put together a fun day in the local community. It was our fourth meeting together and we had not made any significant progress in terms of agreeing the programme for the day, making contact with potential activity providers or advertising it. I was feeling a bit dispirited so during supervision I raised these issues. My supervisor pointed out a number of alternative views that I hadn't considered. The group had met four times. They had shared ideas about what to do. They agreed what needed to be done. My supervisor suggested that, given this group was newly formed, these were some achievements I should recognise.

What can we draw from this example? The major lesson for us appears to be the value of recognising and praising small steps towards a larger goal. In task-oriented groups there is a tendency to focus on the end product as the measure of success. This can distract us from acknowledging the steps in the process that highlight significant learning points.

As facilitators we should use reflective practice to be alert to:

- the development of positive relationships within the group;
- each small step towards achieving a larger goal.

And we should demonstrate pro-social modelling by:

- sharing with and praising the group for the things we observe.

Task 12.7

Discuss the progress of your group with your supervisor or line manager.

- What is working? What 'small steps' have been achieved?
- What is not working? What challenges have the group faced?
- How good is the group at bonding and supporting each other?
- How effective have you been as a facilitator?

---

5) Closing

Many groups are time-bound and ultimately come to an end when the goals have been attained. This period might be termed 'closing'. We need to be sensitive to how the closure of a group may impact upon relationships, particularly if these have developed in a positive way as a result of the group. We might also consider how the successes of attaining a goal may be followed by feelings of uncertainty or disappointment that new goals cannot be set. We should also acknowledge that some groups may continue to thrive independently.

Some things to consider when closing a group include:

- how we identify and celebrate the success of the group as a whole;
- how we acknowledge and celebrate the role of individuals within the group;

- how we identify what learning has occurred throughout the groupwork process;
- how we support the group to move forwards or close as it desires;
- how we provide a bridging role to others if we are unable to continue our engagement.

Celebration of a group's closure might come in the form of the end goal being achieved. For example, the delivery of a particular activity or event that the group has planned may be enough for members to feel like they have achieved what they set out to do. In other cases, youth workers might plan specific events to acknowledge the group's performance and the contribution of individual members:

> I worked with a group in a school who developed a guide to tackling bullying for other students. At the end of the process, we'd produced the guide and decided to launch it at a special assembly. We gave each of the students a certificate for their contribution to the group and these were presented by a local sports celebrity who was an anti-bullying champion.

Our commitment to evaluating the group requires us to think about not only how the group has performed but also what learning has occurred through the process. Inviting participants to engage in evaluating the group at the end gives them the opportunity to reflect on what they have enjoyed, what they might do differently and what knowledge and skills they might have gained from being involved.

Finally, we will want to consider how we support the group if it decides to move on. In the context of working on placement we might find that our role as facilitator has to come to an end. In all aspects of work that is time-bound, providing a good 'handover' is important:

> I had spent a number of months supporting a residents group to get off the ground. The residents did not know each other before they came together and we spent a lot of time focusing on building the group. As my placement came to an end I was really worried that the group would flounder or would feel unsupported so in the last two weeks, I asked a part-time community worker to co-facilitate the group with me. This meant that the group had a chance to build a relationship with my colleague and I could exit knowing that she would be there to support its ongoing development.

Task 12.8

Discuss the issues raised in this section of the chapter with your supervisor or line manager.

- If the group plans to close, how can you celebrate what has been achieved?
- How will you enable the group to evaluate its learning?
- Will the group continue without you? If yes, what handover strategies can you use?

Conclusion

Youth workers primarily work with groups because they provide the space for fostering collaborative learning, association and democracy. Understanding why and how groups work together is vital for their success. This chapter has encouraged you first to think about the groups you are a member of and the value you attribute to these. It has also encouraged you to support young people in thinking about their own groups. In doing so, the chapter has set out some practical strategies for both understanding groups and effectively facilitating them.

It is incumbent on all practitioners to recognise that groups can be places where people flourish but that they can also reinforce exclusion and oppression. Thus the role of a good facilitator should not be understated. A commitment to reflection, evaluation and pro-social modelling will help us all to be better at helping groups to thrive.

13 Effective communication

Introduction

Once upon a time, a lecturer sat down to interview a prospective applicant for a youth work course. The exchange went something like this . . .

> *Lecturer: You've said on your application form that you're a good communicator. Can you give me an example of one communication skill that you feel you have developed well?*

> *Student: Well, I'm an excellent listener. Everyone always comes to me for advice; I give them great advice and talk about how my experiences are similar to theirs. They like to hear stories that they can relate to, it makes it easier for us to build a relationship together so I tell them bits about my own life.*

The example above illustrates that what we perceive to be our most developed skills (e.g. 'an excellent listener') may not be as good as we would like to think. The student here has described talking and giving advice as examples, the very opposite of active listening. Similar scenarios happen all the time. David Brent, the central character in the sitcom *The Office*, was notoriously bad at recognising how his poor communication (verbal and non-verbal) impacted negatively upon those around him. Yet, he believed in his heart that his communication skills were amongst his best assets.

We like to think of ourselves as good communicators but how often do we allow ourselves the time and reflective space to think about what constitute good communication skills? How do we judge whether we are good or less good at certain types of communication? How might we build on our skills to be more effective in communicating with a diverse range of people?

This chapter provides an overview of some key aspects of communication. It defines some of the key factors that underpin the context of communication and some of the problems inherent in how we interact with young people. It then introduces an overarching strategy that can aid good and purposeful communication with young people and concludes by offering good practice approaches to two key communication skills: listening and asking questions.

Communication, meaning and context

Communication can be defined as the sending and receiving of 'messages' between two or more people. The messages that we send out to young people, peers, supervisors and lecturers are situated within the context of our relationships, and carry *meanings* that are 'decoded' by others (Fulcher and Scott 1999). These meanings may be influenced by a number of factors, not least in how our 'own background, assumptions and perspectives . . . influence our approach to others' (Taylor 2003: 26). In Chapter 3, we explored the importance of understanding ourselves in order to understand and work with others. This 'does not involve pretending to be what we are not' (Taylor 2003: 27), it means recognising how our own identity and experiences can either enhance or hinder our work with young people. Our own identity therefore influences how we relate to other people but also how they perceive us. Before we look at some of the key skills of communication in practice, we need to consider how wider contextual factors influence the communication we have with others.

Power

The relationship between communication and power is pervasively strong. A command of language combined with confidence in verbal and non-verbal communication can be a powerful tool in forming networks and building relationships. In our work, we may nurture communication skills because we believe them to be key life skills that young people should develop in order to progress in their own personal or social development goals. As a tool for empowerment, we may support isolated individuals to use language for 'creating social relationships and realising the self involved in those relationships' (Rees 1991: 95 in Dalrymple and Burke 1995). Rees's point here is that through interactions with others, our own self-identity can be reinforced – confidence and assertiveness through collective identities can replace feelings of exclusion.

As practitioners, we start from a position of elevated power when we work with young people. We are often the initiators of communication and the guardians of communication 'rules'. For instance, we will usually be the first to pro-actively engage with young people and we may insist that they do not use language that we determine to be unacceptable. Our interactions may be set within formal contexts where institutional power supports us in our role. For example, a young person at risk of exclusion meeting us within a school setting for the first time is likely to approach the encounter with particular prejudices about our role and how we might engage with them.

Clearly, the most obvious and common issue of power in our relationship with young people is linked to 'age'. Children and young people are often characterised as 'possessions' belonging to parents and other adults, or as 'subjects' in need of protection (Lloyd-Smith and Tarr 2000). Approaches to communicating with young people will therefore reflect these dominant ideas: they can be 'told off', 'told what to do', 'seen and not heard' and so on. At the point of our first encounter with young people, they are likely to be very experienced at hearing how adults talk to and about them but limited in their capacity to have a powerful voice of their own.

Youth workers therefore attempt to redress power imbalances through empowering, participatory practice that seeks to reposition young people as 'participants' and 'citizens' (Lloyd-Smith and Tarr 2000), better equipped to communicate their needs and make decisions. It follows that the communication approaches we use need to avoid falling into the trap of reinforcing negative constructions of children and young people. We seek to value young people's contributions (Fleming and Hudson 2009) and ensure that the 'foundations of anti-ageist practice should be a high priority for workers in this field' (Thompson 2001: 89). This sometimes requires 'tipping [the] balances of power in favour of young people' (Davies 2005: 10) but certainly requires that the practitioner 'understands their personal, professional, political and organisational *power and influence* and uses it ethically and effectively' (Tyler 2009: 243).

Respectful communication strategies may not completely redress the power imbalance but they at least enable young people to question why such imbalances may exist. Linking the 'subjective experience of [young] people and the objective social conditions' (Dalrymple and Burke 1995: 12) enables individuals to see how systems of power (through communication) may work against them. This is central to youth work practice: 'Youth work should encourage young people to question ideas, attitudes and standards – and not only their own but others' as well . . . Such questioning and critical reflection is, in fact, part of the essential purpose of youth work' (Young 1999: 6).

Language

Language is the means through which most communication happens and is therefore the 'indicator' of power. Many areas of our life and work demonstrate the interconnections between power and language. Professionals, for example, have their own systems of shared language that mark them out as 'experts' in particular fields and exclude those on the outside. Picture the scene of the doctor who describes to the patient that they might have a tension-type, cluster or other trigeminal autonomic cephalalgias. You and I might refer to this as a 'headache'.

In relation to our own work, we have a whole suite of terminology and jargon available to us to describe what we do in ways that may not connect to people we come into contact with. For example, you would be unwise on your first meeting with young people to describe the work you intend to engage in with them as 'anti-oppressive, empowering and participatory informal education practice'! Professional terminology is also used by individuals when they attend multi-agency meetings, by way of ensuring that they are taken seriously in order to redress feelings of powerlessness (see Chapter 8). A university education helps to reinforce the power of language and if unchecked can distance you from the very groups you wish to engage with.

Young people operate within their own systems of shared language. The use of particular slang, phrases or street talk enables young people to simultaneously identify with a group (their peers) and reject wider groups (e.g. adults). This in turn contributes to a sense of pride as young people feel good in the shared use of their particular terms. We can all recount stories of trying to understand what a young person might mean when they refer to something as 'sick' (good) or talk about their 'but' (mate) looking 'peng' (good). Schools and other institutions may work hard to reduce such language and have powerful instruments at their disposal to help them do so. Like professionals using language in the multi-agency settings, schools seek to instil language skills in young people so that they can play their part in the dominant discourses of society.

Finding the right language to use in the right situations is therefore important. The first step though is to understand how language and power can interact, either reinforcing or redressing young people's exclusion.

History

Every communication we have with young people and others comes on the back of previous communication experiences. Imagine a particular day when you interact with a number of different people for different reasons. On any given day, you will have been asked or told to do things, been humoured or patronised, encouraged or empathised with, laughed at or laughed with. You may have spoken to family members, friends, colleagues, a doctor, a former partner, the city council's less than helpful helpline . . . the list goes on. Now put this day into the context of other days and you begin to see how our lives are made up of interactions with others. Understanding this and applying it to our work with young people will enable us to start with some basic assumptions:

- Young people will have had lots of contact with other adult professionals. Some of this contact will have been positive, some negative.
- In some cases, young people may have been disappointed or let down by their contact with other adults.
- Some young people may have been on the receiving end of negative language through discipline or other uses of power.
- Certain phrases and gestures may hold particular significance for young people if they have been used in a particular way before.

Seeing communication in the context of history is important as it helps us to understand where we 'fit' within the perceptions and experiences of people we seek to work with. There is the potential for every conversation we have with young people to either reinforce or challenge a negative or positive prior experience, or to provide new means of 'extending ourselves' (Crosby 2005). Understanding the 'personal biography' (Kemshall 2009) of young people enables us to use communication strategies that connect with the individual context of young people's lives. For example, we might avoid extolling the virtues of a university education if a young person chose to leave university due to disappointment. We may never ask whether a young man has a girlfriend, since we would not make the assumption that the young man is heterosexual. Extending ourselves means being open to the individuality of the young people we work with and this is mainly informed by understanding their historical narrative. As Crosby (2005: 96) says, 'each person . . . has a unique set of perceptions and experiences but, too often, informal educators do not take the time to learn about these'.

Good communication as a process

We have established that all communication can be linked to power and that the language we use reflects this. If we allow power to provide a negative influence on our communication, this forms a block between us and the young people we seek to work with. Some of the key principles and values discussed throughout this book will enable us to guard against this. As the above section also demonstrated, communication can be empowering: it can enable young people to 'come to voice' (Batsleer 2008), particularly where young people feel marginalised or excluded. Where possible, we should avoid various 'roadblocks' that can reinforce the powerful role of authority over children and young people. Gordon (1974) identified these as:

- ordering/commanding
- warning/threatening
- moralising/preaching
- advising/giving solutions
- persuading with logic
- judging/blaming
- praising/agreeing
- name-calling/ridiculing
- analysing/diagnosing
- reassuring/sympathising
- probing/questioning
- diverting/sarcasm.

Undoubtedly some of these have their place, and in a positive sense, young people may sometimes look to us to provide praise and agreement or to help analyse a problem they might be facing. What we should avoid at all costs is the 'automatic response', where we reach into our own experience pot to provide a ready-made solution to some of the challenges that young people face. This approach fails to demonstrate openness; it presupposes that all young people respond in the same way. So how do we ensure that we remain open, and what process can help us to use communication as a tool for empowering young people?

We wish to focus on two elements of effective communication:

- listening
- questioning.

Listening

In Chapter 9, we argue that assessment is an all-important component of youth work practice since the more we are able to 'know' about the young people we work with, the more straightforward and effective our planning and interventions will be. Good communication practice begins with the same assumption: the question 'what's going on?' invites us to develop a good understanding of the individual stories of the young people we work with. The priority here is to develop a deep and rich understanding of those we work with. Our own stories, perspectives and values are repressed in favour of *listening* to those we work with. The first stage is therefore concerned with providing the space and time for the young person to tell their *story* in their own way, and to be fully heard and acknowledged. It is also about gently helping them lift their head to see the wider picture and other perspectives, and to find a point from which to go forward with hope. How do we enable someone to tell their story effectively, without allowing our own 'automatic response' to minimalise or shut down the contributions they wish to make? The first part of this process requires us to use good active listening skills.

Being an active listener is arguably the most important communication skill we have to offer young people, since it is probably true that plenty of adults will *talk to* or *talk about* young people but very few will *listen to them*. Listening enables us to 'see behind the facade of the stories we adults tell about [a young person] . . . we are that much closer to hearing their version of the truth' (Ungar 2006: 42). Often, we rely on adult accounts of young people's lives to help determine our approach to addressing particular challenges young people may be facing. How many times for example do we refer to young people by an externally imposed label ('I'm working with this teenage parent') or begin our work after reading a risk assessment or referral form? School mentors may often take accounts of a young person's behaviour from the perspective of teachers. As the opening section of this chapter demonstrated, good communication with young people enables us to understand young people's feelings, attitudes and behaviours through their perspective and in the context of their own experiences.

What does it take to be an active listener? Like other forms of communication, listening is a skill that can be developed and there are a number of important elements that help us to become ever better at listening.

Reflection 13.1

Think of the people who *listen* to you. Who would you consider to be an active listener? How do you *know* they are a good listener? What particular techniques and skills do they use? Invite one of your peers or colleagues to also undertake this reflection and then share your findings. Did you identify any common skills or attributes?

We might describe a number of qualities that are linked to how the person encourages us to talk, takes time to let us finish what we have to say and positively reinforces a focus on us through their verbal and non-verbal 'cues'. But above all, being a good listener involves actually *listening*! This sounds fairly obvious but sometimes, whether intentionally or not, we may act as if we are listening rather than really genuinely listening. Think of the times you have heard the phrase 'you're not listening to me' and try to picture the scenario in which this might have been said. In most cases, the person doing the talking feels or knows that the person listening is not taking in what is being said. More often than not, the listener is not focused on the conversation or is not being attentive enough. Recently, one of the authors of this book attended a supervision session with a manager:

> *We sat down for a conversation about how I was getting on. I hadn't seen my manager for at least two months so there was a lot I wanted to talk about. The manager started the session by asking how it was going, a very general question, so I started by talking generally about how I was feeling. Within a few minutes, he was looking down at his tablet computer, checking emails and nodding occasionally to model interest in what I was saying.*

There are a number of difficulties we can identify in the above exchange. For one, the supervisor did not *seem* to be interested in what the individual wanted to talk about. This may not necessarily mean that the person was not interested, but they did not convey the right message to indicate otherwise. It is also impossible to really listen to someone if distractions interfere with the exchange between two people. In this case, the tablet computer proved to be a tempting distraction that was hard to resist, but other distractions may be somewhat outside of our control.

Reflection 13.2

Imagine you are in a busy youth club session and a young man comes up to you who you know has lately been quieter than usual – you've suspected he's been having a few problems. You are one of three staff managing a busy session and you're currently in the sports hall. The young man begins to talk and you find yourself listening as best as you can whilst also keeping one eye on a rowdy group playing basketball . . .

In this situation, what could you do to listen to what the young person has to say?

For many of us, encountering young people in these contexts is more common than having a quiet space for people to talk, free of distractions. The environment obviously matters and where possible, practitioners should find quiet and uninterrupted spaces to enable active listening. For instance, the worker might have asked for someone else on the staff team to provide cover for the sports hall but this may not have been possible and the encounter between the young person and the worker may be disturbed by changing the environment. In this case then, the environment cannot be changed, but whether or not this is the case, some key techniques help us to show that we are listening. These include:

- focus on actually listening rather than on acting as if you are listening;
- be attentive – concentrate;
- maintain eye contact – but don't stare;
- acknowledge any distractions and ask the person to repeat what they were saying;
- if you have not understood or heard properly, say so – don't pretend;

- make it clear that the young person can talk to you again;
- clarify;
- restate;
- reflect back;
- summarise.

(Youth Justice Board 2004)

Questioning

In Chapters 5 and 9, we demonstrate that questions are important components of our approach to conversation with young people. We would contend that the use of effective, thoughtful questions can do more to empower young people than imparting sage advice. If used effectively, questions can be purposeful; they encourage people to open up and tell stories about their lives. Questions can enable us to dig deep into issues, to provide exploration of 'current' and 'preferred' scenarios and can help young people to identify the steps required to move from one to the other (Egan 2010). However, questions are only useful if we are aware of the different forms they can take and the limitations and benefits of each type.

Consider this common scenario:

> *The sound of the door slamming alerted Mum to the fact that Jimmy was home from school. She saw him rush through the front room, head down and looking visibly unhappy. He threw his bag down on the floor and slumped in the armchair making an audible sigh . . .*

From the way that Jimmy entered the house, we can perhaps deduce that he has not had the best of days at school, and many parents or carers in this situation will instantly want to know why. Here are some possible questions that Jimmy's mum might ask:

- Did you have a bad day at school?
- What went wrong today?
- What did you do wrong today?
- Why are you in such a huff?
- Do you want to talk about it?

Consider these questions and reflect on which of them might elicit information from Jimmy. Admittedly, we do not have much information about Jimmy's relationship with his mum, but it was telling that he chose to sit down in the room with her – perhaps indicating that he did want his bad mood to be acknowledged. Some of the questions posed by his mum might instantly result in Jimmy feeling threatened or blamed for something that he has not yet even had a chance to get off his chest (e.g. 'What did *you* do wrong today?'). Some might come across as unintentionally downplaying a problem (e.g. 'Why are you in such a huff?'). Others might invite a conversation (e.g. 'Do you want to talk about it?').

The quality of our questions relates directly to the quality of answers we get back. The most common types of questioning style are outlined in Table 13.1.

Table 13.1 Seven styles of questioning

Type	Purpose	Example
CLOSED	The number of possible answers is small and predictable, can be useful in verifying what has been done, said or thought, and for getting a decision.	*Did someone send you here to see me?*
OPEN	The number of possible answers is great. Its most basic form is, *Tell me* . . . In essence, the more open the questions you ask, the greater the quantity of information you will get. Typically, open questions start with the words: *WHAT? WHY? HOW?*	*Tell me about what happened in the classroom today* . . .
REFLECTIVE	These are powerful, making the person feel that he/she is in control of the conversation. Each question is based on the previous answer and reflects its content.	*So you think that the teacher was overly harsh on you. What may have prompted her to act in the way she did?*
PROBING	Useful when you want to pursue a particular line of conversation.	*What do you think about what happened? Tell me more about that.*
LEADING	Can be used to great effect when you want to influence someone else. This is seldom an appropriate style of question in working with young people.	*Don't you think that it's important to have behaviour policies in school?*
MULTIPLE	Of little real use at any time. Most people can only handle one question at a time and will either be confused by multiple questions or only answer the part of the question that suits them.	*How do you feel this session has gone – was it good, bad, was it fun or was it difficult, did you enjoy working with others or did they put you off, do you think we should do things differently next time?*
COMBINA-TIONS	A sequence of questions, which you may find useful, is: closed, open and probing. A sensible use of all three can provide a progressive build-up, which eventually leads to a deeper understanding of the real problem.	*How are you today?* (Response) *Tell me more* . . . (Response) *Why did you feel this way?* (Response)

If we are genuinely interested in learning more about young people, their stories and how we might best be able to support them, then we should argue for more emphasis on questioning styles that are open, reflective and probing than those that are closed or confusing. We might also use questions to enable young people to develop their own reflective thinking. The use of the 'why' question can be a powerful tool in this respect, as can the act of 'challenging' young people.

Challenging is *not* about confrontation. We use challenge to provide a form of feedback to young people, aiding further self-reflection. Challenging means:

- Using questions to explore different perspectives (How do others see it? Is there anything you have overlooked? What does he/she think/feel? What would he/she say about all this?).
- Using questions to overcome obstacles in thinking (Why do you feel this way? In what ways does thinking like this help you? In what ways might this have an impact on others?).

Good questions should involve the opportunity for young people to challenge themselves, to change their way of thinking and acting that keeps them 'stuck' and prevents them from identifying and developing opportunities.

Task 13.1

In this task, we are going to invite you to test your active listening and questioning skills. Form a group of three and nominate one person to be the speaker, one to be a listener and one to be an observer.

Part one:
1) The speaker will talk to the listener for five uninterrupted minutes on a subject they are interested in or about an experience they have recently had.
2) The listener will only speak to encourage the speaker, using questions to elicit further information and invite deeper contributions from the speaker.
3) The observer will remain silent throughout, making notes about their observations of the interaction. The observer should also be responsible for keeping time.

Part two:
At the end of the five-minute interaction, the listener should provide a one-minute summary of what the speaker talked about.

Part three:
Following this, each member of the group should offer their reflections:

1) For the speaker: How easy was it to talk? How helpful was the listener in encouraging you to talk? What strategies did the listener use that were

---

particularly helpful? Did the listener accurately summarise what you discussed?

2) For the listener: How easy was it to listen? What strategies did you use to remain focused? What questioning techniques did you use to encourage the speaker to talk?

3) For the observer: What comments do you have on the overall interaction? What particular things did you observe that could be indicative of good practice or areas to develop?

Conclusion

Good communication skills underpin our work with young people. Whether we are focusing on developing our skills as informal educators and group workers or developing our approaches to challenging oppression, we need to develop both our listening and questioning strategies. This chapter has briefly reviewed these two common elements of communication. In doing so, it has only provided a very brief insight into the importance of communication as a key skill of youth workers. We must also be aware of how young people's communication styles will vary considerably according to their own needs.

As with all aspects of good reflective practice, developing communication requires us to step away from what we might assume we are good at. Rather, we need to invest the time and commitment to develop communication as a *skill* to be practised, refined and reviewed throughout our work with young people.

14 Challenging oppression

Introduction

Practitioners working in a wide range of social and health occupations will inevitably come into contact with people who are on the wrong side of the unequal. The powerful combination of oppressive socio-economic forces, personal prejudice and resulting discriminatory behaviour can reinforce already difficult circumstances. Youth and community workers have a professional duty to challenge discrimination within a moral, legal and ethical framework.

There is a significant body of work that engages with theoretical perspectives of prejudice, discrimination and oppression, and this chapter does not seek to do more than revisit some key definitions. The main focus of this chapter is on practice: how can we as practitioners engage with issues of discrimination and oppression to begin to make a difference? To do so requires us to think about the qualities of the anti-oppressive practitioner on the one hand, and some of the practical strategies that can be deployed on the other. This chapter seeks to enable the reader to consider how they can challenge individual discriminatory attitudes and behaviour, and 'interrupt' oppressive group norms.

Defining oppression

Reflection 14.1

When and how have you tried to deal with discrimination/oppression either in your personal life or professional life? How effective did you feel this was? Have there been times when you have recognised discrimination but have not taken action? Why was this?

The terms prejudice, discrimination and oppression are routinely and interchangeably used in youth work practice, and it is not the intention of this chapter to extensively explore what each means in any detail. In brief, prejudice refers to those pre-judgements we often make about people based on characteristics we assume they embody based on their identities, circumstances or other factors. To prejudge is to be human: instinctive judgements about certain situations may be important to us when avoiding danger. However, our prejudices can also be underpinned by false judgements since their origins may be rooted in problematic stereotypes. These prejudices may falsely ascribe aspects of behaviour we expect from individuals based on their 'race', gender, sexuality, class and so on. The roots of these may have come from messages we have received from our families, our friends or wider influences such as sections of the media; messages that we may have consciously or subconsciously subscribed to. To outsiders, certain prejudices may seem irrational. For example, watching debates about certain religious attitudes towards gay, lesbian and bisexual equality can invite incredulous disbelief. For those who have lived all their lives with such prejudices supported by the religions they follow, they may believe the alternative to be irrational.

Discrimination is the 'act' of using prejudice to treat people differently and usually negatively. It can manifest in a number of ways, through employment, education, leisure and so on. For instance, the personal prejudices of a teacher linked to 'race' may deter them from offering the same levels of support, encouragement or engagement with certain groups of young people. An employer may refuse to take seriously the application of a woman for a senior post based on their own prejudices about the role of women in society. Discriminatory actions stem from prejudice but require the degrees of power or authority to act.

Our focus in this chapter is on oppression, and the distinction between anti-oppressive and anti-discriminatory practice is important to note. Whilst anti-discriminatory practice is concerned with challenging specific forms of discrimination, anti-oppressive practice is concerned with 'minimising the power differences in society' (Dalrymple and Burke 1995: 3). Thinking about oppression enables us to consider how the socio-economic structures and systems in society reinforce power divisions, since power is the main source through which inequality is maintained. It also helps us to see individual views and discriminatory behaviours in a broader context. If we rely solely on tackling prejudice and discrimination, we may find ourselves laying the blame for inequality at the level of the individual we are working with. As this chapter demonstrates, inequality is far more systemic, and whilst our challenges will occur 'locally', we must be mindful that we are contributing to a broader effort to tackle injustice. Anti-oppressive practice is therefore about 'Recognising power imbalances and working towards the promotion of change to redress the balance of power . . . challenging assumptions, recognising that we all have rights and challenging the institutional practices that oppress and so systematically disempower those with whom we work' (Dalrymple and Burke 1995: 15).

How does oppression manifest itself? Mullaly (2002: 42–9) draws on Young's five categories of oppression, and these are explored below.

Exploitation

According to Mullaly (2002: 42), exploitation 'refers to those social processes whereby the dominant group is able to accumulate and maintain status, power, and assets from the energy and labour expended by subordinate groups'. Exploitation in this sense is intimately linked with capitalism, since inequalities of wealth, ownership and power are necessary for a competitive society. Society is divided by class, 'race' and gender, whereby groups with comparatively less power will usually assume roles that are either materially poorer or more dangerous than those with power. For instance, a young man in London is responsible for undertaking cleaning duties that regularly bring him into contact with hazardous chemical products. He is paid less than the recommended amount for the living wage and routinely cleans the office of a highly paid executive, hours before he attends work. The executive works long hours but receives pay at a rate of 300 per cent higher than the cleaner and is rarely exposed to such hazards. Similar stories can be found in everyday life, where those in power face fewer risks than those in positions of less power. This process of exploitation is manifested both in material differences (the difference in wealth) and health (the proximity to risk).

Marginalisation

Society functions on the basis of inclusion and exclusion, with certain groups either permanently or temporally 'confined to the margins of society' (Mullaly 2002: 43). Marginalisation can be linked to material deprivation, where financial resources can prohibit 'useful and meaningful participation' (Mullaly 2002: 43), but increasingly other forms of 'capital' are seen to be as important when thinking about the extent to which certain individuals or groups are excluded. For instance, older people may have a reasonable standard of material well-being but may spend many weeks in isolation without connection to others. In cases where the state does take action to address material deprivation, this can still contribute to marginalisation. For example, the experience of many who are in receipt of welfare assistance from the state through their entitlements or benefits can often be characterised as lacking dignity and respect, with state officials or departments interfering with basis rights of 'privacy, respect and autonomy' (Mullaly 2002: 44). Young people often experience temporal forms of marginalisation with active policies designed to exclude them from public spaces or media portrayals that reinforce negative stereotypes that inflate public fears. This may be more confounded or longer term where, along with age, a young person's 'race', gender, mental or physical health, sexuality or class are also used to exclude them.

Powerlessness

The dominance of hierarchical and patriarchal structures in society ensure, as we have said above, that power inequality is maintained. At the very start of our lives, power relationships are often structured in an unequal way as children find themselves at the mercy of adult direction. When we intervene in young people's lives, we do so as professionals who have authority over others and belong to a group in society that experiences positive forms of 'status privilege' (Mullaly 2002: 44). Factors that contribute to powerlessness can result in '*experiences* of powerlessness, such as exclusion, rejection or being treated as inferior, which lead to feelings of inadequacy, helplessness and dependency' (Dalrymple and Burke 1995: 15).

Cultural imperialism

As Mullaly identifies, much of what we have discussed so far concerns relations of power in terms of work, and, we would suggest, financial capital more generally. Cultural imperialism has also been identified by anti-racist and feminist thinkers and activists, who have argued that oppression occurs when 'the state promotes a single national culture' (Parekh Report 2000). Osler and Starkey (2010) argue that states create an 'imagined community' underpinned by myths of a 'monolithic common narrative of national culture based on a national history and mythology' (2010: 88). Processes of globalisation have challenged the legitimacy of these narratives, especially through increasing the 'cosmopolitan' transformation of communities that are 'increasingly diverse . . . we live alongside people with many different belief systems. Cosmopolitanism requires us to engage with difference, rather than create the illusion that it is possible to live parallel lives' (Osler 2008b: 457).

Violence

Violence is systematically experienced by oppressed groups. Women are more likely to be at risk of sexual harassment, domestic abuse and sexual assault. Violence on the grounds of racism or religious hatred is a common experience for Black and other so-called minority ethnic groups. Surveys of lesbian, gay and bisexual young people show high levels of homophobic bullying in and outside of schools, despite significant progress in the equalisation of legal rights (Guasp 2012).

Young's categories are helpful in identifying how oppression manifests itself, but rather than thinking of each category as isolated from the others, it is more useful to consider their interrelatedness. If oppressed, a person is most likely to experience most if not all of the five forms. Challenging oppression therefore requires us to challenge all experiences of injustice.

Internalisation and 'voice'

Questioning who are 'the oppressed' is a challenging, frustrating and unrewarding process. Whatever our own position of power or otherwise, declaring that *others* are oppressed might be met by those we are talking about with a mixture of incredulity or hostility. How we describe *others* might appear to be patronising at the very least. For example, as a white, heterosexual, able-bodied, middle-class male, might it not be disingenuous to engage with a group of unemployed Black young men on the basis that *you tell them* that *they* are oppressed? Worse, perhaps, that you seek to *help* them because they are oppressed. In addition, individuals may not accept or identify with the label of 'oppressed' and there are a number of complex reasons for this. The concept of 'internalisation' is one reason worthy of exploration. This concerns the acceptance of norms or values that are often powerful and oppressive.

Internalisation operates at all levels in society and provides an important function. We regulate our own behaviours according to the norms established, agreed and reinforced by the institutions, laws and moral or cultural codes of conduct that we come into contact with. At the very extreme end of this, most of us would adhere to a number of codes that, if broken, would have a negative impact upon society: not committing violent acts, for example. Laws and other systems of governance ensure that these norms are upheld, resulting in the presence of a 'status quo'. The effect of these systems is for people to regulate their own moral codes, and by and large this is successful. For example, *most* people believe that paid work is *normal*. This is further explored in the discussion on ideology (Chapter 7).

If we explore internalisation in respect of oppression, we can begin to make sense of why both the powerful and the powerless play an equal role in maintaining the status quo. The seminal and inspirational work by Brazilian educator Paulo Freire is often credited as one of the best articulations of this. Freire argues that oppression can only succeed when both oppressor and oppressed accept and adhere to the unequal relationship they find themselves in. As he states:

> Cultural conquest leads to the cultural inauthenticity of those who are invaded; they begin to respond to the values, the standards, and the goals of the invaders . . . For cultural invasion to succeed, it is essential that those invaded become convinced of their intrinsic inferiority.
>
> (Freire 1996: 134)

Freire's point here is that in order for oppression to succeed, it requires those without power to accept their circumstances without serious question. They 'internalise' norms that may in fact be doing harm. Freire also argues that the oppressor internalises a position of power based on a series of damaging belief systems about superiority.

Internalisation operates at a number of different levels. Carrington's (2000) work around 'race' looked at how leading Black British athletes reacted to questions about racism. Frank Bruno, who was at the time a famous boxer and popular cultural icon, often appeared to dismiss suggestions that racism was a problem beyond a 'minority of people':

> As far as Laura and I are concerned . . . (Racism) has never mattered. If there is a problem, it is in the minds of other people. The world's problems would be settled if we could all be mixed together in a great big melting pot.
>
> (Bruno 1992: 95)

Carrington (2000: 151) critiques Bruno's position, arguing that he adopted: 'Conservative ideologies and the assimilationist model of "race relations", which in the current climate amounts to little more than disavowal of Black cultural identity and any notion of Black empowerment.'

The critique reflects the seminal work by Franz Fanon, who argued that when the Black man denies and internalises oppression, he 'becomes whiter as he renounces his blackness, his jungle' (1986: 18) and 'the most eloquent form of ambivalence is adopted toward them by the native, the one-who-never-crawled-out-of-his-hole' (1986: 19). Similarly, feminists have engaged critically and extensively in understanding how women seemingly 'accept' gendered roles, lower pay and, in some cases, their victim-hood at the hands of domestic abuse. People writing about sexuality show how inter-nalisation can lead to lesbian, gay, bisexual and transgendered denial or repression of sexual identity.

Informal educators use Freire's ideas to address internalisation to engage in a process of raising consciousness. If oppression depends on the acceptance of myths or misinformation on both sides, then the task of the educator is to encourage people to think critically in order to challenge these. Young (1999: 89) argues that this process represents real and meaningful 'empowerment': 'Each individual's ability to transcend the internalised lies, myths and misinformation which keep us corralled in our own sense of powerlessness'.

Being an anti-oppressive practitioner

Whilst legal frameworks and practice 'tips' can be useful in tackling discriminatory or oppressive behaviours, they are in themselves merely 'tools' that enable us to do a job. We would argue that *being* an anti-oppressive practitioner requires much more than simply adhering to instrumental requirements. This is where a restatement of *values* is important. Professional values act as lamplights for us, a set of principles that guide us through dealing with difficult and contentious issues (Tyler 2009). Values require a higher level of commitment and this is demonstrated beyond merely 'doing' the right thing. They require us to think critically and reflectively about how our own identities, histories, belief systems and attitudes can themselves reinforce oppression (being reflective). This is turn requires us to think about how we project these in our behaviours and interactions with others (being a role model).

Being reflective

Reflective practice is extensively discussed throughout this book because we believe it is impossible to be an effective youth worker without continuous attention to it. Who we are, where we come from and what we believe are facets of our identity that invariably impact upon our view of the world (Chapter 3). Yet, we too often take such things for granted. We may stand in judgement of things that we believe to be unjust whilst at the same time holding true to beliefs or values that may impact negatively on others. Our identity not only shapes our view of the world, it shapes how others might see us. Conscious and deliberate reflection can help us to unpick or challenge things that we might otherwise let go, or take for granted. A youth work practitioner offered this example of when he had been particularly challenged to consciously reflect on his approach to anti-oppressive practice:

> *A number of years ago, I used to lead training sessions for youth workers. I was a popular trainer, well liked by groups, and I considered myself to be a critical thinker who encouraged participants to challenge their values and approaches to practice. When we came to evaluate my sessions, I received a really negative comment from a female participant who was tired of me making references to my adoration of a female pop star. She described my language as oppressive and inappropriate as I was objectifying a woman. I was shocked.*

In this case, the youth worker reflected on an important point of learning. He had clearly espoused a commitment to anti-oppressive practice and accounted for several examples of actively challenging himself and others to think and act differently about issues. However, his choice of language when describing how much he adored a pop star was open to challenge. Whilst most of the group enjoyed his humour, he had not even considered that his comments may have caused offence. Through his reflection, he was able to see how his identity (in this case, his gender) both helped define his choice of subject matter and the offensive outcome (in this case, for someone of an opposite gender). It also helped him to see how comments may be endorsed by a majority (evidenced by the group's enjoyment) with serious implications for those in a minority.

An additional layer of reflection considers the interplay of *theory*. The youth worker had to transcend his thinking from the encounter with his group to thinking about sexism more generally. Using theory in reflective practice is important as we are able to operate at two levels of thinking:

- consider the isolated experience, our learning, feelings and possible alternative perspectives;
- consider the experience in the wider social and cultural context.

Theories of sexism help us to understand how humour acts as a mechanism through which subconscious or hidden attitudes can be transmitted (Thompson 2006). Whilst we might actively challenge overt sexism, for example by intervening when someone makes a derogatory comment about a woman, we may at the same time reinforce sexist attitudes through casual language.

Being a role model

The example above invites us to consider the importance of behaviour in being an anti-oppressive practitioner. Our interactions with young people are built upon an immutable power relationship whether we choose it or not. We are therefore adults who are active in role modelling; the question becomes, what kind of role model do we want to be?

Role modelling can help to reinforce or challenge the dominant ideas that young people are exposed to on a regular basis. At times, we might find ourselves in congruence with other role models, reinforcing behaviours that have been established by others. For instance, we may impart similar messages to parents when addressing challenging behaviour. At other times, we may offer ways that are significantly different from other role models, for example, we may challenge young people to think differently from their parents on particular issues. Being consciously aware of this is important as it enables us to begin to think about both the content of the issues we are addressing and the methods we adopt. Our goal as practitioners is to link the two to actively demonstrate what is commonly termed 'pro-social modelling'.

Pro-social modelling is most often used in the training of probation workers or other practitioners who work with clients in a non-voluntary relationship. Here the role includes 'modelling pro-social values, reinforcing [clients'] pro-social expressions and actions' (Trotter 2009: 142). The emphasis is on modelling: the practitioner both demonstrating and rewarding the patterns of behaviour expected in others. Examples of how pro-social modelling works are numerous, but some straightforward ones might include:

- encouraging people to turn up on time for sessions *and* always being on time yourself;
- challenging swearing *and* not swearing yourself;
- promoting physical health *and* undertaking healthy activities;
- encouraging people to thank others for their work *and* thanking others for their work.

Being a role model in this work often means motivating young people and encouraging them to participate in activities or opportunities that they might not normally have access to. The most motivating youth workers are often those who are popular with young people. They may be energetic in their encounters with young people by telling jokes, joining in sports or being able to cite up-to-date cultural references. However, popularity alone is not the best element of a good role model: it is what is done with that popularity that matters. The example of the contrasting youth workers in the introductory chapter shows how someone who is seen as less popular can in fact make more of a difference to young people's attitudes and behaviour by offering an alternative perspective. In the case of being an anti-oppressive practitioner, this means taking a stand on issues where injustice is likely to occur if no action is taken.

Practical strategies

Consider this experience from a youth worker:

> We worked with some white young people who held quite racist views in the youth club. We decided to take the group to watch the lights get switched on at the Diwali

festival – they had never been before and we thought this might provide us with an opportunity to challenge attitudes. Before the group left, one youth worker banned some young people from the trip who were expressing racist views.

What do you think happened as a result of the intervention taken in this case?

In a memorable scene from the Danny Boyle film *The Beach*, a character who was mortally wounded in a shark attack is left to die, far away from the crowd so that his cries do not disrupt the sense of 'paradise' the rest of the group enjoys. The scenes in the film remind us how true the phrase 'ignorance is bliss' can be. Removing a problem from its immediate context can seem like a reasonable solution, and it has long been a technique used by some youth workers who argue that racist, sexist, homophobic or other discriminatory attitudes should be silenced. However, like the shark attack victim, ignorance does not alter that fact that the problem is still there – it has just been displaced. The case study above shows how excluding discriminatory behaviour can result in negative consequences.

The youth worker who banned the young people from the trip hopefully did this for noble reasons, and certainly based on a desire to instil a sense of intolerance for racist views. However, such an approach seems like the path of least resistance: the problem of racism is still there, it is just not in a place where we can do something about it. The example also had further consequences:

> *When we returned to the club, the tensions between the two groups from either end of the estate were very high and the same youth worker didn't think the groups should mix again.*

We often have to disrupt the norms of a group and challenge their belief systems (Chapter 5) but must do so on the basis that we are going to make a positive difference. The values of youth and community work signal that we are committed to working in ways that can support 'human flourishing' (Jeffs and Smith 2011). In this case, by separating the two groups, tensions arose and this further confirmed the youth worker's desire to segregate and isolate the racist views the group held. In the end, the student youth worker worked with her colleagues to enable them to see that the point of the trip was to challenge racism, and that banning people from it was counterproductive.

Reflection 14.2

In certain circumstances, it may be necessary to 'ban' a young person from attending provision to protect others. When might this be the case? What other courses of action might you try first?

Ultimately, we have a duty of care over those we work with and need to promote the health, welfare and safety of young people, colleagues and ourselves. In certain situations, where verbal or physical aggression accompanies the discriminatory views described above, we may need to act quickly to reduce potential hazards. It is our view that these circumstances should be treated as exceptions since our primary responsibility in dealing with discriminatory or oppressive behaviour and attitudes is to engage with and seek to challenge them.

The importance of being open to the views and experiences of others is a theme that is consistent throughout this book. Chapter 3 showed how important it is to understand ourselves before we attempt to engage with others, and Chapter 5 described the importance of conversation as the underpinning method of informal education.

These principles are most tested when it comes to hearing and responding to views that are contrary to our own values or principles. Such views can invoke painful or difficult reactions in us, a feeling that might be even more acute if we identify with the group that is targeted in discriminatory ways. For example, a gay youth worker may struggle to engage with a group that consistently makes homophobic comments. Whilst being open is not easy, silencing or shutting down views does little to challenge and change: at best, it displaces the problem; at worst it can add to it. A further problematic approach that can occur is the idea of trivialising or ignoring when something goes wrong. For example, practitioners may dismiss sexist or racist comments as 'banter' or the casual use of the word 'gay' to describe things in a negative way as 'just a way that young people express themselves'. In adopting this approach, the practitioner condones the negative language and as a result reinforces it.

We have established the importance of not displacing the problem of oppression and not ignoring it when it occurs. However, this does not mean rushing to action when something we disagree with causes discomfort. Comments that cause us or others offence might provoke us into responding quite forcefully, either through dismissing the contributor or by using our power to present our own account. This 'do something now' pressure to act (Collander-Brown 2010: 53) can sometimes cause us to lose the calmness and reassurance we need in order to respond effectively to young people and may shut down further potential opportunities for conversation. As Wolfe (2001: 134) notes, conversations are contextualised: 'each one is necessarily informed by previous conversations, and exerts an influence on future ones'.

Wolfe's point is very helpful, not just in terms of thinking about how we best respond to young people but also in how we think about the historical context of the conversation we are having with them (as we discussed in Chapter 13). If we follow Thompson's (2006) analysis that oppression operates and is maintained at personal (P), cultural (C) and structural (S) levels, and that as practitioners we can have the most impact at the P and C levels, then we need to examine the role that 'cultural' or 'communal' norms play in the groups we work with. Personal belief systems do not operate in a vacuum; they are the result of various cultural, collective and social influences, each one helping to uphold the other. Understanding how young people's views are shaped is a good step towards thinking about how we can interrupt difficult norms. Following this understanding, there are a number of potentially difficult steps we can take to challenge oppressive attitudes or behaviours.

Disrupting humour

Collective humour is one way through which normative ideas are communicated and endorsed. Sexist, racist or homophobic jokes can betray deeply held prejudices that, through laughter, are reinforced rather than checked. A student once described their difficult experience of being at family events where his parents, uncles and aunts would sit round telling jokes that made him feel deeply uncomfortable. He described his experience as being made to feel like an outsider and without the confidence to challenge dominant adult views. In a youth club setting, it can be common for jokes or derogatory views to be expressed with the endorsement, real or otherwise, coming from laughter. Take this example:

> *When I started working at a youth club, I noticed that all of the young people there referred to things they didn't like or agree with as 'gay'. Almost all of the young people used this language. I felt that I didn't have the right to silence them since it was a shared code that I was not part of. Instead, I began to ask questions. Why did they refer to things or people they didn't like as 'gay'? What did they think other people would make of this?*

When we 'disrupt' humour or oppressive language, we seek to introduce alternative ways of thinking. As the example above demonstrates, we must do all we can to avoid telling people that their views are wrong since we are effectively 'outsiders'. Asking questions gives us a way to invite young people to express why they believe certain things or use forms of language that may not be appropriate. Through questioning, young people might examine, justify and defend their language, or they might be encouraged to think about the impact of their language on other people. The youth worker again:

> *I found some resources from a campaign website that demonstrated the effects of homophobic bullying. When I met the group of young people again, I used these resources to stimulate discussion about why the word 'gay' when used in a derogatory way could be harmful.*

The worker made a choice here to be more directive in encouraging young people to think about their language. He accessed materials that would stimulate further discussion (instead of leaving the conversation at the questioning stage) and ultimately sought to raise consciousness about an issue that young people perhaps had not fully considered.

Reflection 14.3

What strategies do you and can you use to disrupt humour and derogatory language? How can you encourage young people to make the link between what they say and the potential harm it can have on others?

Changing the environment

Our environments help to reinforce behaviours. Just as the set-up in a classroom maintains the power divide between a teacher and students, the choice of how walls are decorated in a youth club can reinforce the acceptability of oppressive norms. At one youth centre, the walls of the snooker room were decorated with posters from men's magazines of women in their underwear. It was unsurprising that young men tended to congregate in that room and young women met elsewhere. Spence's classic chapter on gender and youth work highlighted the broader 'masculine' focus of much youth work practice. She argued that the dominant focus on 'keeping the kids off the street' (Spence 1990: 75) reinforced an emphasis on the problems that young men present with and that responses for young women are often an afterthought. Consequently, 'clubs, coffee bars and drop-in projects are continuously subject to takeover by able-bodied, local male groups . . . when young women and girls do use [buildings] they are forced to seek out their own "safe" spaces' (Spence 1990: 77).

If we merely interpret equality as providing access to all, we are in danger of reproducing dominant environments that reinforce societal patterns of exclusion and oppression. Instead, practitioners need to take active steps to ensure the environment is an active component of nurturing anti-oppressive practice.

Reflection 14.4

Look around at the environment you work in. To what extent do you think it is inclusive? What aspects suggest that it is inclusive? Are any groups sidelined or excluded? If so, why do you think this is?

New experiences

In Chapter 12 we discussed the importance of social capital in young people's lives. Recent research has emphasised how networks play a role in the formation of young people's identities (Boeck 2009). Bonded networks (those that are comparatively closed and help us to 'get by') might limit our exposure to diversity and difference, whereas bridging networks can bring us into contact with a whole range of different groups. In theory, at least, the more diverse the networks the more likely it is that young people can experience 'difference' in a positive way:

If people are able to connect and communicate with others from a diversity of backgrounds, abilities and outlooks, they are likely to respond more positively to different views and be better able to manage their lives within the complex and dynamic matrix of interactions which underpins our experience of society.

(Gilchrist 2001: 117)

The example we offered earlier in this chapter described how a worker wanted to use the Diwali festival as an opportunity to open up new experiences as a mechanism for challenging racism amongst young white people. This approach has often formed part of what has been termed multi-cultural education, making seemingly distant cultures more proximate to individuals. The approach has obvious benefits, not least in terms of making cultural diversity an exciting and engaging learning experience. Yet, on its own it is unlikely to challenge deeply held prejudices. Critics have argued that multi-culturalism focuses on celebrating difference through cultural exchange at the expense of tackling racism: the 'romantic' form of multi-culturalism (Osler 2008a). Rather, those involved in anti-racist practice should seek to challenge the structural, cultural and personal dimensions of oppression (Ashrif 2001) and accept that such a process is necessarily uncomfortable since it is far easier to celebrate the exotic than challenge the problematic. In sum, we would not argue against the positive benefits of widening experience. We would however suggest that these need to be located within efforts to challenge assumptions and prejudices.

Conclusion

In this chapter, we have explored the concept of anti-oppressive practice as a defining feature of youth work. The values inherent to and the practice methods of youth work both suggest the need to encourage young people to think critically about their own views and the views of those around them. We caution against silencing, ignoring or silencing views that we would regard as oppressive. Rather, the more difficult task for the youth worker is to see and use these as educational opportunities. In so doing, we are more likely to make a lasting impression on those we work with. In turn, this enables us to make a small but significant contribution to social justice.

15 | Enhancing participatory practice

Introduction

Young people are active partners in the process of youth work. Unlike many other professional interventions, encouraging active participation has long been a cornerstone of youth work theory and practice. Practitioners seek to help move young people from a position of passive 'consumers' or 'beneficiaries' to active participants in shaping the design, delivery and evaluation of services. Through informal education, they seek to enable young people not only to think critically about situations or circumstances but also to take action as drivers for change. To do this requires a commitment to genuine, meaningful participatory practice.

This chapter explores the relationship between young people, youth work and active participation. It briefly sets out some of the key tenets on which participatory practice is based before inviting the reader to consider how to develop participatory approaches to working with young people. In doing so, it encourages a 'thick' version of understanding participation – beyond what Fleming and Hudson rightfully dismiss as 'tokenistic' attempts to engage young people (2009). Rather than simply provide the steps for integrating participatory practice, we encourage you to consider why, how and to what extent participation already features in young people's lives and how you as a practitioner can build on these prior experiences using a responsive framework.

Youth work and participatory practice

The past two decades have seen considerable developments in increasing the participation of children and young people in mainstream policy and practice, so much so that it is now 'widely accepted, supported by statute and enhanced by specific practice guidance' (Gunn 2008: 253) and is certainly 'a near hegemonic practice in youth work' (Farthing 2012: 71). The word participation is used to cover a variety of activities. These include everything from consultation, 'where young people's views are gathered to be used in decision making' (Faulkner 2009: 89), to young people leading whole processes of change and securing greater influence in society.

The move towards participatory practice has been underpinned by a number of key shifts at both a global and national level. A key driver has been the increasing attention paid to the United Nations' Convention on the Rights of the Child (CRC), which was ratified by the United Kingdom in 1991. Global conceptions of human rights are a powerful framework for strengthening young people's opportunities to be heard, since they offer an international legal guarantee of participation. Indeed, Lundy (2007) argues that the case for the increased involvement of young people in decision making is most compelling when framed within a human rights perspective. Article 12:

> Can make a unique and powerful contribution to the creation of a children's rights culture . . . one way of sustaining the existing momentum [of involvement] might be to reframe the discourse to reflect the fact that pupil involvement in decision making is a permanent, non-negotiable human right.
>
> (Lundy 2007: 940)

An equally powerful factor that has contributed to the growth of participatory practice can be found in changes to social policy and welfare since the late 1970s. These include various policy initiatives designed to make people more responsible for tackling social problems through encouraging 'active citizenship' in place of traditional government-led responses (Wood 2012). Programmes of active citizenship education were designed to install greater levels of personal, social, civic and moral responsibility, often with young people as the key targets. These shifts were reflected in global changes in the provision and uptake of welfare. They also built upon the increasing importance of the 'consumer' and 'markets' in the context of welfare, essentially individuals having more power over the nature and quality of services. In current English social policy, this trend continued in recent times with a focus on notions of increased community participation through reforms aimed at reducing the role of the state in addressing social problems and empowering individuals and communities to take more of an active role. The welfare changes briefly described here have been extensively criticised, not least for their failure to recognise that communities may not have the resources and capacity required to address social problems (Wood 2010b, 2012).

Youth work has a long association with participation and the encouragement of young people as 'partners'. One of the key statements of purpose that underpinned local authority youth work in the United Kingdom for some time was that set out in a ministerial conference on youth work in the early 1990s. Here participation was framed as a partnership between practitioners and young people, and through 'empowerment', youth workers support 'young people to understand and act on the personal, social and political issues which affect their lives, the lives of others and the communities of which they are a part' (NYB 1991: 16).

In his review of how youth work promotes active citizenship, Rowe (1999) found that many practitioners engaged regularly in forms of rights-based education and were in favour of strategies that sought to emphasise responsibilities to self and others as 'vital to the achievement of a tolerant and humane society' (Rowe 1999: 59). In line with the wider 'turn' towards citizen engagement in public services (Andrews *et al.* 2008), one significant reform of youth services in 2002 indicated a commitment to the active involvement of young people. *Transforming Youth Work* stipulated that local authorities should ensure the 'active participation of young people in the specification, governance, management, delivery and quality assurance of youth services' (DfES 2002: 9). As a result, local authorities began 'investing in the active involvement of young people as part of a drive to modernise local government' (Merton 2002: 19). Later reforms, including *Youth Matters* and the ten-year youth strategy initiated by the Treasury (*Aiming High for Young People*) both contained specific proposals for extending the active involvement of young people in youth services. The first policy statement of the coalition government *Positive for Youth* set out commitments to involve young people at all stages of commissioning youth services:

> Involving young people does not only lead to better decisions and a greater sense of ownership by young people. It also offers an opportunity to those engaged directly for personal and social development and the development of skills for employment and further education. It also sends a clear message about the valued and positive place of young people in their community.
>
> (Department of Education 2011: Para 5.12)

In practice, youth workers often interpret participation through process models where practitioners work with young people to increase the 'level' of involvement they have in, say, the running of a local youth club. Huskins (2003) visualised this as a 'curriculum development model' where young people progress through seven stages of empowerment, from the limited end of 'making contact' through to 'leading' projects. These stages were accredited through the *Youth Achievement Awards* promoted by the charity *UK Youth*. Another common way of illustrating youth work participation is in the form of a 'ladder' where participation is progressed through 'steps' towards greater autonomy (Simpkin 2004). Such approaches are rightly criticised for their tendency to see participation in simplistic and linear terms, and critically the 'danger of creating some sense of failure if the high rung on the ladder is not reached' (Simpkin 2004: 15).

Other common criticisms stem from a fundamental question: Who benefits from participatory practice? There is much debate about the extent to which participation includes all young people or whether it is only focused on *certain* young people (perhaps those already with the capacity or resources to have their say). Others suggest that adult models of participation have been all too readily transposed to young people, which fails to recognise that young people can and do participate in ways that are different from the structures that adults favour. An example often seen is when councils merely open their committees to young participants but continue to run their meetings in the same format as they would have done prior to young people's engagement.

Given these criticisms, we would argue that it would be unwise to begin any form of participatory practice without first understanding young people's own perceptions and experiences of active involvement. Young people can and do play significant roles in shaping their own lives and taking action where it is needed. There is much evidence to suggest that young people are already active participants within their communities and schools and within a wide range of political movements. The duty to consult young people placed upon local authorities and the rise of school youth councils are just two examples of the many formalised ways in which young people can have a say. Perhaps more important is the wide range of evidence available that suggests young people participate in 'informal' voluntary and community action on a day-to-day basis.

For example, Lister *et al.* (2002) investigated the day-to-day experience of young people and found a range of socially constructive practices that included formal voluntary work as well as 'neighbourliness, informal political action, and other forms of social participation' (2002: 10). Wood's (2009b) study found that young people could readily identify a wide range of 'responsibilities' that they exercised within their neighbourhoods and schools.

Both studies offer examples of a common theme in the youth citizenship and participation literature: young people do generally participate and are engaged in a wide range of activities that, at the very least, suggest they are politically or socially minded.

Therefore, as a starting point to incorporating participatory practice in our work, it is incumbent on us to understand the extent to which young people *are already engaged*. We can do this through examining:

- the extent to which young people feel they have influence over their circumstances;
- the extent to which they can link their day-to-day actions with a broader understanding about their social, political and civic rights and responsibilities;
- their visions for what needs to change;
- the opportunities we have for enabling them to exercise their influence.

Each of these is now discussed in turn.

Mapping young people's spheres of influence

If evidence of active citizenship and participation includes understanding and acting on personal, social and political issues (NYB 1991), it follows that we should seek to understand whether, how and to what extent young people do this in their daily lives. This requires us to explore the interplay of influence, decision making and the degrees of control young people can exercise over situations or circumstances they encounter. This is commonly known as agency: the capacity to act independently, make choices and influence situations. Analysis of young people's agency enables us to consider how structures (factors that limit or determine someone's decisions, experiences and so on) help or hinder young people in acting on the issues that affect them.

In Wood's (2009b) study, young people were asked about the extent to which they felt they could make decisions about issues that affected their lives. 'Decision making' was seen by young people as a key signifier of active participation since, as one young man suggested, 'if you are going to be an active citizen, you need to be able to make decisions about things otherwise you are not a leader' (Wood 2009b: 219).

For many of us, we make decisions in a number of different contexts and these decisions have varying degrees of impact. Some may only affect our immediate and personal situations. For example, we might make a decision about how to change the environment in which we live by painting a wall a different colour or we might decide to change our personal appearance in some way. Others may have more influence beyond this, for example encouraging the council to take action about the litter problems in a local park. Young people are no different to anyone else in this respect: sometimes they feel that they can influence and shape situations, other times they feel powerless to affect change.

Figure 15.1 and the accompanying explanation below provides a framework for examining the extent to which young people can evidence decision making and influence at different levels.

The *proximate* context refers to the most immediate networks in young people's lives, including household family members, the extended family and close peer groups. This is often the place where most young people identify that they can make decisions about issues that affect them, but there is some evidence to suggest that these decisions have limited influence on others. For example, in Wood's (2009b) study, most young people related decision making to choices of clothes and make-up, hair styles, music, how to spend leisure time and which groups of friends to identify with. These decisions were either exercised solely by young people, and peers or family members sometimes helped to make, support or oppose the decision. Decisions taken within the family context tended to concern the use of private space or having private time with or away from the family. Common types also concerned the distribution and uptake of household jobs (such as what day a young person would be responsible for cleaning) and having a say in the layout of the household environment.

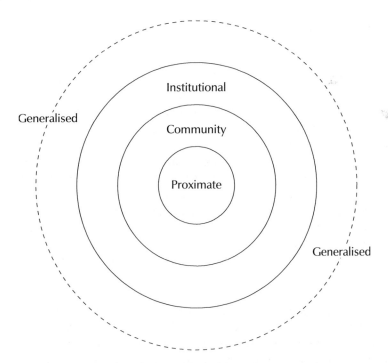

Figure 15.1 Active citizenship across contexts

Source: Wood (2009b: 294)

The *community* context refers to groups that young people identify as neighbours, extended peer networks, associates and other local people outside of their immediate family and peer networks. The label 'community' also includes the geographical spaces that young people occupy: the neighbourhood, the estate and other synonyms for local area. In contrast with the discussions around making decisions in personal, family and peer contexts, young people in Wood's study (2009b) were less able to articulate evidence of making decisions in a community context. Decision making in the wider contexts of young people's lives was felt to be the capacity to influence and change circumstances. One young person highlighted why many felt they had no influence in their local community: 'To make decisions you need power. Young people haven't got any power. That's right isn't it . . . Think about all the people who make decisions for us, they've all got power' ('Bruno', cited in Wood 2009b: 266).

The *institutional* context refers to the various institutions that interact with young people. These include schools and other educational providers, youth clubs, health services, advice and information services and so on. The young people you work with will all have some experience of being in an institutional context. It is within this context that some measures may exist to increase and formalise opportunities for young people to have influence. We have already set out in this chapter the various policy developments that have sought to integrate citizenship education and participatory practice into different organisations. However, as a practitioner we need to look beyond the surface and ask whether such opportunities are meaningful and likely to result in any change. For example, schools remain adult managed, hierarchical, anti-democratic institutions (Evans 2008). Educational programmes (with school councils as an example) end up reproducing a 'reflection of existing societal patterns' (Evans 2008: 523) through established teaching and learning methods. More positive examples might be identified though. For instance, it may be interesting to see the extent to which young people exercise influence within the youth provision that you are working with. In some cases, young people can be active partners, able to make decisions about the aims, funding and evaluation of youth projects.

Why do we engage in the work that we do? What is the point of encouraging young people to participate? Does the work we do link to any broader ideas about young people's position in society? The outer sphere in the diagram (*generalised*) helps us to think about how actions at the proximate, community or individual level relate to a set of principles or values about active citizenship that we would want to draw a link to. To explore this we will use two examples from Wood's (2009b) study, starting with a youth grant funding panel:

> *Members of a local youth grants panel were appointed by a local charity funding body to help them make decisions about which youth projects should be funded. Ten young people served on the panel. The panel met once a month for funding decision meetings and group building work. They also participated in a range of leisure activities together. Young people in the youth grants panel held principled views about the need to promote children and young people's rights and were in positions of comparative power to be able to distribute funds to support the implementation of these principles.*

In this example, we can see a group of young people engaged in a series of actions that were designed to strengthen the voice of young people in influencing funding decisions. What is particularly interesting about the case is that they were also able to locate this work within a broader agenda to promote the rights of children and young people. During interviews, they were able to express how they would apply what they had learnt on the grants panel to other contexts in their life. Many of the young people talked about being 'more involved in campaigns' or helping others to make sense of participatory practice. We might therefore conclude that young people in this case could demonstrate a clear relationship between their instrumental actions and a wider awareness of why participation matters.

Let us now consider another example:

> A school council was based in a mixed community college for 11–16 year olds with approximately 950 students. Set up as a response to an inspection report that called for the improvement of relationships between staff and students, the council provided a forum for greater student involvement. The school council was a formal body of ten elected students who represented school students in making decisions about the school. They had formal meetings once a month, during lunch breaks, and met occasionally at other times. The council had successfully campaigned to have a breakfast club restarted within their school. However, this positive example was accompanied by a failure to secure support from the school to develop a basketball area for young men. In the case of the breakfast club, there was evidence of strong parental and teacher support for the initiative whereas in the case of the basketball court, 'there wasn't the same kind of support' (Member, School Council). Furthermore, the reasons for the rejection of the basketball idea were not communicated to the council members.

In the case of the school council, we can clearly see evidence of young people making a difference by securing the reintroduction of a breakfast club. However, we can also determine two underpinning problems with this case. The first problem appears to be that young people cannot achieve things without the explicit support and approval of adults – approval for a breakfast club, no approval for the basketball area – reflecting 'existing societal patterns' (Evans 2008: 523). It was clear when interviewing the young people that they did not expect the council to always get what it wanted. However, this links to a second problem. Adults in this case have also failed to effectively communicate with young people about *why* certain things could be pursued and others not. This left young people confused and uncertain. For Boyden and Ennew (1997), this represents the difference between 'taking part' and 'knowing that one's actions are taken note of and may be acted upon' (1997: 33). These issues demonstrate that on the face of it, the school can hold up examples of actively involving young people (through the breakfast club), but when further investigation is undertaken, these can be defined as quite limited and not within a wider ethos of supporting young people to understand both the processes and problems of active participation.

Informal education concerns the 'enlargement of experience' with an emphasis on learning from experience in everyday, real-world situations. Enabling young people to draw a link between their own day-to-day actions and a wider set of principles should underpin our approach to participatory practice. In order to do this, we need to consider both for ourselves and with the young people we work with:

- why being an active participant can make a difference;
- how our work reproduces or challenges the relative power position of young people in society (Chapter 7);
- how the experiences we engage in might result in transferable knowledge, skills and resources for young people;
- how different young people might experience participation in different ways, both positively and negatively.

Task 15.1

The above model can be a useful tool for helping young people to think about how much power and influence they have at each of the different levels (proximate, community, institutional) and what views they have on the broader principles of why active participation matters (generalised).

Using the model, work with a group of young people to:

- provide examples of the decisions they make at each of the three levels;
- discuss the extent to which they feel they have power and influence at each of the levels;
- discuss whether they think their experiences are similar or different to those of young people more generally.

Visioning change

Participatory practice seeks to extend opportunities for young people to 'come to voice' and be 'heard' by understanding and taking action on issues that affect their lives (Batsleer 2008). It is both a 'process' insofar as participation is a *method* relying on particular ways of working *with* young people. It is also a concept underpinned by particular *values* or *beliefs* we hold about the capacity of young people to be partners in decision making, to hold us and others to account and to exercise their own rights to self-determination (Lloyd-Smith and Tarr 2000). Participation should therefore have a *purpose* beyond merely being a way of working. It follows that we need to ask not just *how we do* participatory practice but also *to what end*? Whilst the skills acquisition associated with engaging in the method is no doubt important for young people, we should also be concerned with the question 'why bother'?

The concept of 'visioning' is useful here. Visioning is an exercise whereby young people are encouraged to think collaboratively about challenges, problems, barriers or difficulties that they face and to imagine alternatives. Often used in community development or engagement work, visioning enables 'people to work through their different perspectives and interests, create new knowledge to make more informed decisions, and empower [young people] to take on the challenging issues' (Ayres 2012: 17).

Visioning depends on the quality of the relationship you have built up with young people, your skills as a group work facilitator (Chapter 12) and your role in helping to guide conversations (Chapter 5). It emphasises 'a commitment to inclusiveness, open communication, mutual respect for all' and crucially 'a focus on understanding *interests* that move beyond *positions* [in] an effort to create consensus' (Ayres 2012: 22). In the same way that Socratic dialogue (discussed in Chapter 4) seeks to move groups towards shared ethical principles, visioning aims for consensus both in terms of prioritising challenges and seeking collective, participative solutions. Visioning should also focus on the proximate, community and institutional spheres set out above as it purposefully seeks to enable young people to not only understand opportunities, issues or challenges but also to identify steps they might take to act upon these.

Visioning follows much the same path as those steps identified by Egan (2010). It invites the facilitator to guide the group through a series of stages:

- *What is going on?* Here, we might ask young people to talk about what it is like to grow up in their neighbourhood or what it is like to go to their school. The facilitator will rely on their skills at fostering open dialogue where a range of views can be heard. Young people use this stage to explore what is good, what is bad and why they feel this way.
- *What do we want instead?* Here young people are invited to imagine alternatives. The facilitator asks questions about 'how could things be better' and 'what needs to change?' This stage may still be open, with often quite ambitious or seemingly unattainable goals expressed. Again, the time and space needs to be nurtured by the facilitator to ensure that these views and ideas are given a good hearing.
- *How do we get there?* The final stage of the visioning process is to identify the steps that the group can take to make a change. Here, the facilitator will encourage the group to move towards more specific steps in response to the issues identified in the first two stages. They will encourage action plans, roles and responsibilities for the groups, and ways of supporting the group to act on what they have identified.

Visioning requires a creative approach to really engage young people in the process. A variety of techniques can be used, and some of the examples discussed elsewhere in this book could easily be applied. By way of an illustration, we show here how photos and other media can be used in a positive way to help with a visioning exercise:

- *What is going on?* Young people are given disposable cameras for a week, during which they are asked to take photos that represent what they like and dislike about living in their neighbourhood. They can take any photos that best express these issues from their perspective and ideally the exercise is undertaken individually. The only caveats are that photos should be legal and should not put the young person in a position of vulnerability or embarrassment. At the end of the week, the group comes together to discuss why they took their particular photos and what they mean.

- *What do we want instead?* In the second week, young people are asked to capture images or stories from a range of media that represent what they would like to see instead. Sources of media might include traditional media such as magazines, newspapers or a variety of new media such as online videos. The unifying theme of this collected media is that it should connect to the first step – so, in this case, different visions for their neighbourhood.
- *How do we get there?* In the final week, the group meets to look at the two sets of media. A workshop using the 'listing, grouping and prioritising needs' approach (discussed in Chapter 9) helps the group to identify the types and priority of actions that could be taken to move from Step 1 to Step 2.

Whichever technique is used, the general principle is to move the group from open dialogue and general thinking to very specific issues and possible responses. Taking this approach is likely to increase the opportunities for young people to participate and take action in specific and meaningful ways.

An example of the staged process described above shows how the steps can result in positive change:

> *A youth worker met with a group of Black young men living in an area where a number of difficult and persistent social and economic challenges exist. During the visioning exercise, the young people identified a number of things they liked about growing up in the area, including their friendship groups and the places where they could meet, especially during the summer. However, their relationships with the police were seen as very negative and many young people expressed concerns about being stopped and searched on a regular basis. The group talked about some of the things they would like to change including a better relationship between the police and the community. As a result of the exercise, the group identified a series of steps they could take to work towards the changes they wanted to see. This included attending the police station, en masse, to complain about the excessive stop and search, and setting up a forum for young people to talk directly to senior police officers about their concerns. Some members of the group went on to play an even more active role in influencing local police policy and practice by having regular meetings with senior command and contributing to community safety events.*

Case studies such as this one can provide good practical examples of how visioning can result in positive action. However, they are too brief to highlight the various stages in detail, not least the conflict or tensions that a group might experience in arriving at their positive solutions. As Ayres (2012) points out, there is a need to move towards shared 'interests' and ultimately shared 'actions'.

In the chapter on groups, we set out a number of 'warnings' to watch for when facilitating groups. These apply to visioning exercises and can guard against things going awry. They enable the group to focus, to work on agreed terms and, ultimately, to focus on how to identify collective ways forward based on consensus. In addition to these general groupwork principles, there are other factors that need consideration when thinking about encouraging young people to take action – it is worth reflecting on these with your supervisor and colleagues. At the top of our list is one that comes from young people themselves: the need to be realistic about what can change (Wood 2009a). Young people may identify a number of issues that are beyond their control, such as the precarious state of employment in their city or other macro issues. Research with young people has shown that they understand and do not expect things to always change in their favour, but that unrealistic promises made by youth workers was a contributory factor to further disengagement (Wood 2009a).

Task 15.2

Using the three stages set out above design a groupwork activity that will support young people to undertake a visioning exercise. During Stage 3 of the exercise, identify the practical ways in which young people can take positive action to work towards addressing the issues they have identified. Reflect, with your supervisor, tutor or peers, on:

- the extent to which these steps are realistic and achievable;
- the support that young people will need;
- who or what might be affected by young people taking action;
- what might, or might not, change as a result.

Other ways of bringing participation to life

In this chapter, we have identified a number of different steps that enable you to encourage young people to think and act in a participatory way. We would argue that working in a participative way with young people should extend beyond particular projects or activities: where possible, it should be an integral method to your way of working. Our own institutions are often the best testing grounds both for increasing participation but also in identifying the various barriers that may inhibit this way of working. The ways in which young people can be active partners in their own learning have been discussed throughout this book and we would now like to turn briefly to how they might be more active as partners in shaping the wider provision.

Participation in your daily practice should take the form of identifying opportunities for young people to be involved in the co-production of what is undertaken by the organisation. Co-production refers to a collaborative way of working that aims to 'put principles of empowerment into practice, working *with* communities and offering communities greater control' (Durose *et al.* 2010: 2). In practice, this means working with young people to collaboratively design, deliver and evaluate forms of youth work practice. Increasing the roles and responsibilities of young people can result in a number of benefits for themselves and the organisations that work with them. Simply by listening more effectively to young people's ideas and concerns, organisations can become more adept at being more responsive. Through encouraging young people to be active partners, they are also likely to see more meaningful and sustained engagement.

Organisations can encourage democratic co-production through the opportunities they create for young people to participate. For example, youth clubs might offer young people the opportunity to collaborate in the planning, delivery and evaluation of events or activities such as a trip with their peers. Youth participation might be formalised through a youth council, responsible for governing youth service funding decisions or holding staff to account.

Given the various different organisational contexts you might be working in, it is worth reflecting on some general questions to assist in identifying opportunities for young people to participate:

- What opportunities are there for young people to shape and influence the organisation's work?
- How do young people feel about participation?
- What evidence is there that participatory practice has been part of the work of the organisation?
- What mechanisms or approaches are used to listen to young people?
- How might my own work be enhanced if I adopt a co-production approach?
- What barriers might limit young people's opportunities to influence the organisation?
- How might young people have a say beyond the organisation?

If you are working with a locally elected youth council, you might expect to see some very positive examples of young people exercising influence (though not always). In contrast, young people in restrictive settings may not have much say in how their day-to-day lives are managed. At the outset then, we recognise the inherent difficulties in trying to describe how to introduce participatory practice in the same way in every context. Yet, starting with these reflective questions and discussing them with your supervisor and colleagues is a good way to begin to identify if and how participatory practice can become more developed in your work.

Task 15.3

In discussion with your supervisor and using the general questions set out above, reflect on:

- whether and to what extent the organisation currently engages young people as active participants;
- whether this should develop and how;
- what actions need to be taken to develop participatory practice.

Conclusion

There has been a growing and positive emphasis on encouraging young people's active participation and citizenship, with an increasing recognition of the value of listening to and working in partnership with young people. Too often, policy approaches to citizenship education emphasise the deficits that young people possess, whether in terms of their political disengagement or their perceived antipathy towards local communities. We would challenge these policy notions by emphasising the importance of starting from where young people are at in terms of understanding their existing patterns of social participation. This chapter has provided one framework to enable you to work with young people in a way that encourages them to think about their current experiences, how things might change and the steps they need to take to get there. It is hoped that by modelling participatory practice, we can draw a much more effective relationship between daily actions and wider awareness.

References

Adams, L. (undated) 'Learning a New Skill is Easier Said than Done', available at www.gordontraining.com/free-workplace-articles/learning-a-new-skill-is-easier-said-than-done/ (last accessed 17/12/13).

Alcock, P. (2008) *Social Policy in Britain* (3rd edition), Palgrave Macmillan: Basingstoke.

Andrews, R., Cowell, R. and Downe, J. (2008) 'Support for Active Citizenship and Public Service Performance: an empirical analysis of English local authorities', *Policy and Politics*, 36 (2), pp. 225–43.

Armstrong, D. (2004) 'A Risky Business? Research, policy, governmentality and youth offending', *Youth Justice*, 4 (2), pp. 100–16.

Ashrif, S. (2001) 'Questioning the Concept of Democracy and its Relationship to "Civilised" Behaviour', available at http://youthworkcentral.tripod.com/sashrif_citizens.htm (last accessed 15/12/13).

Avineri, S. and de-Shalit, A. (1992) 'Introduction', in S. Aveneri and A. de-Shalit (eds) *Communitarianism and Individualism*, Oxford: Oxford University Press.

Ayres, J. (2012) 'Essential ingredients in successful visioning', in N. Walzer and G.F. Hamm (eds) *Community Visioning Programs: processes and outcomes*, Abingdon: Routledge.

Baim, C., Brookes, S. and Mountford, A. (2002) *The Geese Theatre Handbook: drama with offenders and people at risk*, Hampshire: Waterside Press.

Banks, S. (2004) *Ethics, Accountability and the Social Professions*, Basingstoke: Palgrave.

Banks, S. (2010a) 'Ethics and the Youth Worker', in S. Banks (ed.) *Ethical Issues in Youth Work* (2nd edition), Abingdon: Routledge.

Banks, S. (ed.) (2010b) *Ethical Issues in Youth Work*, Abingdon: Routledge.

Batsleer, J. (2008) *Informal Learning in Youth Work*, London: Sage.

Batsleer, J. and Davies, B. (eds) (2010) *What is Youth Work?*, Exeter: Learning Matters.

Beckett, C. and Taylor, H. (2010) *Human Growth and Development* (2nd edition), London: Sage.

Benson, J. (2000) *Working More Creatively with Groups*, London: Routledge.

Berger, P.L. and Luckmann, T. (1966) *The Social Construction of Reality: a treatise on the sociology of knowledge*, New York: Anchor Books.

Berry, G., Briggs, P., Erol, R. and van Staden, L. (2011) *Effectiveness of Partnership Working in a Crime and Disorder Context: a rapid evidence assessment*, London: Home Office.

Blaine, Bruce E. (2007) *Understanding the Psychology of Diversity*, London: Sage.

Boeck, T. (2009) 'Young People and Social Capital', in J. Wood and J. Hine (eds) *Work with Young People: theory and policy for practice*, London: Sage.

Boltanski, L. and Chiapello, E. (2005) *The New Spirit of Capitalism*, London: Verso.

Borton, T. (1970) *Reach, Touch and Teach*, London: Hutchinson.

Boud, D., Cohen, R. and Walker, D. (eds) (1993) *Using Experience for Learning*, Buckingham: SRHE and Open University Press.

Boud, D., Keogh, R. and Walker, D. (1985) *Reflection: turning experience into learning*, London: Kogan Page.

Boyden, J. and Ennew, J. (1997) *Children in Focus: a manual for participatory research with children*, Stockholm: Radda Barnen.

Boylan, J. and Dalrymple, J. (2009) *Understanding Advocacy for Children and Young People*, Maidenhead: Open University Press.

Bradford, S. (2005) 'Modernising Youth Work: from the universal to the particular and back again', in R. Harrison and C. Wise (eds) *Working with Young People*, London: Sage.

Bradley, G. and Hojer, S. (2009) 'Supervision Reviewed: reflections on two different social work models in England and Sweden, *European Journal of Social Work*, 12 (1), pp. 71–85.

Brechin, A., Brown, H. and Eby, M.A. (eds) (2000) *Critical Practice in Health and Social Care*, London: Sage.

Brookfield, S. (1995) *Becoming a Critically Reflective Teacher*, San Francisco: Jossey Bass.

Brown, A. and Bourne, I. (1996) *The Social Work Supervisor*, Buckingham: Open University Press.

Brown, R. (2010) *Prejudice: its social psychology* (2nd edition), New York: John Wiley & Sons.

Bruno F. (1992) *The Eye of the Tiger: my life*, London: Weidenfeld & Nicolson.

Burkitt, I. (2008) *Social Selves: theories of self and society* (2nd edition) London: Sage.

Burney, E. (2002) 'Talking Tough, Acting Coy: what happened to the Anti-Social Behaviour Order?', *The Howard Journal*, 41 (5), pp. 469–84.

Butler, P. (2013) 'If Only Cuts to Youth Services were Fantasy', *The Guardian*, 30 April.

Carrington, B. (2000) *Double Consciousness and the Black British Athlete*, in K. Owusu (ed.) *Black British Culture and Society*, London: Routledge.

Carter, C. (2013) 'Nick Hurd Says Young People Lack Skills for Workplace', *The Telegraph*, 21 August.

Carter, P., Jeffs, T. and Smith, M.K. (eds) (1995) *Social Working*, London: Macmillan.

Carvel J. (2006) 'Memberships Soar as Average Briton Joins 17 Organisations', *The Guardian*, 7 November, available at www.guardian.co.uk/uk/2006/nov/07/british identity.johncarvel (last accessed 17/07/14).

The Children's Society (2012) *The Good Childhood Report 2012: a review of our children's well-being*, London: The Children's Society.

Chouhan, J. (2009) 'Anti-Oppressive Practice', in J. Wood and J. Hine (eds) *Work with Young People: theory and policy for practice*, London: Sage.

Claxton, G. (1999) *Wise Up: the challenge of lifelong learning*, London: Bloomsbury.

Coleman, J., Catan, L. and Dennison, C. (2004) 'You're the Last Person I'd Talk To', in J. Roche, S. Tucker, R. Thomson and R. Flynn (eds) *Youth in Society* (2nd edition), London: Sage.

Collander-Brown, D. (2010) 'Being with an Other as a Professional Practitioner: uncovering the nature of working with individuals', in T. Jeffs and M.K. Smith (eds) *Youth Work Practice*, Basingstoke: Palgrave.

Crosby, M. (2001) 'Working with People as an Informal Educator', in L. Deer Richardson and M. Wolfe (eds) *Principles and Practice of Informal Education*, London: Routledge Falmer.

Crosby, M. (2005) 'Working with people as an informal educator', in R. Harrison and C. Wise (eds) *Working with Young People*, London: Sage.

Crow, G. and Allan, G. (1994) *Community Life: an introduction to local social relations*, Hemel Hempstead: Harvester Wheatsheaf.

Dalrymple, J. and Burke, B. (1995) *Anti-Oppressive Practice: social care and the law*, Buckingham: Open University Press.

Davies, B. (2005) 'Youth Work: a manifesto for our times', *Youth and Policy* (88), pp. 5–28.

Davies, B. (2010) 'Policy Analysis: a first and vital skill of practice' in Batsleer, J.R. and Davies, B. (eds) *What is Youth Work?*, Exeter: Learning Matters.

Davies, N. (2009) *Flat Earth News*, London: Vintage.

Davys, A. and Beddoe, L. (2010) *Best Practice in Professional Supervision: a guide for the helping professions*, London: Jessica Kingsley Publishers.

Deacon, A. (1994) 'Justifying Workfare: the historical context of the workfare debates', in M. White (ed.) *Unemployment and Public Policy in a Changing Labour Market*, London: Public Services Institute.

Delanty, G. (2003) *Community*, Abingdon: Routledge.

Department for Education and Skills (DfES) (2002) *Transforming Youth Work: resourcing excellent youth services*, London: DfES.

Department of Education (2011) *Positive for Youth: a new approach to cross-government policy for young people aged 13–19*, London: DoE.

Department of Education (2012) 'The CAF Process', available at www.education.gov.uk/childrenandyoungpeople/strategy/integratedworking/caf/a0068957/the-caf-process (last accessed 23/07/13).

Dewey, J. (1933) *How We Think: a restatement of the relation of reflective thinking to the educative process* (revised edition), Boston: D.C. Heath.

Doel, M. (2010) *Social Work Placements*, Abingdon: Routledge.

Dunlosky, J. and Metcalfe, J. (2009) *Metacognition*, London: Sage.

Durose, C., Beebeejaun, Y., Rees, J., Richardson, J. and Richardson, L. (2010) *Towards Co-Production in Research with Communities*, London: AHRC.

Dwyer, P. (2000) *Welfare Rights and Responsibilities: contesting social citizenship*, Bristol: The Policy Press.

Dwyer, P. (2004a) *Understanding Social Citizenship: themes and perspectives for policy and practice*, Bristol: The Policy Press.

Dwyer, P. (2004b) 'Creeping Conditionality in the UK: from welfare rights to conditional entitlements?', *Canadian Journal of Sociology*, 29 (2), pp. 265–87.

Egan, G. (2010) *The Skilled Helper: a problem-management and opportunity development approach to helping* (9th edition), Belmont, California: Brooks/Cole Cengage Learning.

Etzioni, A. (1993) *The Spirit of Community: the reinvention of American society*, New York: Touchstone.

Evans, M. (2008) 'Citizenship Education, Pedagogy, and School Contexts', in J. Arthur, I. Davis and C. Hahn (eds) *The Sage Handbook of Education for Citizenship and Democracy*, London: Sage.

Fanon, F. (1986) *Black Skin, White Masks*, London: Pluto.

Farthing, R. (2012) 'Why Youth Participation? Some justifications and critiques of youth participation using New Labour's youth policies as a case study', *Youth and Policy*, 109, pp. 71–97.

Faulkner, K.M. (2009) 'Presentation and Representation: youth participation in ongoing public decision-making projects', *Childhood* 16 (1), pp. 89–104.

Feaviour, K., Trelfa, J. and Watkins, K. (2002) 'The Five Phase Supervision Relationship' in Connexions (2003) *The Process of Supervision: developing the reflective practitioner: introduction*, Sheffield: Crown Copyright.

Fenwick, T. (2009) 'Making to measure? Reconsidering assessment in professional continuing education', *Studies in Continuing Education*, 31 (3), pp. 229–44.

Findlay, L. (2008) 'Reflecting on "Reflective Practice"'. A discussion paper prepared for PBPL CETL (www.open.ac.uk/pbpl), available at www.open.ac.uk/cetl-workspace/cetlcontent/documents/4bf2b48887459.pdf (last accessed 02/04/2012).

Fleming, J. and Hudson, N. (2009) 'Young People and Research: participation in practice', in J. Wood and J. Hine (eds) *Work with Young People: theory and policy for practice*, London: Sage.

Flynn, N. (1997) *Public Sector Management* (3rd edition), London: Prentice Hall.

Forsyth, D.R. (2006) *Group Dynamics* (4th edition), Belmont, CA: Thomson Wadsworth Publishing.

France, A. (1996) 'Youth and Citizenship in the 1990s', in *Youth and Policy*, 53, pp. 28–43.

France, A. (2007) *Understanding Youth in Late Modernity*, Maidenhead: Open University Press.

Frazer, E. (1999) *The Problems of Communitarian Politics: unity and conflict*, Oxford: Oxford University Press.

Freire, P. (1996) *Pedagogy of the Oppressed*, Penguin Books.

French, S. and Swain, J. (2004) 'Young Disabled People' in J. Roche, S. Tucker, R. Thomson and R. Flynn (eds) *Youth in Society* (2nd edition), London: Sage.

Fulcher, J. and Scott, J. (1999) *Sociology*, Oxford: Oxford University Press.

Furlong, A. and Cartmel, F. (2007) *Young People and Social Change: new perspectives* (2nd edition), London: Sage.

Furlong, A. and Cartmel, F. (2011) 'Social Change and Political Engagement Among Young People: generation and the 2009/2010 British Election Survey', *Parliamentary Affairs*, 65 (1), pp. 13–28.

George, V. and Wilding, P. (1994) *Welfare and Ideology*, London: Harvester and Wheatsheaf.

Gilchrist, A. (2001) 'Working with networks and organisations', in L.D. Richardson and M. Wolfe (eds) *Principles and Practice of Informal Education: learning through life*, London: Routledge.

Glassman, W.E. and Hadad, M. (2013) *Approaches to Psychology* (6th edition), Berkshire: Open University Press.

Goffman, E. (1959) *The Presentation of Self in Everyday Life*, USA: Anchor Books.

Gordon, T. (1974) *Teacher Effectiveness Training*, New York: Wyden.

Green, L. (2010) *Understanding the Life Course: sociological and psychological perspectives*, Cambridge: Polity Press.

Grice, A. (2013) 'Nearly a Million Under-25s still Unemployed despite Growth', *The Independent*, 13 November.

Guasp, A. (2012) *The School Report: the experiences of gay young people in Britain's schools*, London: Stonewall.

Gunn, R. (2008) 'The Power to Shape Decisions? An exploration of young people's power in participation', *Health and Social Care in the Community*, 16 (3), pp. 253–61.

Hall, T., Coffey, A. and Williamson, H. (1999) 'Self, Space and Place: youth identities and citizenship', *British Journal of Sociology of Education*, 20 (4), pp. 501–13.

Hawkins, P. and Shohet, R. (2006) *Supervision in the Helping Professions* (3rd edition), Milton Keynes: Open University Press.

Hawkins, P. and Shohet, R. (2007) 'Towards a Learning Culture', in R. Harrison, C. Benjamin, S. Curran and R. Hunter (eds) *Leading Work with Young People*, Milton Keynes: Open University Press.

Hawtin, M. and Percy-Smith, J. (2007) *Community Profiling: a practical guide* (2nd edition), Milton Keynes: Open University Press.

Hill, M. (2003) *Understanding Social Policy* (7th edition), Oxford: Blackwell Publishing.

Hine, J. (2009) 'Young People's Lives: taking a different view' in J. Wood and J. Hine (eds) *Work with Young People: theory and policy for practice*, London: Sage.

Hine, J. and Wood, J. (2009) 'Working with Young People: emergent themes', in J. Wood and J. Hine (eds) *Work with Young People: theory and policy for practice*, London: Sage.

HM Government (1998) Crime and Disorder Act, London: HMSO.

HM Government (2006) Education and Inspections Act, London: HMSO.

Hobbs, V. (2007) 'Faking it or Hating it: can reflective practice be forced?', *Reflective Practice*, 8(3), pp. 405–17.

Hoggarth, L., Merton, B. and Tyler, M. (2009) *Managing Modern Youth Work*, Exeter: Learning Matters.

Hoggett, P. (ed.) (1997) *Contested Communities: experiences, struggles, policies*, Bristol: Policy Press.

Holland, J., Reynolds, T. and Weller, S. (2007) 'Transitions, Networks and Communities: the significance of social capital in the lives of children and young people', *Journal of Youth Studies*, 10 (1), pp. 97–116.

Home Office (1998) *The Crime and Disorder Act: inter-departmental circular on establishing youth offending teams*, London: Home Office.

House of Commons Education Select Committee (2011) *Services for Young People: third report of session 2010–12*, London: The Stationery Office.

Hudson, B. (1999) 'Joint Commissioning Across the Primary Health Care–Social Care Boundary: can it work?', *Health and Social Care in the Community*, 7 (5), pp. 358–66.

Hughes, G. and Follett, M. (2006) 'Community Safety, Youth, and the Anti-Social', in B. Goldson and J. Muncie (eds) *Youth Crime and Justice*, London: Sage.

Hughes, E., Kitzinger, J. and Murdock, G. (2006) 'The Media and Risk', in P. Taylor-Gooby and J. Zinn (eds) *Risk in Social Science*, Oxford: Oxford University Press.

Huskins, J. (2003) *Youth Work Support for Schools*, Bristol: John Huskins.

Illeris, K. (2011) *The Fundamentals of Workplace Learning*, Abingdon: Routledge.

Ipsos MORI (2011) *Children's Wellbeing in UK, Sweden and Spain: the role of inequality and materialism*, London: Ipsos MORI.

Jeffs, T. and Smith, M.K. (1999) *Informal Education: conversation, democracy and learning*, London: Education Now.

Jeffs, T. and Smith, M.K. (2011). 'What is Informal Education?', *The Encyclopaedia of Informal Education*, available at http://infed.org/mobi/what-is-informal-education/ (last accessed 30/04/14).

Jenkins, R. (2008) *Social Identity* (3rd edition), Abingdon: Routledge.

Johns, C. (2009) *Becoming a Reflective Practitioner* (3rd edition), London: John Wiley & Sons.

Jones, O. (2011) *Chavs: the demonization of the working class*, London: Verso.

Kadushin, A. (1976) *Supervision in Social Work*, New York, Columbia University Press.

Kelly, P. (2003) 'Growing Up as Risky Business? Risks, surveillance and the institutionalized mistrust of youth', *Journal of Youth Studies*, 6 (2) pp. 165–80.

Kemshall, H. (2002) *Risk, Social Policy and Welfare*, Buckingham: Open University Press.

Kemshall, H. (2009) 'Risk, Youth and Social Policy', in J. Wood and J. Hine (eds) *Work with Young People: theory and policy for practice*, London: Sage.

Kemshall, H., Mackenzie, G., Wood, J., Bailey, R. and Yates, J. (2005) *Strengthening the Multi-Agency Public Protection Arrangements*, London: Home Office.

Kolb, D.A. (1984) *Experiential Learning Experience as a Source of Learning and Development*, New Jersey: Prentice Hall.

Kolb, A.Y. and Kolb, D.A. (2009) The Learning Way: meta-cognitive aspects of experiential learning. *Simulation Gaming* Vol 40, p. 297, available at https://weatherhead.case.edu/departments/organizational-behavior/workingPapers/wp-08-02.pdf (last accessed August 2011).

Liddle, A.M. and Gelsthorpe, L. (1994) *Crime Prevention and Inter-Agency Co-Operation, Police Research Group Crime Prevention Unit Series: Paper no. 53*, London: Home Office.

Lifelong Learning UK (2008) *National Occupational Standards for Youth Work*, London: Lifelong Learning UK.

Lister, R., Middleton, S., Smith, N., Vincent, J. and Cox, L. (2002) *Negotiating Transitions to Citizenship*, London: ESRC.

Lizzio, A., Wilson, K. and Que, J. (2009) 'Relationship Dimensions in the Professional Supervision of Psychology Graduates: supervisee perceptions of process and outcomes', *Studies in Continuing Education*, 31 (2), pp. 127–40.

Lloyd-Smith, M. and Tarr, J. (2000) 'Researching Children's Perspectives: a sociological perspective', in A. Lewis and G. Lindsay (eds) *Researching Children's Perspectives*, London: Sage.

Lundy, L. (2007) '"Voice" is Not Enough: conceptualising Article 12 of the United Nations Convention on the Rights of the Child', *British Educational Research Journal*, 33 (6), pp. 927–42.

Marken, M. and Payne, M. (eds) (1987) *Enabling and Ensuring: supervision in practice*, Leicester: National Youth Bureau.

Marshall, T.H. (1992) *Citizenship and Social Class, and Other Essays*, London: Pluto Press.

May, V. (2011) 'Self, belonging and social change', *Sociology*, 45 (3), pp. 363–78.

McGill, I. and Brockbank, A. (2009) *The Action Learning Handbook*, Abingdon: Routledge.

McKenzie, N. (2005) 'Community Youth Justice: policy, practices and public perception', in J. Winstone and F. Pakes (eds) *Community Justice: issues for probation and criminal justice*, Cullompton: Willan.

McNair, A. (1944) *Teachers and Youth Leaders: The McNair Report*, London: Crown Copyright.

McVeigh, T. (2013) 'No Grit? Today's Young are Tougher than They are Ever Given Credit for', *The Observer*, 25 August.

Merton, B. (2002) *So, What's Happening? Innovation in youth work*, Leicester: National Youth Agency.

Mezirow, J. (1997) 'Transformative Learning: theory to practice, *New Directions for Adult and Continuing Education*, 74, pp. 5–12.

Mizen, P. (2004) *The Changing State of Youth*, Palgrave: Basingstoke.

Moon, J.A. (2004) *A Handbook of Reflective and Experiential Learning Theory and Practice*, London: RoutledgeFalmer.

Moore, S., Neville, C., Murphy, M. and Connolly, C. (2010) *The Ultimate Study Skills Handbook*, London: Open University Press/McGraw-Hill Education.

Mullaly, B. (2002) *Challenging Oppression: a critical social work approach*, Buckingham: Open University Press.

Muncie, J. (2004) 'Youth Justice: responsibilisation and rights', in J. Roche, S. Tucker, R. Thomson and R. Flynn (eds) *Youth in Society* (2nd edition), London: Sage.

National Youth Agency (NYA) (2004) *Ethical Conduction in Youth Work: a statement of values and principles from the National Youth Agency*, Leicester: NYA.

National Youth Bureau (NYB) (1991) *Towards a Core Curriculum – The Next Step: report of the second ministerial conference*, Leicester: NYB.

Ord, J. (2007) *Youth Work Process, Product and Practice: creating an authentic curriculum in work with young people*, Lyme Regis: Russell House.

OSDE (Open Spaces for Dialogue and Enquiry) (undated), available at www.osde methodology.org.uk (last accessed 21/02/2012).

Osler, A. (2008a) 'Citizenship Education and the Ajegbo Report: re-imaging a cosmopolitan nation', *London Review of Education*, 6 (1), pp. 11–25.

Osler, A. (2008b) 'Human Rights Education: the foundation of education for democratic citizenship in our global age', in J. Arthur, I. Davies and C. Hahn (eds) *The Sage Handbook of Education for Citizenship and Democracy*, London: Sage.

Osler, A. and Starkey, H. (2010) *Teachers and Human Rights Education*, Stoke on Trent: Trentham Books.

Page, S. and Wosket, V. (2001) *Supervising the Counsellor: a cyclical model*, Brunner-Routledge: East Sussex.

Palmer, Parker. J. (1998) *The Courage to Teach: exploring the inner landscape of a teacher's life*, San Francisco: Jossey-Bass.

Parekh, B. (2000) *The Future of Multi-Ethnic Britain: the Parekh Report*, London: Profile Books.

Parker, J. and Bradley, G. (2010) *Social Work Practice: assessment, planning, intervention and review* (3rd edition), Exeter: Learning Matters.

Payne, M. (2005) 'Working with Groups', in R. Harrison and C. Wise (eds) *Working with Young People*, London: Sage.

Payne, M. (2009) 'Modern Youth Work: purity or common cause?', in J. Wood and J. Hine (eds) *Work with Young People: theory and policy for practice*, London: Sage.

Percy-Smith, J. (2006) 'What Works in Strategic Partnerships for Children: a research review', *Children and Society*, 20 (4), 313–23.

Philippart, F. (2003) 'Using Socratic Dialogue', in S. Banks and K. Nøhr (eds) *Teaching Practical Ethics for the Social Professions*, Copenhagen: FESET.

Power, A., Willmot, H. and Davidson, R. (2011) *Family Futures: childhood and poverty in urban neighbourhoods*, Bristol: Policy Press.

Proctor, B. (1987) 'A Co-Operative Exercise in Accountability', in M. Marken and M. Payne (eds) *Enabling and Ensuring – Supervision in Practice*, Leicester: National Youth Bureau.

Proctor, B. (2001) 'Training for Supervision Attitude, Skills and Intention', in J. Cutcliffe, T. Butterworth and B. Proctor (eds) *Fundamental Themes in Clinical Supervision*, London: Routledge.

Pugh, C. (2010) 'Sustaining Ourselves and Our Enthusiasm', in T. Jeffs and M.K. Smith (eds) *Youth Work Practice*, Basingstoke: Palgrave.

Reay, D. and Lucey, H. (2000) '"I Don't Really Like It But I Don't Want to be Anywhere Else": children and inner city council estates', *Antipode*, 32 (4), pp. 410–28.

Rees, K.L. (2007) 'The Lived Experience of Final Year Student Nurses of Learning through Reflective Processes'. PhD thesis. Bournemouth University.

Remen, R. N. (2006) *Kitchen Table Wisdom: stories that heal*, New York: Riverhead Books.

Reynolds, M, and Vince, R. (eds) (2004) *Organizing Reflection*, London: Ashgate.

Restorative Justice Council (2012) 'What is Restorative Justice?', available at www. restorativejustice.org.uk/what_is_restorative_justice/ (last accessed 17/12/13).

Rogers, C.R. (1980) *A Way of Being*, Boston: Houghton Mifflin.

Roker, D., Player, K. and Coleman, J. (1999) 'Young People's Voluntary and Campaigning Activities as a Source of Political Education', *Oxford Review of Education*, 25 (1/2), pp. 185–98.

Rolfe, G., Jasper, M. and Freshwater, D. (2011) *Critical Reflection in Practice: generating knowledge for care* (2nd edition), Basingstoke: Palgrave.

Rowe, D. (1999) *Youth Work and the Promotion of Citizenship*, London: Citizenship Foundation.

Sampson, R. (1999) 'What Community Supplies', in R. Ferguson (ed.) *Urban Problems and Community Development*, Washington, DC: Brookings Institution.

Sapin, K. (2009) *Essential Skills for Youth Work Practice*, London: Sage.

Scaife, J.M. (2009) *Supervision in Clinical Practice: a practitioner's guide* (2nd edition), East Sussex: Routledge.

Schön, D. (1983) *The Reflective Practitioner: how professionals think in action*, London: Temple Smith.

Schön, D. (1987) *Educating the Reflective Practitioner*, San Francisco: Jossey-Bass.

Secker, J. and Hill, K. (2001) 'Broadening the Partnerships: experiences of working across community agencies', *Journal of Interprofessional Care*, 15 (4), pp. 341–50.

Selznick, P. (1998) 'The Communitarian Persuasion', in E.A. Christodoulidis (ed.) *Communitarianism and Citizenship*, Aldershot: Ashgate.

Sercombe, H. (2010) *Youth Work Ethics*, London: Sage.

Shohet, R. and Wilmot, J. (1991) 'The Key Issue in the Supervision of Counsellors: the supervisory relationship' in W. Dryden and B. Thorne (eds) *Training and Supervision for Counselling in Action*, London: Sage.

Shohet, R. (ed.) (2008) *Passionate Supervision*, London: Jessica Kingsley Publishers.

Simpkin, B. (2004) 'Participation and Beyond: a collaborative research project investigating examples of participative and empowering youth work', PhD thesis submitted to De Montfort University.

Smith, M.K. (1994) *Local Education: community, conversation, praxis*, Buckingham: Open University Press.

Smith, M.K. (2008) 'What is a group?', *The Encyclopaedia of Informal Education*, available at: www.infed.org/mobi/what-is-a-group/ (last accessed 23/10/12).

Smith, M.K. (2011) 'Introducing informal education', *The Encyclopaedia of Informal Education*, available at: www.infed.org/i-intro.htm (last accessed: 24/01/12).

Spence, J. (1990) 'Youth Work and Gender', in T. Jeffs and M. Smith (eds) *Young People, Inequality and Youth Work*, Basingstoke: Macmillan.

Spence, J. (2005) 'Concepts of youth'. In *Working with Young People*. Harrison, R. and Wise, C., London: The Open University in association with Sage Publications.

Spence, J. and Wood, J. (2011) 'Editorial: youth work and research', *Youth and Policy*, 107, pp. 1–16.

Spicker, P. (1995) *Social Policy: themes and approaches*, Bristol: Policy Press.

Staeheli, L.A. (2008) 'Citizenship and the Problem of Community', *Political Geography*, 27 (1), pp. 5–21.

Stenhouse, L. (1975) *An Introduction to Curriculum Research and Development*, London: Heinemann.

Stephen, D. and Squires, P. (2004) '"They're Still Children and Entitled to be Children": problematising the institutionalised mistrust of marginalised youth in Britain', *Journal of Youth Studies*, 7 (3), pp. 351–69.

Sutton, C. (1999) *Helping Families with Troubled Children: a preventative approach*, Chichester: Wiley.

Taylor, A.M. (2003) *Responding to Adolescents: helping relationship skills for youth workers, mentors and other advisers*, Lyme Regis: Russell House.

Thompson, N. (2001) *Anti-Discriminatory Practice* (3rd edition), Basingstoke: Palgrave.

Thompson, N. (2005) 'Reflective Practice' in R. Harrison and C. Wise (eds) *Working with Young People*, London: Sage.

Thompson, N. (2006) *Anti-Discriminatory Practice* (4th edition), Basingstoke: Palgrave.

Thompson, N. (2007) 'Using Supervision', in R. Harrison, C. Benjamin, S. Curran and R. Hunter (eds) *Leading Work with Young People*, London: Sage.

Thompson, S. and Thompson, N. (2008) *The Critically Reflective Practitioner*, Basingstoke: Palgrave Macmillan.

Tiffany, G. (2009) *Community Philosophy: a project report*, York: Joseph Rowntree Foundation.

Titmuss, R.M. (1968) *Commitment to Welfare*, London: George Allen and Unwin.

Trotter, C. (2009) 'Pro-Social Modelling', *European Journal of Probation*, 1 (2), pp. 142–52.

Tuckman, B.W. (1965) 'Developmental Sequence in Small Groups', *Psychological Bulletin*, 63 (6), pp. 384–9.

Tyler, M. (2009) 'Managing the Tensions', in J. Wood and J. Hine (eds) *Work with Young People: theory and policy for practice*, London: Sage.

Ungar, M. (2006) *Strengths Based Counselling with At-Risk Youth*, London: Sage.

Unicef (2007) 'The State of the World's Children', available at www.unicef.org/sowc07/ (last accessed April 2014).

Upson, A. (2006) *Perceptions and Experiences of Anti-Social Behaviour: findings from the 2004/05 British Crime Survey*, London: Home Office.

Vaughan, J.C. (1990). Foreword in R.C. Clift, W.R. Houston, and M.C. Pugach (eds), *Encouraging Reflective Practice in Education: an analysis of issues and programs*, New York: Teachers College Press.

Weller, S. (2007) *Teenagers' Citizenship: experiences and education*, Abingdon: Routledge.

Whitaker, D.S. (1989) *Using Groups to Help People*, London: Routledge.

Whyte, W.F. (1943) *Street Corner Society: social structure of an Italian slum*, Chicago: University of Chicago Press.

Wolfe, M. (2001) 'Conversation', in L.D. Richardson and M. Wolfe (eds) *Principles and Practice of Informal Education: learning through life*, London: Routledge.

Wood, J. (2009a) 'Education for Effective Citizenship', in J. Wood and J. Hine (eds) *Work with Young People: theory and policy for practice*, London: Sage.

Wood, J. (2009b) 'Young People and Active Citizenship: an investigation,' PhD thesis submitted to De Montfort University, available at http://hdl.handle.net/2086/3234 (last accessed 15/12/13).

Wood, J. (2010a) 'Young People as Activists: ethical issues in promoting and supporting active citizenship', in S. Banks (ed.) *Ethical Issues in Youth Work* (2nd edition), Abingdon: Routledge.

Wood, J. (2010b) '"Preferred Futures": active citizenship, government and young people', *Youth and Policy*, 105: pp. 50–70.

Wood, J. (2012) 'The University as a Public Good: active citizenship and university community engagement', *International Journal of Progressive Education*, 8 (3), pp. 15–31.

Wood, J. and Hine, J. (2009) 'The Changing Context of Work with Young People' in J. Wood and J. Hine (eds) *Work with Young People: theory and policy for practice*, London: Sage.

Wood, J. and Kemshall, H. (2008) 'Risk, Accountability and Partnerships in Criminal Justice: the case of Multi-Agency Public Protection Arrangements (MAPPA)' in B. Stout, J. Yates and B. Williams (eds) *Applied Criminology*, London: Sage.

Woods, J. (2001) 'Using Supervision for Professional Development', in L. Deer Richardson and M. Wolfe (eds) *Principles and Practice of Informal Education*, London: Routledge.

World Health Report (WHO) 2008 – Primary Health Care (Now More Than Ever), available at www.who.int/whr/2008/en/index.html (last accessed 21/02/2012).

Yates, J. (2009) 'Youth Justice: moving in an anti-social direction', in J. Wood and J. Hine (eds) *Work with Young People: theory and policy for practice*, London: Sage.

Yates, S. (2009) 'Good Practice in Guidance: lessons from Connexions', in J. Wood and J. Hine (eds) *Work with Young People: theory and policy for practice*, London: Sage.

Young, J. and Matthews, R. (2003) 'New Labour, Crime Control and Social Exclusion', in R. Matthews and J. Young (eds) *The New Politics of Crime and Punishment*, Cullompton: Willan.

Young, K. (1999) *The Art of Youth Work*, Lyme Regis: Russell House.

Young, K. (2006) *The Art of Youth Work* (2nd edition), Lyme Regis: Russell House.

Young Foundation (The) (2012) *An Outcomes Framework for Young People's Services*, London: The Young Foundation.

Youth Justice Board (2004) *Mental Health: certificate in effective practice*, London: Youth Justice Board.

Youth Justice Board for England and Wales (2013) *Modern Youth Offending Partnerships: guidance on effective youth offending team governance in England*, London: Ministry of Justice.

Zeldin, T. (1994) *An Intimate History of Humanity*, London: Vintage.

Index